DRESSMAKING
step by step

DRESSMAKING
step by step

Alison Smith

LONDON, NEW YORK, MUNICH, MELBOURNE,
AND DELHI

DK UK
PROJECT EDITOR Laura Palosuo
SENIOR EDITOR Hilary Mandleberg
SENIOR ART EDITOR Glenda Fisher
PRE-PRODUCTION PRODUCER Rebecca Fallowfield
SENIOR PRODUCER Ché Creasey
CREATIVE TECHNICAL SUPPORT Sonia Charbonnier
MANAGING EDITOR Penny Smith
MANAGING ART EDITOR Marianne Markham
PUBLISHER Mary Ling
ART DIRECTOR Jane Bull

DK INDIA
SENIOR EDITOR Dorothy Kikon
EDITOR Janashree Singha
SENIOR ART EDITOR Ivy Roy
ART EDITORS Vikas Sachdeva, Zaurin Thoidingjam
MANAGING EDITOR Alicia Ingty
MANAGING ART EDITOR Navidita Thapa
PRODUCTION MANAGER Pankaj Sharma
PRE-PRODUCTION MANAGER Sunil Sharma
SENIOR DTP DESIGNER Jagtar Singh
DTP DESIGNERS Anurag Trivedi, Satish Chandra Gaur

Material first published in *Dressmaking*, 2012

This edition first published in Great Britain in 2015 by
Dorling Kindersley Limited
80 Strand, London WC2R ORL

A Penguin Random House Company

1 2 3 4 5 6 7 8 9 10
001–256404– Feb/2015

A CIP catalogue record for this book is available from the British Library.

ISBN: 978-1-4093-5261-7

Printed and bound in China by Hung Hing.

Colour reproduction by Altaimage UK.

Discover more at www.dk.com/crafts

CONTENTS

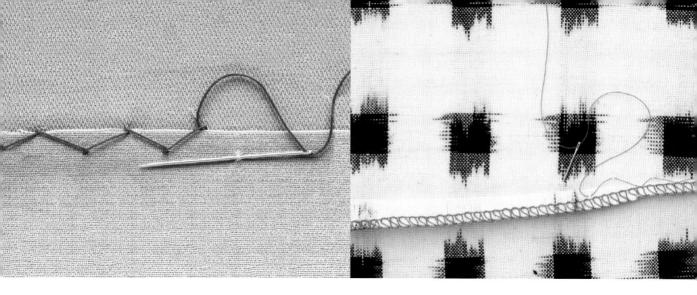

Introduction

Making your own clothes is really rewarding. With so many terrific fabrics on sale, you can choose just what you like and up with a garment that is totally you. And as well as making something that you won't find in the shops, you can also save money. What's not to like about that? But the question beginners always ask themselves is: where to start? This book is your perfect introduction. It shows you all you need to know to make a basic collection of clothes – five skirts, five dresses, two stylish pairs of trousers, one pair of shorts, three go-anywhere tops, and three must-have jackets to give your outfits the perfect finishing touch.

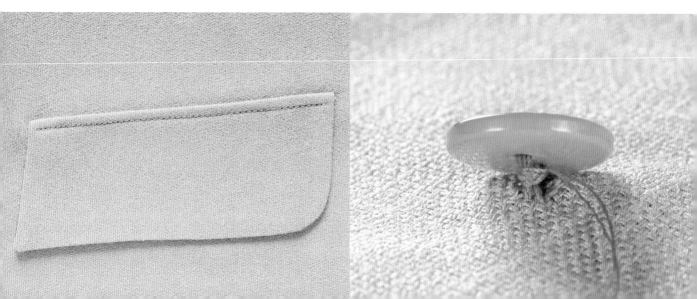

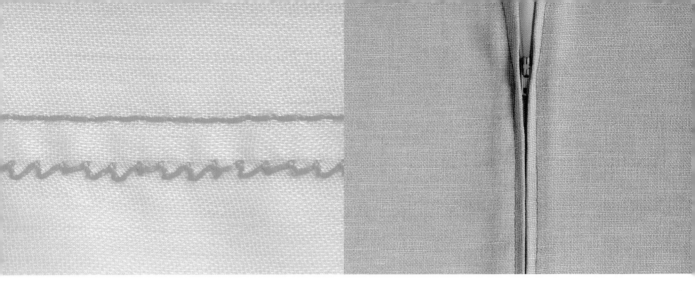

In the book's first section you'll find clear pictures of all the kit a beginner sewer requires, followed by detailed instructions for the sewing techniques you need to make the garments to a professional standard. Next come the garments themselves, with photographs of how they'll look when they're finished, together with fabric suggestions for each. The clear step-by-step instructions that follow will take you right from cutting out your fabric to sewing on the last button. The final section of the book is the key to it all – the twelve garment patterns. Each of these has been drawn up in a range of sizes, so you'll also find full instructions for choosing the correct size for you as well as for scaling the patterns up and transferring them to paper. So all you need to do now is choose your fabric and get started. Happy sewing!

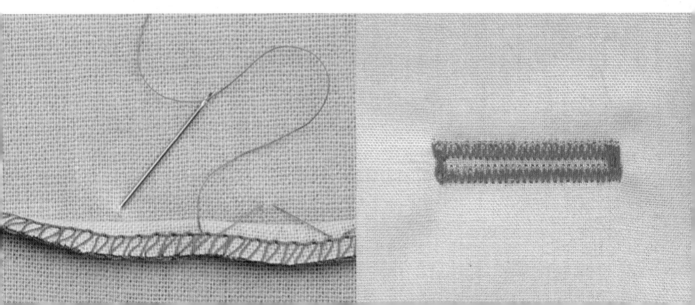

Tools and techniques

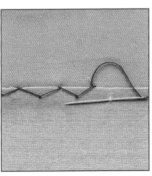
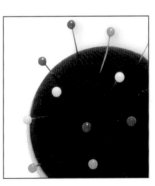

Basic sewing equipment

A well-equipped sewing kit will include all the items shown below and more, depending on the type of sewing that you do regularly. Use a suitable container to keep your tools together, so that they will be readily to hand and to keep them tidy.

Pins
Needed by every sewer to hold the fabric together prior to sewing it permanently. There are different types of pins for different types of work.

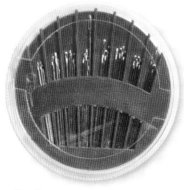

Needles
A good selection of different types of needles for sewing by hand. They will enable you to tackle any hand-sewing project.

Tape measure
Essential, not only to take body measurements, but also to help measure fabric, seams, etc. Choose one that gives both metric and imperial. A tape made of plastic is best as it will not stretch.

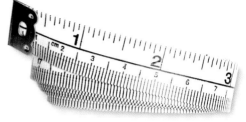

Pin cushion
To keep your needles and pins safe and clean. Choose one that has a fabric cover and is firm.

Haberdashery
All the odds and ends a sewer needs, including everything from buttons and snaps to trimmings and elastic. A selection of buttons and snaps in your basic kit is useful for a quick repair.

Ironing board
Essential to iron on. Make sure the board is height-adjustable.

Iron
A good-quality steam iron is a wonderful asset. Choose a reasonably heavy iron that has steam and a shot of steam facility.

Pressing cloth
Choose a cloth made from silk organza or muslin as you can see through it. The cloth stops the iron marking the fabric and prevents burning delicate fabrics.

Threads
A selection of threads for hand sewing and machine/overlocker sewing in a variety of colours. Some threads are made of polyester, while others are cotton or rayon.

Safety pins
In a variety of sizes. Useful for emergency repairs as well as for threading elastics.

Tailor's ham
A ham-shaped pressing cushion that is used to press darts.

Cutting tools

There are many types of cutting tools, but one rule applies to all: buy good-quality products that can be re-sharpened. When choosing cutting shears, make sure that they fit the span of your hand so that you can comfortably open the whole of the blade with one action. This is very important to allow clean and accurate cutting lines. Shears and scissors of various types are not the only cutting tools required – everyone will at some time need a seam ripper to remove misplaced stitches or to unpick seams for mending.

Cutting shears
The most popular type of shear, used for cutting large pieces of fabric. The length of the blade can vary from 20–30cm (8–12in) in length.

Snips
A very useful, small, spring-loaded tool that easily cuts the ends of thread. Not suitable for fabrics.

Trimming scissors
These scissors have a 10cm (4in) blade and are used to trim away surplus fabric and neaten ends of machining.

Embroidery scissors
Small and very sharp scissors used to get into corners and clip threads close to the fabric.

Seam ripper
A sharp, pointed hook to slide under a stitch, with a small cutting blade at the base to cut the thread. Various sizes of seam ripper are available, to cut through light to heavyweight fabric seams.

Buttonhole chisel
A smaller version of a carpenter's chisel, to cut cleanly and accurately through buttonholes. As this is very sharp, use it with a chopping board underneath.

Pinking shears
Similar in size to cutting shears but with a blade that cuts with a zigzag pattern. Used for neatening seams and decorative edges.

Paper scissors
Use these to cut around pattern pieces – cutting paper will dull the blades of fabric scissors and shears.

Bent-handled shears
This type of blade has an angle between the blade and the handle, which enables the shears to sit flat on the table when cutting out. Popular for cutting long, straight edges.

Sewing machine

A sewing machine will speed up any sewing job. Most of today's machines are aided by computer technology, which enhances stitch quality and ease of use. Always try a sewing machine before you buy, to really get a feel for it.

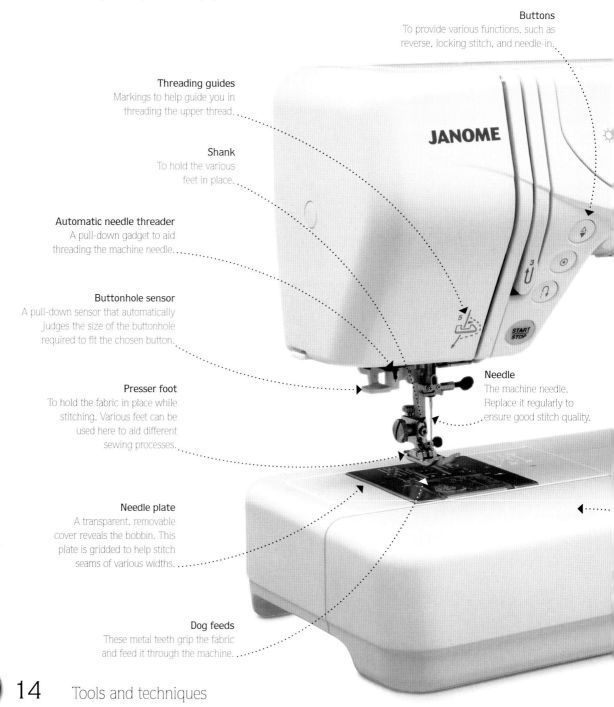

Buttons
To provide various functions, such as reverse, locking stitch, and needle-in.

Threading guides
Markings to help guide you in threading the upper thread.

Shank
To hold the various feet in place.

Automatic needle threader
A pull-down gadget to aid threading the machine needle.

Buttonhole sensor
A pull-down sensor that automatically judges the size of the buttonhole required to fit the chosen button.

Presser foot
To hold the fabric in place while stitching. Various feet can be used here to aid different sewing processes.

Needle plate
A transparent, removable cover reveals the bobbin. This plate is gridded to help stitch seams of various widths.

Needle
The machine needle. Replace it regularly to ensure good stitch quality.

Dog feeds
These metal teeth grip the fabric and feed it through the machine.

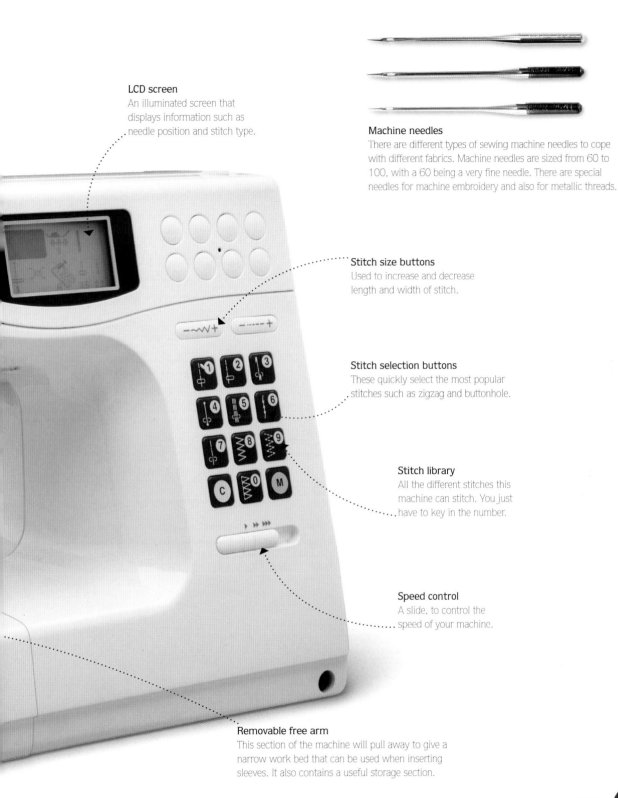

LCD screen
An illuminated screen that displays information such as needle position and stitch type.

Machine needles
There are different types of sewing machine needles to cope with different fabrics. Machine needles are sized from 60 to 100, with a 60 being a very fine needle. There are special needles for machine embroidery and also for metallic threads.

Stitch size buttons
Used to increase and decrease length and width of stitch.

Stitch selection buttons
These quickly select the most popular stitches such as zigzag and buttonhole.

Stitch library
All the different stitches this machine can stitch. You just have to key in the number.

Speed control
A slide, to control the speed of your machine.

Removable free arm
This section of the machine will pull away to give a narrow work bed that can be used when inserting sleeves. It also contains a useful storage section.

Overlocker

Use this to neaten the edges of your fabric, giving your work a very professional finish. It can also be used for seams on stretchy fabrics. It has two upper threads and two lower threads (the loopers), as well as integral knives that remove the surplus fabric as you overlock.

Overlocker accessories

You can purchase additional feet for the overlocker. Some will speed up your sewing by performing tasks such as gathering.

Overlocker needles
The overlocker uses a ballpoint needle, which creates a large loop in the thread for the loopers to catch and produce a stitch. If a normal sewing machine needle is used it could damage the overlocker.

Overlocker foot
The standard foot used for most processes. Other feet are available for gathering and cording.

Overlocker stitches

As the overlocker works, the threads wrap around the edge to give a professional finish. The 3-thread stitch is used primarily for neatening. A 4-thread stitch can also be used for neatening, but its fourth thread makes it ideal for constructing a seam on stretch knits.

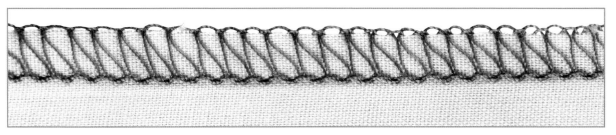

3-THREAD OVERLOCK STITCH

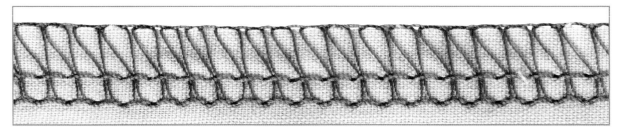

4-THREAD OVERLOCK STITCH

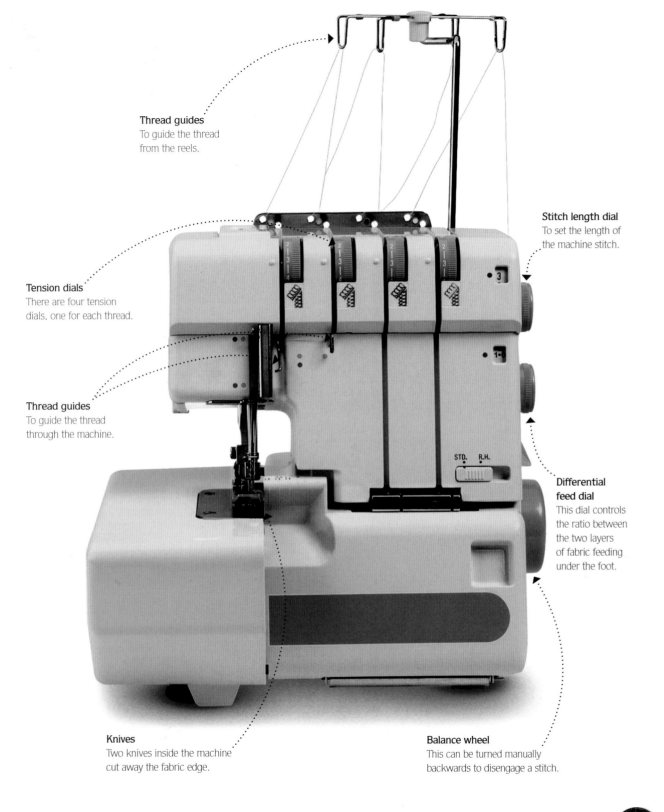

Thread guides
To guide the thread from the reels.

Stitch length dial
To set the length of the machine stitch.

Tension dials
There are four tension dials, one for each thread.

Thread guides
To guide the thread through the machine.

Differential feed dial
This dial controls the ratio between the two layers of fabric feeding under the foot.

Knives
Two knives inside the machine cut away the fabric edge.

Balance wheel
This can be turned manually backwards to disengage a stitch.

Useful extras

You can buy many more accessories to help with your sewing but knowing which products to choose can be daunting. The items you need will depend on the type of sewing you are doing but all of these would be useful for making the garments in this book. Most are relatively inexpensive, so why not ask friends and family for one or two as a birthday present?

Thimble

An essential item for many sewers, to protect the middle finger from the end of the needle. There are many types of thimble, so choose one that fits your finger comfortably.

Wire needle threader

A handy gadget, especially useful for needles with small eyes. Also helpful in threading sewing-machine needles.

Sewing gauge

A small tool about 15cm (6in) long, marked in centimetres and inches, with a sliding tab. Use as an accurate measure for small measurements such as hems.

Tweezers

These can be used for removing stubborn tacking stitches that are caught in the machine stitching. Also an essential aid to threading the overlocker.

Tracing wheel and carbon paper

These two items are used together to transfer markings from a paper pattern or a design on to fabric. Not suitable for all types of fabric though, as marks may not be easily removable.

Dressmaker's dummy
An adjustable form that is useful when fitting garments as it can be adjusted to personal body measurements. Excellent to help in the turning up of hemlines. Available in female, male, and children's shapes and sizes.

Water/air-soluble pen
This resembles a felt marker pen. Marks made can be removed from the fabric with either a spray of water or by leaving to air-dry. Be careful – if you press over the marks, they may become permanent.

Chalk pencil
Available in blue, pink, and white. As it can be sharpened like a normal pencil, it will draw accurate lines on fabric.

Cutting out

Cutting out can make or break your project. But first you need to examine the fabric in the shop, looking for any flaws, such as a crooked pattern, and checking to see if the fabric has been cut properly from the roll – that is at a right angle to the selvedge. If it has not been cut properly, you will need to straighten the edge before cutting out. If the fabric is creased, press it; if washable, wash it to avoid shrinkage later. After this preparation, you will be ready to lay the pattern pieces on the fabric, pin in place, and cut out.

Fabric grain and nap

It is important that pattern pieces are cut on the correct grain; this will make the fabric hang correctly. The grain is the direction in which the yarns or threads that make up the fabric lie. The majority of pattern pieces need to be placed with the straight of grain symbol running parallel to the warp yarn. Some fabrics have a nap due to the pile, which means the fabric shadows when it is smoothed in one direction. A fabric with a one-way design or uneven stripes is also described as having a nap. Fabrics with nap are generally cut out with the nap running down, whereas those without nap can be cut out at any angle.

GRAIN ON WOVEN FABRICS

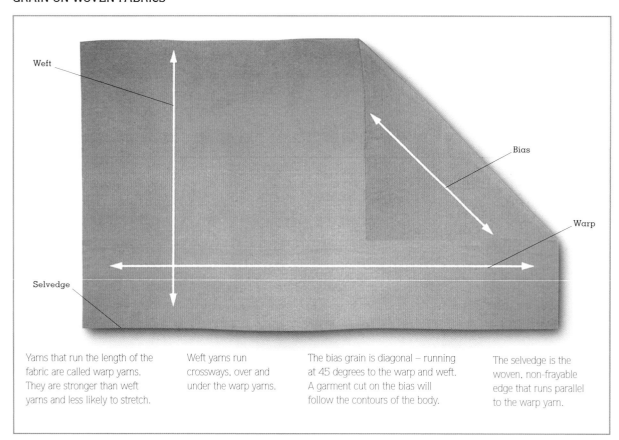

Weft

Bias

Warp

Selvedge

Yarns that run the length of the fabric are called warp yarns. They are stronger than weft yarns and less likely to stretch.

Weft yarns run crossways, over and under the warp yarns.

The bias grain is diagonal – running at 45 degrees to the warp and weft. A garment cut on the bias will follow the contours of the body.

The selvedge is the woven, non-frayable edge that runs parallel to the warp yarn.

Pattern layout

For cutting out, fabric is usually folded selvedge to selvedge. With the fabric folded, the pattern is pinned on top, and both the right- and left-side pieces are cut out at the same time. If pattern pieces have to be cut from single layer fabric, remember to cut matching pairs. If a fabric has a design, lay the fabric design-side upwards so that you can arrange the pattern pieces to show off the design. If you have left- and right-side pattern pieces, they are cut on single fabric with the fabric right-side up and the pattern right-side up.

PINNING THE PATTERN TO THE FABRIC

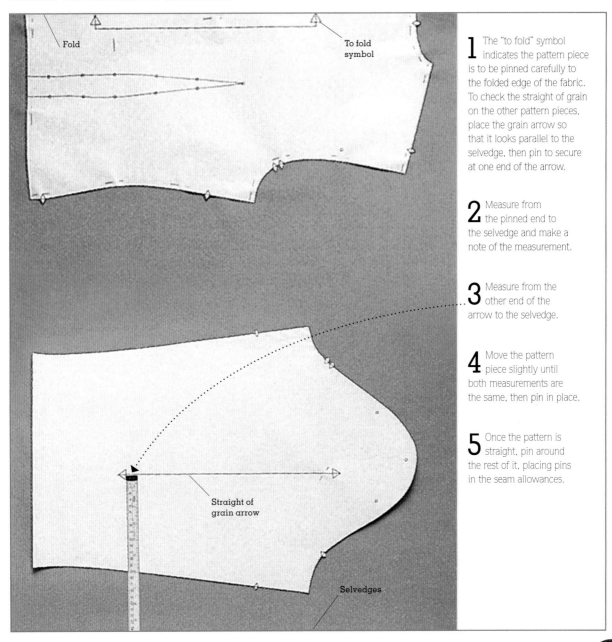

Fold

To fold symbol

Straight of grain arrow

Selvedges

1 The "to fold" symbol indicates the pattern piece is to be pinned carefully to the folded edge of the fabric. To check the straight of grain on the other pattern pieces, place the grain arrow so that it looks parallel to the selvedge, then pin to secure at one end of the arrow.

2 Measure from the pinned end to the selvedge and make a note of the measurement.

3 Measure from the other end of the arrow to the selvedge.

4 Move the pattern piece slightly until both measurements are the same, then pin in place.

5 Once the pattern is straight, pin around the rest of it, placing pins in the seam allowances.

General guide to layout

Place the pattern pieces on the fabric with the printed side uppermost. Some of the pattern pieces will need to be placed to a fold.

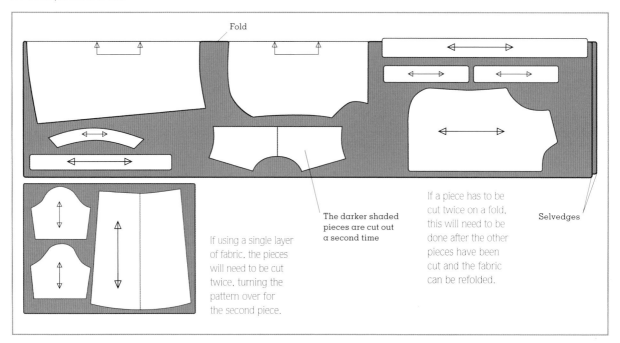

Fold

Selvedges

If using a single layer of fabric, the pieces will need to be cut twice, turning the pattern over for the second piece.

The darker shaded pieces are cut out a second time

If a piece has to be cut twice on a fold, this will need to be done after the other pieces have been cut and the fabric can be refolded.

Layout for fabrics with a nap or a one-way design

If your fabric needs to be cut out with a nap, all the pattern pieces need to be placed so the nap will run in the same direction in the made-up garment.

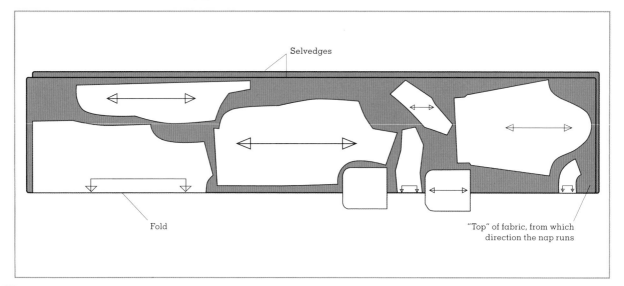

Selvedges

Fold

"Top" of fabric, from which direction the nap runs

Tools and techniques

Stripes and checks

For fabrics with a stripe or check pattern, a little more care is needed when laying out the pattern pieces. If the checks and stripes are running across or down the length of the fabric when cutting out, they will run the same direction in the finished garment. So it is important to place the pattern pieces to ensure that the checks and stripes match and that they run together at the seams. If possible, try to place the pattern pieces so each has a stripe down the centre. With a checked fabric, be aware of the hemline placement on the pattern.

EVEN AND UNEVEN STRIPES

 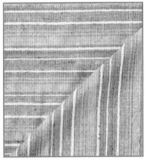

Even stripes When a corner of the fabric is folded back diagonally, the stripes will meet up at the fold.

Uneven stripes When a corner of the fabric is folded back diagonally, the stripes will not match at the fold.

EVEN AND UNEVEN CHECKS

Even checks When a corner of the fabric is folded back diagonally, the checks will be symmetrical on both of the fabric areas.

Uneven checks When a corner of the fabric is folded back diagonally, the checks will be uneven lengthways, widthways, or both.

MATCHING STRIPES OR CHECKS ON A SKIRT

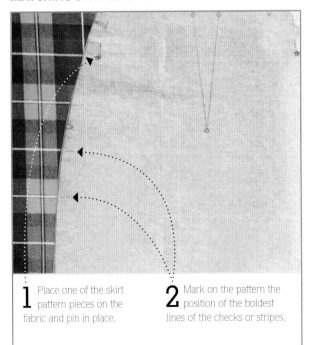

1 Place one of the skirt pattern pieces on the fabric and pin in place.

2 Mark on the pattern the position of the boldest lines of the checks or stripes.

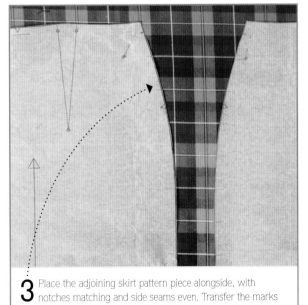

3 Place the adjoining skirt pattern piece alongside, with notches matching and side seams even. Transfer the marks to the second pattern piece and slide it across, matching up the bold lines. Pin in place.

MATCHING STRIPES OR CHECKS AT THE SHOULDER

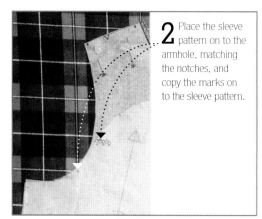

1 Mark the boldest lines of the stripes or checks around the armhole on the front bodice pattern.

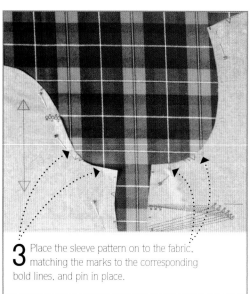

2 Place the sleeve pattern on to the armhole, matching the notches, and copy the marks on to the sleeve pattern.

3 Place the sleeve pattern on to the fabric, matching the marks to the corresponding bold lines, and pin in place.

LAYOUT FOR EVEN CHECKS ON FOLDED FABRIC

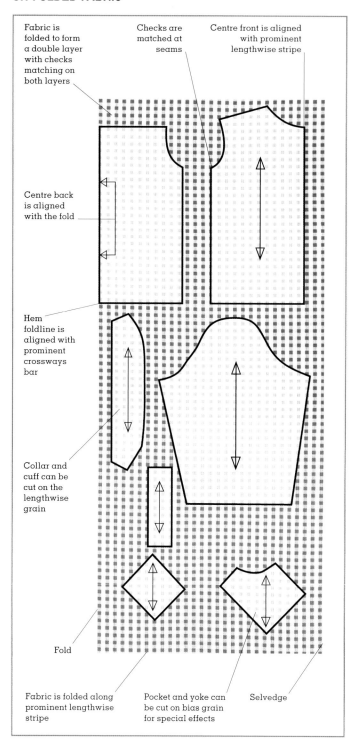

Fabric is folded to form a double layer with checks matching on both layers

Checks are matched at seams

Centre front is aligned with prominent lengthwise stripe

Centre back is aligned with the fold

Hem foldline is aligned with prominent crossways bar

Collar and cuff can be cut on the lengthwise grain

Fold

Fabric is folded along prominent lengthwise stripe

Pocket and yoke can be cut on bias grain for special effects

Selvedge

LAYOUT FOR EVEN STRIPES ON FOLDED FABRIC

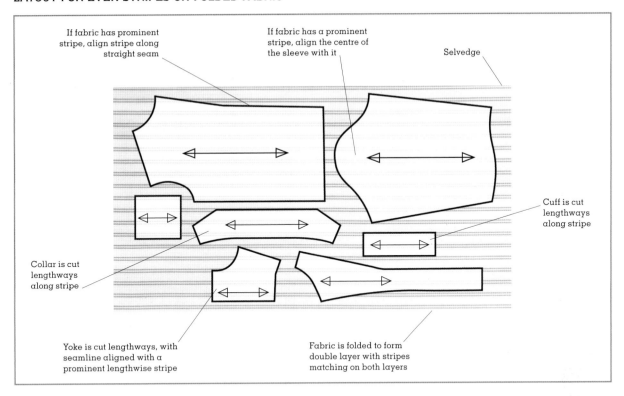

If fabric has prominent stripe, align stripe along straight seam

If fabric has a prominent stripe, align the centre of the sleeve with it

Selvedge

Cuff is cut lengthways along stripe

Collar is cut lengthways along stripe

Yoke is cut lengthways, with seamline aligned with a prominent lengthwise stripe

Fabric is folded to form double layer with stripes matching on both layers

LAYOUT FOR UNEVEN CHECKS OR STRIPES ON UNFOLDED FABRIC

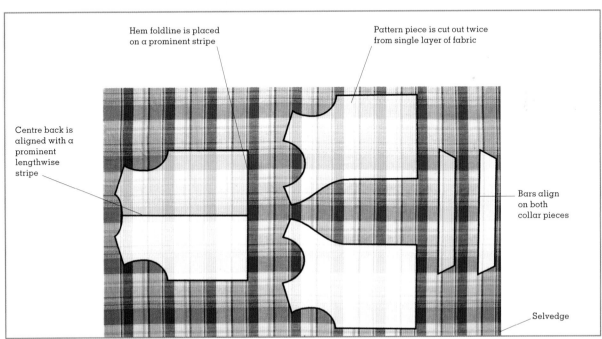

Hem foldline is placed on a prominent stripe

Pattern piece is cut out twice from single layer of fabric

Centre back is aligned with a prominent lengthwise stripe

Bars align on both collar pieces

Selvedge

Cutting out **25**

Cutting out accurately

Careful, smooth cutting around the pattern pieces will ensure that they join together accurately. Always cut out on a smooth, flat surface such as a table – the floor is not ideal – and be sure your scissors are sharp. Use the full blade of the scissors on long, straight edges, sliding the blades along the fabric; use smaller cuts around curves. Do not nibble or snip at the fabric.

HOW TO CUT

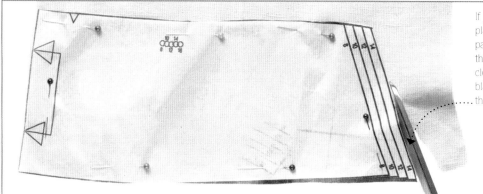

If you are right-handed, place your left hand on the pattern and fabric to hold them in place, and cut cleanly with the scissor blades at a right angle to the fabric.

MARKING NOTCHES

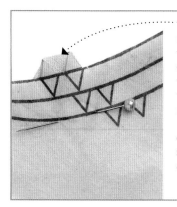

These symbols need to be marked on to the fabric as they are matching points. One of the easiest ways to do this is to cut out the mirror image of the notches in the fabric. Rather than cutting out double or triple notches separately, cut straight across from point to point.

MARKING DOTS

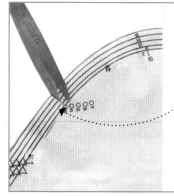

You can cut a small clip into the fabric to mark the dots that indicate the top of the shoulder on a sleeve. Alternatively, these can be marked with tailor's tacks (see opposite).

CLIPPING LINES

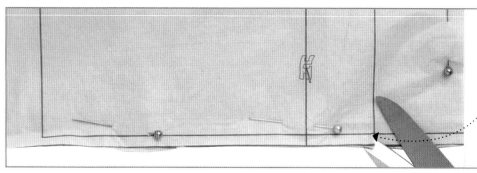

A small clip or snip into the fabric is a useful way to mark some of the lines that appear on a pattern, such as the centre front line and foldlines or notches and dart ends.

Pattern marking

Once the pattern pieces have been cut out, but before you remove the pattern, you will need to mark the symbols shown on the pattern through to the fabric. There are various ways to do this. Tailor's tacks are good for circles and dots, or these can be marked with a water or air-soluble pen. When using a pen, it's a good idea to test it on a piece of scrap fabric first. For lines, you can use trace tacks or a tracing wheel with dressmaker's carbon paper.

TRACE TACKS

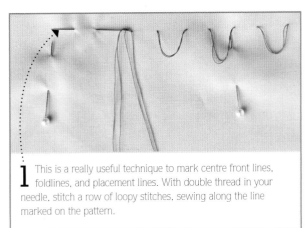

1 This is a really useful technique to mark centre front lines, foldlines, and placement lines. With double thread in your needle, stitch a row of loopy stitches, sewing along the line marked on the pattern.

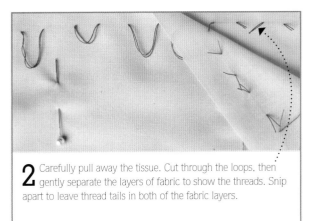

2 Carefully pull away the tissue. Cut through the loops, then gently separate the layers of fabric to show the threads. Snip apart to leave thread tails in both of the fabric layers.

TAILOR'S TACKS

1 As there are often dots of different sizes on the pattern, choose a different colour thread for each dot size. It is then easy to match the colours as well as the dots. Have double thread in your needle, unknotted. Insert the needle through the dot from right to left, leaving a tail of thread. Be sure to go through the pattern and both layers of fabric.

2 Now stitch through the dot again, this time from top to bottom to make a loop. Cut through the loop, then snip off excess thread to leave a tail.

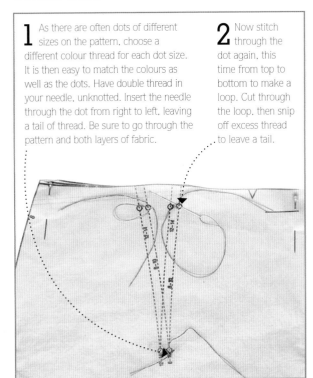

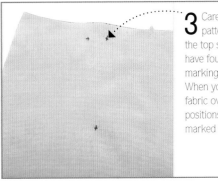

3 Carefully pull the pattern away. On the top side you will have four threads marking each dot. When you turn the fabric over, the dot positions will be marked with an X.

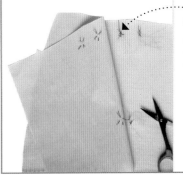

4 Gently turn back the two layers of fabric to separate them, then cut through the threads so that thread tails are left in both pieces of fabric.

DRESSMAKER'S CARBON PAPER AND WHEEL

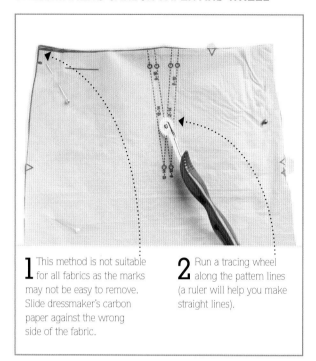

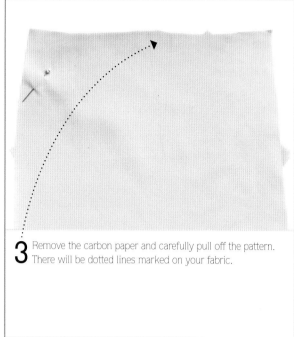

1 This method is not suitable for all fabrics as the marks may not be easy to remove. Slide dressmaker's carbon paper against the wrong side of the fabric.

2 Run a tracing wheel along the pattern lines (a ruler will help you make straight lines).

3 Remove the carbon paper and carefully pull off the pattern. There will be dotted lines marked on your fabric.

MARKER PENS

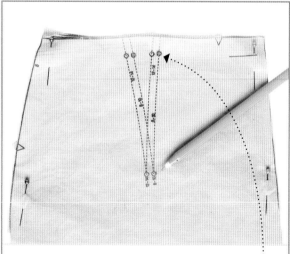

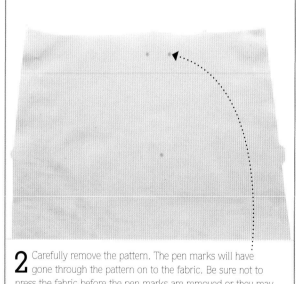

1 This method can only be used with a single layer of fabric. Press the point of the pen into the centre of the dot marked on the pattern.

2 Carefully remove the pattern. The pen marks will have gone through the pattern on to the fabric. Be sure not to press the fabric before the pen marks are removed or they may become permanent.

Stitches for hand sewing

Although modern sewing machines have eliminated the need for a lot of hand sewing, it is still necessary to use hand stitching to prepare the fabric prior to permanent stitching – these temporary pattern-marking and tacking stitches will eventually be removed. Permanent hand stitching is used to finish a garment and to attach fasteners, as well as to help out with a quick repair.

Securing the thread

The ends of the thread must be secured firmly. A knot is frequently used and is the preferred choice for temporary stitches. For permanent stitching a double stitch is a better option.

DOUBLE STITCH

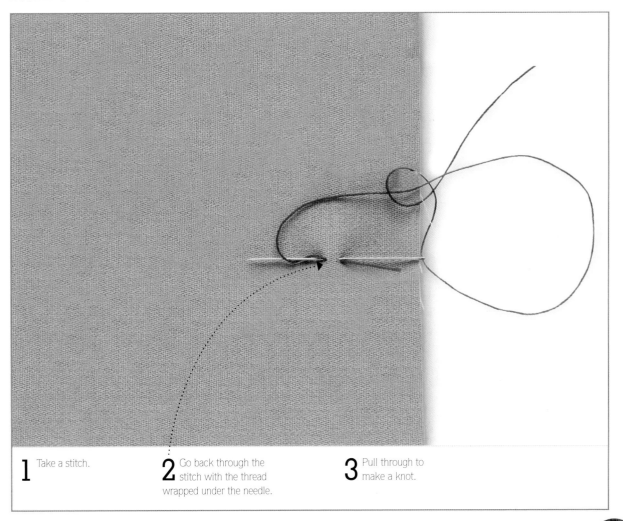

1 Take a stitch.

2 Go back through the stitch with the thread wrapped under the needle.

3 Pull through to make a knot.

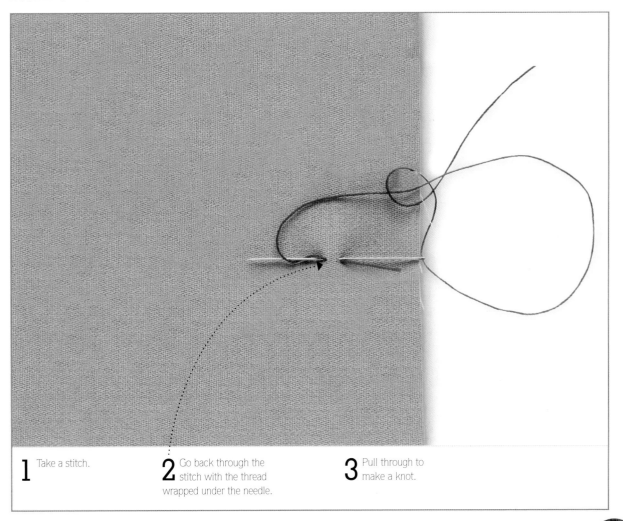

BACK STITCH

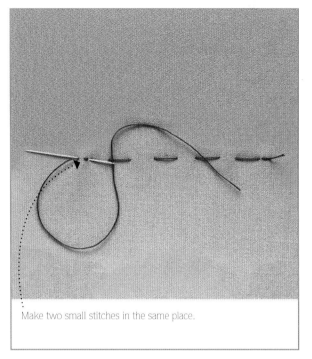

Make two small stitches in the same place.

LOCKING STITCH

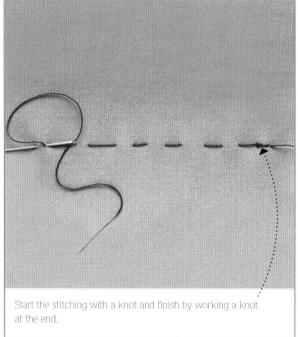

Start the stitching with a knot and finish by working a knot at the end.

Tacking stitches

Each of the many types of tacking stitches has its own individual use. Basic tacks hold two or more pieces of fabric together. Long and short tacks are an alternative version of the basic tacking stitch, often used when the tacking will stay in the work for some time.

BASIC TACKS

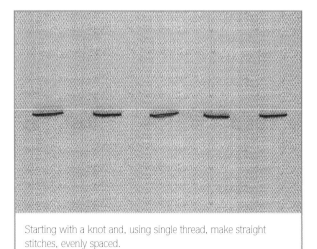

Starting with a knot and, using single thread, make straight stitches, evenly spaced.

LONG AND SHORT TACKS

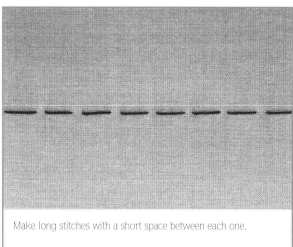

Make long stitches with a short space between each one.

Hem stitches

There are various hand stitches that can be used to hold a hem in place. Whichever of these you choose, ensure the stitches do not show on the right side.

FLAT FELL STITCH

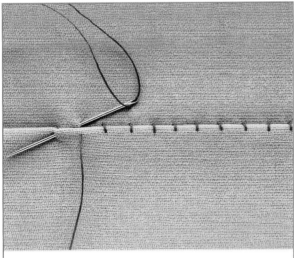

A strong, secure stitch to hold two layers permanently together. As well as being used for hems, this stitch is often used to secure bias bindings and linings. Work from right to left. Make a short, straight stitch at the edge of the fabric.

BLIND HEM STITCH

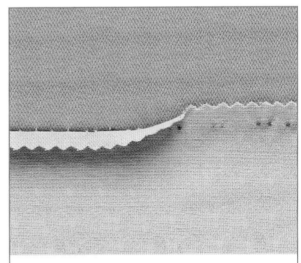

This stitch gives a very discreet finish to a hem. Working from right to left, fold the top edge of the fabric down and use a slip hem stitch (below left).

SLIP HEM STITCH

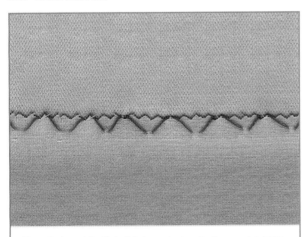

Also called a catch stitch, this is used primarily for securing hems. It looks similar to herringbone (right). Work from right to left. Take a short horizontal stitch into one layer and then the other.

HERRINGBONE STITCH

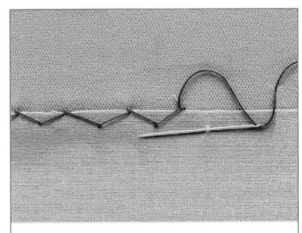

A very useful stitch as it is secure yet has some movement in it. It is used to secure hems and interlinings. Work from left to right. Take a small horizontal stitch into one layer and then the other, so the thread crosses itself.

Machine stitches and seams

When making a garment, fabric is joined together using seams. The most common seam is a plain seam, which is suitable for a wide variety of fabrics and garments. However, there are many other seams to be used as appropriate, depending on the fabric and garment being constructed.

Securing the thread

Machine stitches need to be secured at the end of a seam to prevent them from coming undone. This can be done by hand, tying the ends of the thread, or using the machine with a reverse stitch or a locking stitch, which stitches three or four stitches in the same place.

TIE THE ENDS

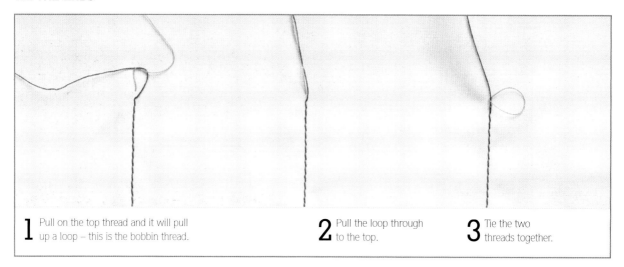

1 Pull on the top thread and it will pull up a loop – this is the bobbin thread.

2 Pull the loop through to the top.

3 Tie the two threads together.

REVERSE STITCH

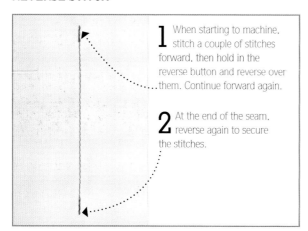

1 When starting to machine, stitch a couple of stitches forward, then hold in the reverse button and reverse over them. Continue forward again.

2 At the end of the seam, reverse again to secure the stitches.

LOCKING STITCH

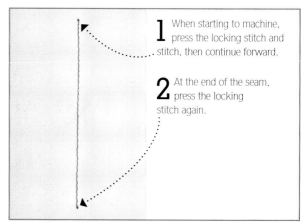

1 When starting to machine, press the locking stitch and stitch, then continue forward.

2 At the end of the seam, press the locking stitch again.

Plain seam

A plain seam is 1.5cm (⅝in) wide. It is important that the seam is stitched accurately at this measurement, otherwise the garment will end up being the wrong size and shape. There are guides on the plate of the sewing machine to help align the fabric correctly.

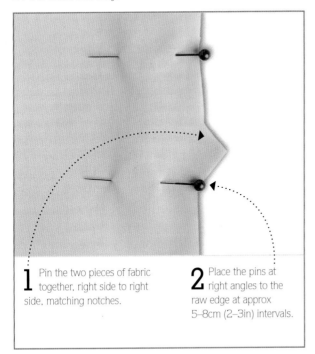

1 Pin the two pieces of fabric together, right side to right side, matching notches.

2 Place the pins at right angles to the raw edge at approx 5–8cm (2–3in) intervals.

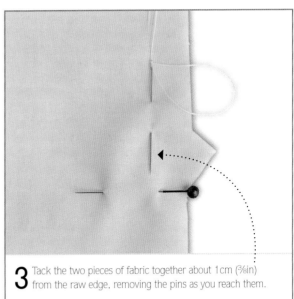

3 Tack the two pieces of fabric together about 1cm (⅜in) from the raw edge, removing the pins as you reach them.

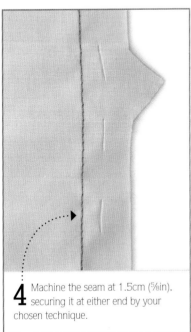

4 Machine the seam at 1.5cm (⅝in), securing it at either end by your chosen technique.

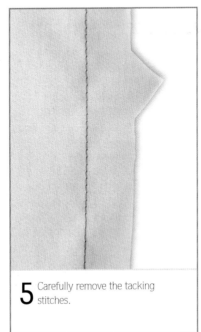

5 Carefully remove the tacking stitches.

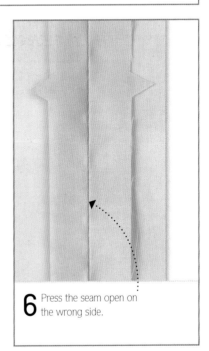

6 Press the seam open on the wrong side.

Seam neatening

It is important that the raw edges of the seam are neatened or finished – this will make the seam hard-wearing and prevent fraying. The method of neatening will depend on the style of garment that is being made and the fabric you are using.

PINKED

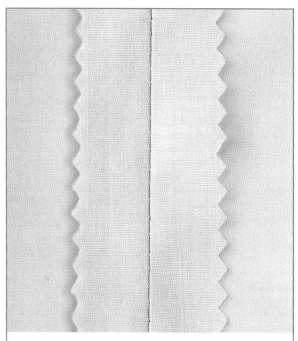

This method of neatening is ideal for fabrics that do not fray badly. Using pinking shears, trim as little as possible off the raw edge.

ZIGZAGGED

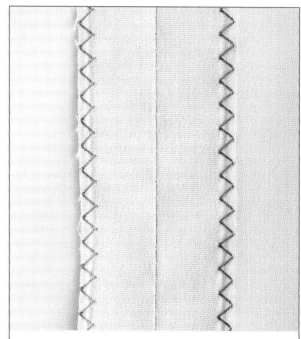

All sewing machines will make a zigzag stitch. It is an ideal stitch for stopping the edges fraying and is suitable for all types of fabric. Stitch in from the raw edge, then trim back to the zigzag stitch. Use a stitch width of 2.0 and a stitch length of 1.5.

3-THREAD OVERLOCK STITCH

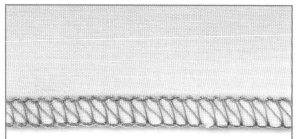

Stitched using three threads on the overlocker. Used to neaten the edge of fabric to prevent fraying.

4-THREAD OVERLOCK STITCH

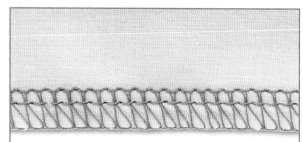

Made using four threads on the overlocker. Used to neaten edges on difficult fabrics or to construct a seam on stretch knits.

Hong Kong finish

This is a great finish to use to neaten the seams on unlined jackets made from wool or linen. It is made by wrapping the raw edge with bias-cut strips.

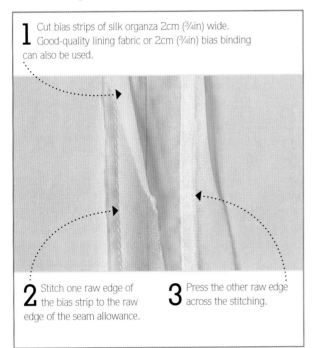

1 Cut bias strips of silk organza 2cm (¾in) wide. Good-quality lining fabric or 2cm (¾in) bias binding can also be used.

2 Stitch one raw edge of the bias strip to the raw edge of the seam allowance.

3 Press the other raw edge across the stitching.

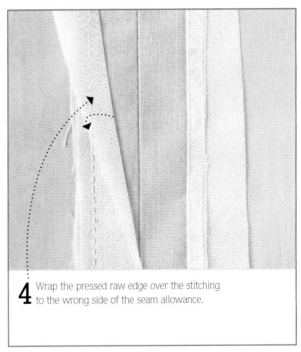

4 Wrap the pressed raw edge over the stitching to the wrong side of the seam allowance.

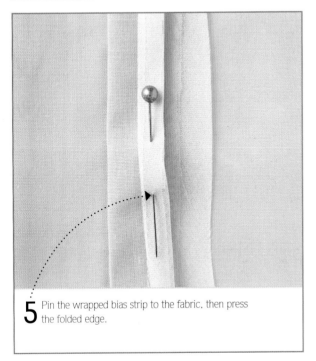

5 Pin the wrapped bias strip to the fabric, then press the folded edge.

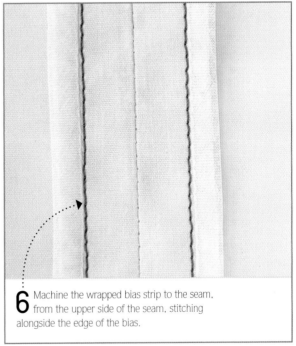

6 Machine the wrapped bias strip to the seam, from the upper side of the seam, stitching alongside the edge of the bias.

A seam for sheer fabrics

Sheer fabrics require specialist care for seam construction because they are very soft and delicate. The seam shown below is very narrow when finished and presses very flat so is less visible on sheer fabrics.

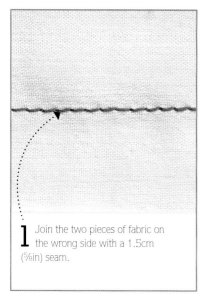

1 Join the two pieces of fabric on the wrong side with a 1.5cm (⅝in) seam.

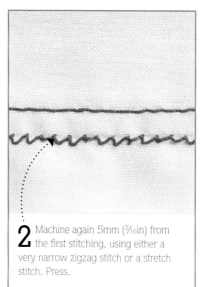

2 Machine again 5mm (³⁄₁₆in) from the first stitching, using either a very narrow zigzag stitch or a stretch stitch. Press.

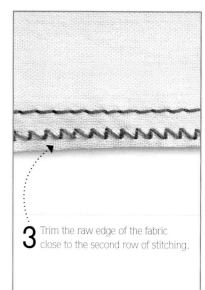

3 Trim the raw edge of the fabric close to the second row of stitching.

Stitching corners

Not all sewing is straight lines. The work will have corners that require negotiation to produce sharp clean angles. The technique for stitching a corner shown below applies to corners of all angles. On a thick fabric, the technique is slightly different, with a stitch taken across the corner.

STITCHING A CORNER

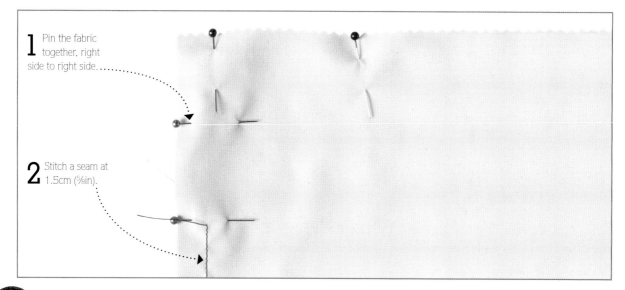

1 Pin the fabric together, right side to right side.

2 Stitch a seam at 1.5cm (⅝in).

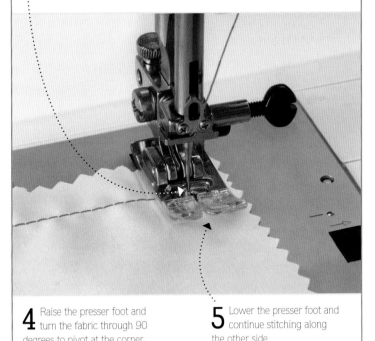

3 On reaching the corner, insert the machine needle into the fabric.

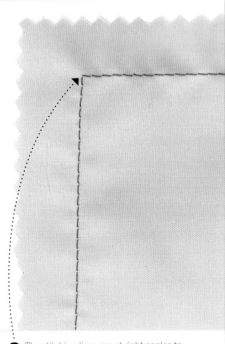

4 Raise the presser foot and turn the fabric through 90 degrees to pivot at the corner.

5 Lower the presser foot and continue stitching along the other side.

6 The stitching lines are at right angles to each other, which means the finished corner will have a sharp point when turned through to the right side.

STITCHING A CORNER ON HEAVY FABRIC

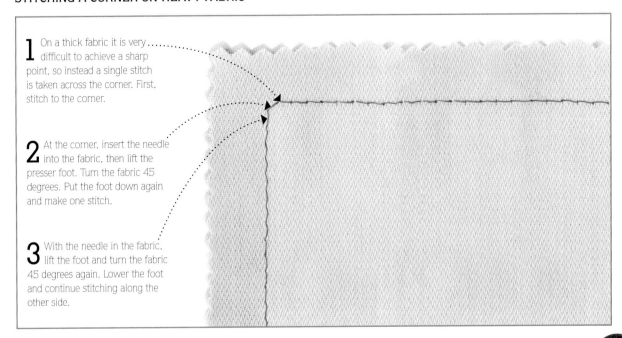

1 On a thick fabric it is very difficult to achieve a sharp point, so instead a single stitch is taken across the corner. First, stitch to the corner.

2 At the corner, insert the needle into the fabric, then lift the presser foot. Turn the fabric 45 degrees. Put the foot down again and make one stitch.

3 With the needle in the fabric, lift the foot and turn the fabric 45 degrees again. Lower the foot and continue stitching along the other side.

Reducing seam bulk

It is important that the seams used for construction do not cause bulk on the right side. To make sure this does not happen, the seam allowances need to be reduced in size by a technique known as layering a seam. They may also require V shapes to be removed, which is known as notching, or the seam allowance may be clipped.

Layering a seam

On the majority of fabrics, if the seam is on the edge of the work, the amount of fabric in the seam needs reducing. Leave the seam allowance that lies closest to the outside of the garment full width, but reduce the seam allowance that lies closest to the body.

Cut along one side of the seam allowance to reduce the fabric in the seam allowance by half to one-third of its original width.

Reducing seam bulk on an inner curve

For an inner curve to lie flat, the seam will need to be layered and notched, then understitched to hold it in place (see p.39).

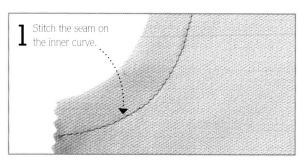

1 Stitch the seam on the inner curve.

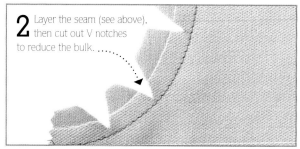

2 Layer the seam (see above), then cut out V notches to reduce the bulk.

3 Turn to the right side and press.

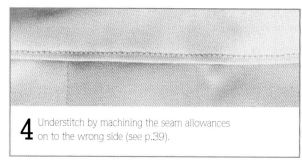

4 Understitch by machining the seam allowances on to the wrong side (see p.39).

Reducing seam bulk on an outer curve

An outer curve also needs layering and notching or clipping to allow the seam to be turned to the right side, after which it is understitched.

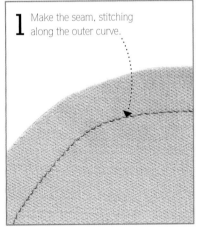

1 Make the seam, stitching along the outer curve.

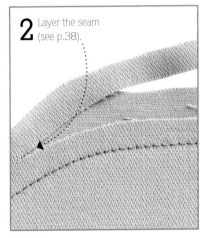

2 Layer the seam (see p.38).

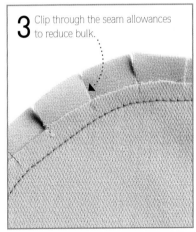

3 Clip through the seam allowances to reduce bulk.

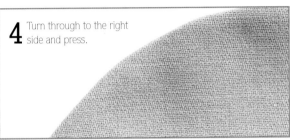

4 Turn through to the right side and press.

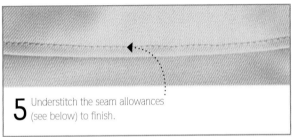

5 Understitch the seam allowances (see below) to finish.

Finishing edges

Topstitching and understitching are two methods to finish edges. Topstitching is meant to be seen on the right side of the work, whereas understitching is not visible from the right side.

TOPSTITCHING

A topstitch is a decorative, sharp finish to an edge. Use a longer stitch length, of 3.0 or 3.5, and machine on the right side of the work, using the edge of the machine foot as a guide.

UNDERSTITCHING

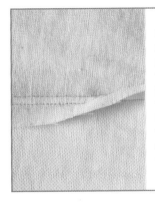

Understitching is used to secure a seam that is on the edge of a piece of fabric. It helps to stop the seam from rolling to the right side. First make the seam, then layer (see p.38), turn to the right side and press. Working from the right side, machine the seam allowance to the facing or to the lining side of the fabric.

Darts

A dart is used to give shape to a piece of fabric so that it can fit around the contours of the body. Some darts are stitched following straight stitching lines and other darts are stitched following a slightly curved line. Always stitch a dart from the point to the wide end as then you will be able to sink the machine needle into the point accurately and securely.

Plain dart

This is the most common type of dart and is used to give shaping to the bust in the bodice. It is also found at the waist in skirts and trousers to give shape from the waist to the hip.

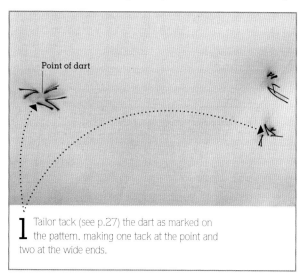

Point of dart

1 Tailor tack (see p.27) the dart as marked on the pattern, making one tack at the point and two at the wide ends.

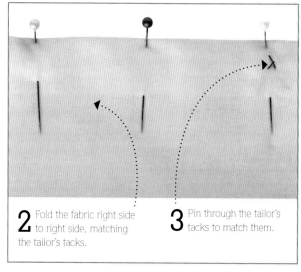

2 Fold the fabric right side to right side, matching the tailor's tacks.

3 Pin through the tailor's tacks to match them.

4 Tack along the dart line, joining the tailor's tacks. Remove the pins.

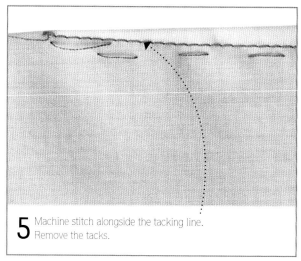

5 Machine stitch alongside the tacking line. Remove the tacks.

6 Sew the machine threads back into the stitching line of the dart to secure them.

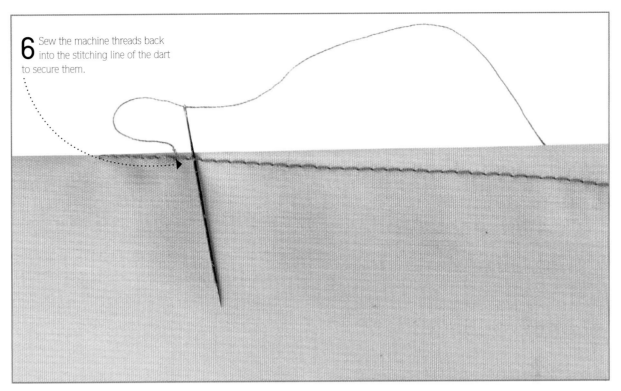

7 Press the dart to one side (see p.43).

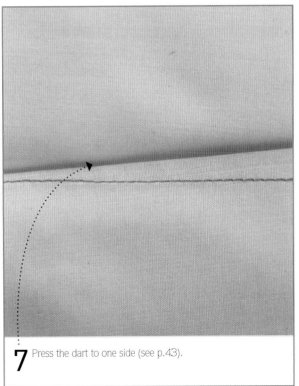

8 The finished dart on the right side.

Shaping darts to fit

Our bodies have curves, and the straight line of the dart may not sit closely enough to our own personal shape. The dart can be stitched slightly concave or convex so it follows our contours. Do not curve the dart by more than 3mm (⅛in) from the straight line.

CONVEX DART

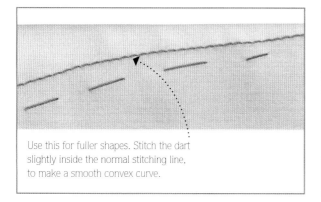

Use this for fuller shapes. Stitch the dart slightly inside the normal stitching line, to make a smooth convex curve.

CONCAVE DART

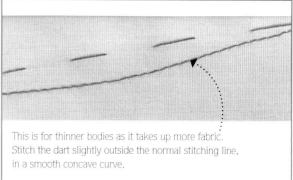

This is for thinner bodies as it takes up more fabric. Stitch the dart slightly outside the normal stitching line, in a smooth concave curve.

Contour or double-pointed dart

This type of dart is like two darts joined together at their wide ends. It is used to give shape at the waist of a dress. It will contour the fabric from the bust into the waist and then from the waist out towards the hip.

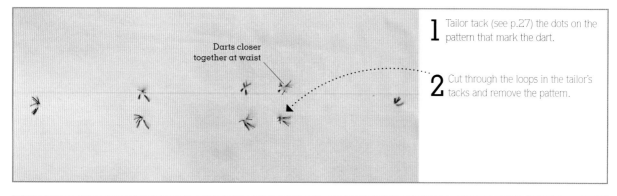

Darts closer together at waist

1 Tailor tack (see p.27) the dots on the pattern that mark the dart.

2 Cut through the loops in the tailor's tacks and remove the pattern.

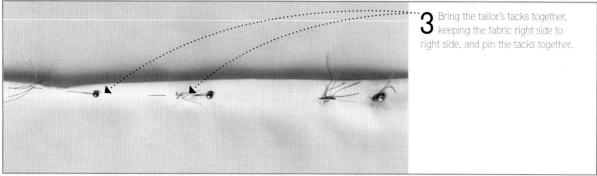

3 Bring the tailor's tacks together, keeping the fabric right side to right side, and pin the tacks together.

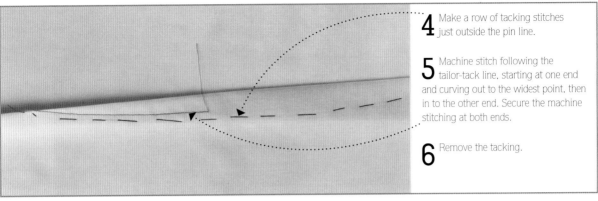

4 Make a row of tacking stitches just outside the pin line.

5 Machine stitch following the tailor-tack line, starting at one end and curving out to the widest point, then in to the other end. Secure the machine stitching at both ends.

6 Remove the tacking.

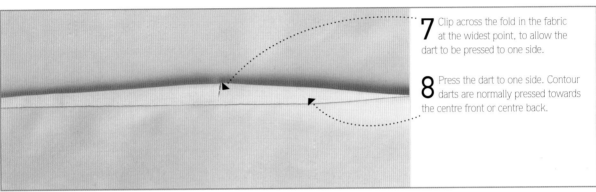

7 Clip across the fold in the fabric at the widest point, to allow the dart to be pressed to one side.

8 Press the dart to one side. Contour darts are normally pressed towards the centre front or centre back.

Pressing a dart

If a dart is pressed incorrectly it can spoil the look of a garment. For successful pressing you will need a tailor's ham and a steam iron on a steam setting. A pressing cloth may be required for delicate fabrics such as silk, satin, and chiffon, and for lining fabrics.

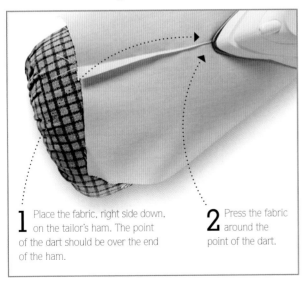

1 Place the fabric, right side down, on the tailor's ham. The point of the dart should be over the end of the ham.

2 Press the fabric around the point of the dart.

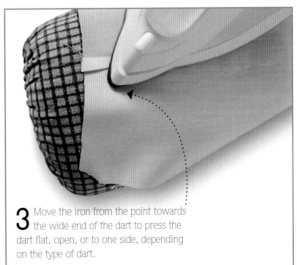

3 Move the iron from the point towards the wide end of the dart to press the dart flat, open, or to one side, depending on the type of dart.

Gathers

Gathers are an easy way to draw up a piece of larger fabric so that it will fit on to a smaller piece of fabric. They often appear at waistlines or yoke lines. The gather stitch is inserted after the major seams have been constructed. Gathers are best worked on the sewing machine using the longest available stitch length. On the majority of fabrics, two rows of gather stitches are required, but for very heavy fabrics it is advisable to have three rows. Try to stitch the rows so that the stitches line up under one another.

Making and fitting gathers

Once all the main seams have been sewn, stitch the two rows of gathers so that the stitches are inside the seam allowance. This should avoid the need to remove them because doing so after they have been pulled up can damage the fabric. In the example below, we attach a skirt to a bodice.

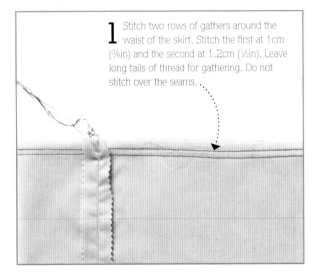

1 Stitch two rows of gathers around the waist of the skirt. Stitch the first at 1cm (⅜in) and the second at 1.2cm (½in). Leave long tails of thread for gathering. Do not stitch over the seams.

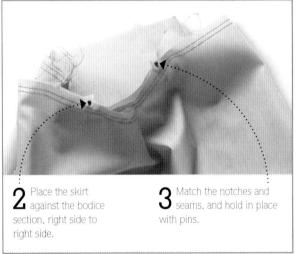

2 Place the skirt against the bodice section, right side to right side.

3 Match the notches and seams, and hold in place with pins.

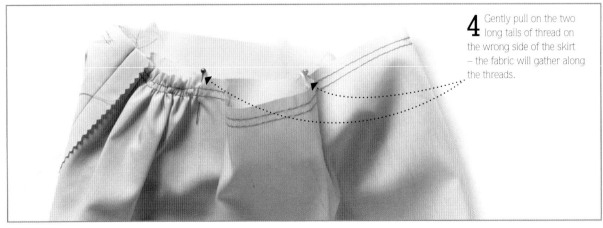

4 Gently pull on the two long tails of thread on the wrong side of the skirt – the fabric will gather along the threads.

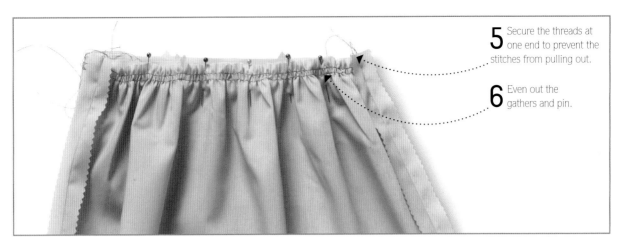

5 Secure the threads at one end to prevent the stitches from pulling out.

6 Even out the gathers and pin.

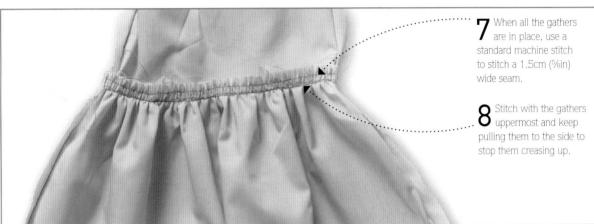

7 When all the gathers are in place, use a standard machine stitch to stitch a 1.5cm (⅝in) wide seam.

8 Stitch with the gathers uppermost and keep pulling them to the side to stop them creasing up.

9 Turn the bodice of the garment inside. Press the seam very carefully to avoid creasing the gathers.

10 Neaten the seam by stitching both edges together. Use either a zigzag stitch or a 3-thread overlock stitch.

11 Press the seam up towards the bodice.

Interfacings

An interfacing may be non-fusible (sew-in) or fusible and is only attached to certain parts of a garment. Parts that are normally interfaced include the collar, cuffs, facings, and waistbands.

Non-fusible interfacings

All of these interfacings need to be tacked to the main fabric around the edges prior to construction of the work or seam neatening.

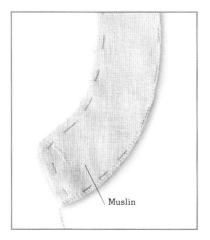

Muslin

Silk organza

Non-woven interfacing

Fusible interfacings

A fusible interfacing is used in the same areas as a sew-in interfacing. To prevent the fusible interfacing from showing on the right side of the work, use pinking shears on the edge of the interfacing.

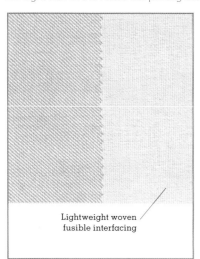

Lightweight woven fusible interfacing

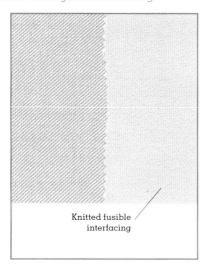

Knitted fusible interfacing

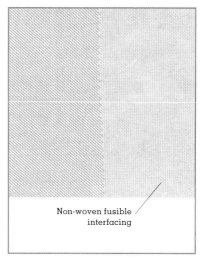

Non-woven fusible interfacing

How to apply a non-fusible interfacing

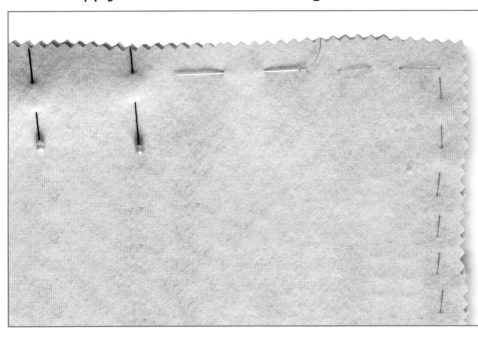

1 Place the interfacing on the wrong side of the fabric, aligning the cut edges. Pin in place.

2 Using a basic tacking stitch, tack the interfacing to the fabric or facing at 1cm (⅜in) within the seam allowance.

How to apply a fusible interfacing

1 Place the fabric on the pressing surface, wrong side up, making sure it is straight and not wrinkled.

2 Place the sticky side (this feels gritty) of the chosen interfacing on the fabric.

3 Cover with a dry pressing cloth and spray the cloth with a fine mist of water.

4 Place a steam iron, on a steam setting, on top of the pressing cloth.

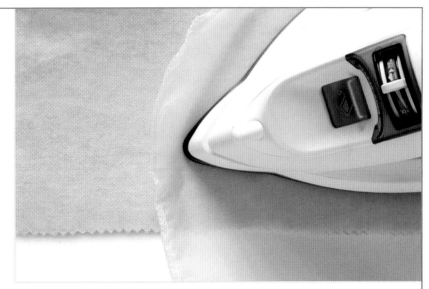

5 Leave the iron in place for at least 10 seconds before moving it to the next area of fabric.

6 Check to see if the interfacing is fused to the fabric by rolling the fabric. If the interfacing is still loose in places, repeat the pressing process.

7 When the fabric has cooled down, the fusing process will be complete. Then pin the pattern back on to the fabric and transfer the pattern markings as required.

Facings

The simplest way to finish the neck or armhole of a garment is to apply a facing. The neckline can be any shape to have a facing applied, from a curve to a square to a V, and many more. Some facings and necklines can add interest to the centre back or centre front of a garment.

Applying interfacing to a facing

All facings require interfacing. The interfacing is to give structure to the facing and to hold it in shape. A fusible interfacing is the best choice and should be cut on the same grain as the facing. Choose an interfacing that is lighter in weight than the main fabric.

INTERFACING FOR HEAVY FABRIC

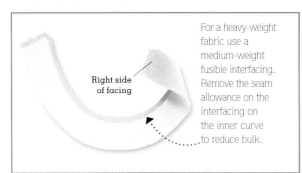

Right side of facing

For a heavy-weight fabric use a medium-weight fusible interfacing. Remove the seam allowance on the interfacing on the inner curve to reduce bulk.

INTERFACING FOR LIGHT FABRIC

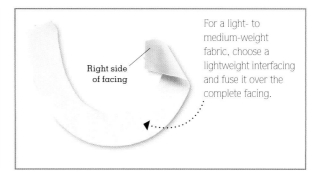

Right side of facing

For a light- to medium-weight fabric, choose a lightweight interfacing and fuse it over the complete facing.

Construction of a facing

The facing may be in two or three pieces in order to fit around a neck or armhole edge. The facing sections need to be joined together prior to being attached. The photographs here show an interfaced neck facing in three pieces.

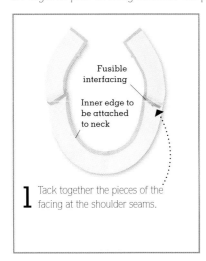

Fusible interfacing

Inner edge to be attached to neck

1 Tack together the pieces of the facing at the shoulder seams.

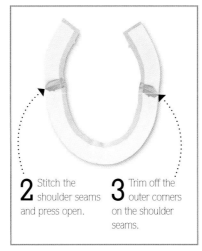

2 Stitch the shoulder seams and press open.

3 Trim off the outer corners on the shoulder seams.

4 The right side of the facing, ready to attach to the neckline.

Neatening the edge of a facing

The following techniques are popular ways to neaten the edge of a facing. The one you choose depends upon the garment being made and the fabric used.

OVERLOCKED

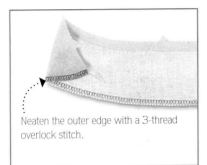

Neaten the outer edge with a 3-thread overlock stitch.

ZIGZAGGED

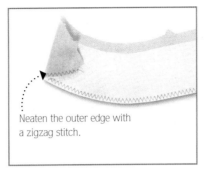

Neaten the outer edge with a zigzag stitch.

PINKED

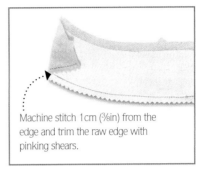

Machine stitch 1cm (⅜in) from the edge and trim the raw edge with pinking shears.

Bias strips

Bias strips are cut on the diagonal grain of the fabric. They have many uses in dressmaking. You can finish a slashed neck or a cuff opening with a bias strip or – for a designer touch inside a garment – use a bias strip to neaten the lower edge of a facing.

CUTTING BIAS STRIPS

1 Fold the fabric on to itself at 45 degrees so the selvedge edges are at right angles to each other. Pin in place.

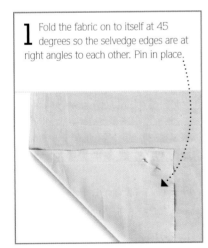

2 Using tailor's chalk and a ruler, mark lines 4cm (1½in) apart. Cut along these lines to make bias strips.

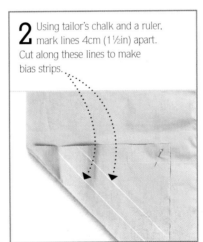

3 Join the strips by placing them together right side to right side at 90 degrees to each other.

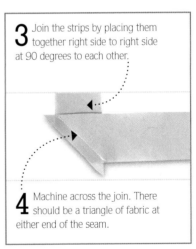

4 Machine across the join. There should be a triangle of fabric at either end of the seam.

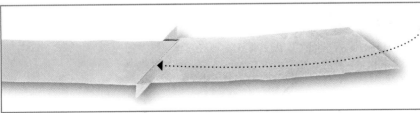

5 Press the seam open. Press under the edges of the bias strip with the iron by running the bias strip through a 25mm (1in) tape maker.

Attaching a neck facing

This technique for attaching a neck facing applies to all shapes of neckline, from round to square to sweetheart.

1 Apply fusible interfacing to the facing and join the three pieces at the shoulder seams (see p.48).

2 Lay the neckline area flat, right side up. Place the facing on top, right side to right side.

3 Match the shoulder seams.

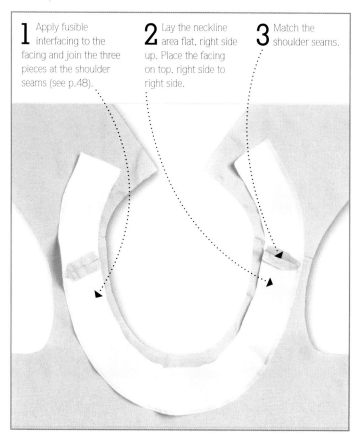

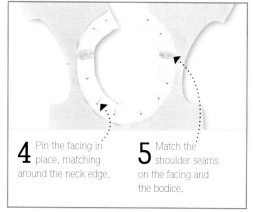

4 Pin the facing in place, matching around the neck edge.

5 Match the shoulder seams on the facing and the bodice.

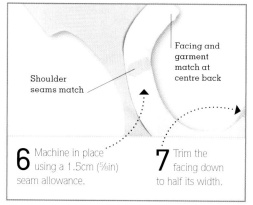

Shoulder seams match

Facing and garment match at centre back

6 Machine in place using a 1.5cm (⅝in) seam allowance.

7 Trim the facing down to half its width.

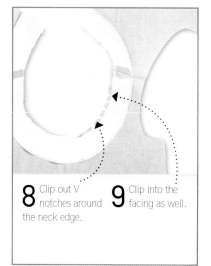

8 Clip out V notches around the neck edge.

9 Clip into the facing as well.

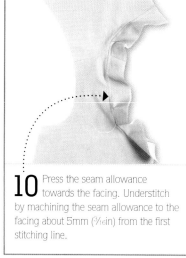

10 Press the seam allowance towards the facing. Understitch by machining the seam allowance to the facing about 5mm (³⁄₁₆in) from the first stitching line.

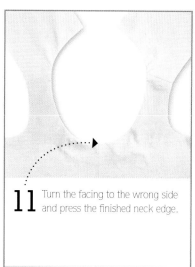

11 Turn the facing to the wrong side and press the finished neck edge.

Attaching a waist facing

Many waistlines on skirts and trousers are finished with a facing, which will follow the contours of the waist but will have had the dart shaping removed to make the facing smooth. A faced waistline always sits comfortably to the body. The facing is attached after all the main sections of the skirt or trousers have been constructed.

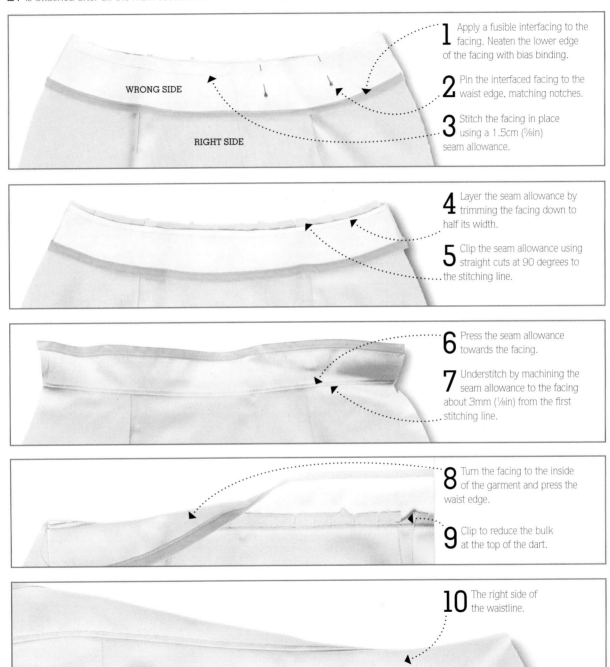

1 Apply a fusible interfacing to the facing. Neaten the lower edge of the facing with bias binding.

2 Pin the interfaced facing to the waist edge, matching notches.

3 Stitch the facing in place using a 1.5cm (⅝in) seam allowance.

4 Layer the seam allowance by trimming the facing down to half its width.

5 Clip the seam allowance using straight cuts at 90 degrees to the stitching line.

6 Press the seam allowance towards the facing.

7 Understitch by machining the seam allowance to the facing about 3mm (⅛in) from the first stitching line.

8 Turn the facing to the inside of the garment and press the waist edge.

9 Clip to reduce the bulk at the top of the dart.

10 The right side of the waistline.

WRONG SIDE

RIGHT SIDE

Waistbands

A waistband is designed to fit snugly but not tight to the waist. Whether it is shaped, straight, or slightly curved, it will be constructed and attached in a similar way. Every waistband will require a fusible interfacing (see p.47) to give it structure and support.

Finishing the edge of the waistband

One long edge of the waistband will be stitched to the garment waist. The other edge will need to be finished, to prevent fraying and reduce bulk inside.

TURNING UNDER

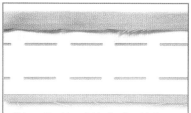

This method is suitable for fine fabrics only. Turn under 1.5cm (⅝in) along the edge of the waistband and press in place. After the waistband has been attached to the garment, hand stitch the pressed-under edge in place.

OVERLOCK STITCHING

This method is suitable for heavier fabrics as it lies flat inside the garment after construction. Neaten one long edge of the waistband with a 3-thread overlock stitch.

BIAS BINDING

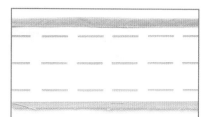

This method is ideal for fabrics that fray badly and can add a feature inside the garment. It lies flat inside the garment after construction. Apply a 2cm (¾in) bias binding to one long edge of the waistband.

Attaching a straight waistband

Special waistband interfacings are available, usually featuring slot lines that will guide you where to fold the fabric. Make sure the slots on the outer edge correspond to a 1.5cm (⅝in) seam allowance. If a specialist waistband fusible interfacing is not available, you can use any medium-weight fusible interfacing.

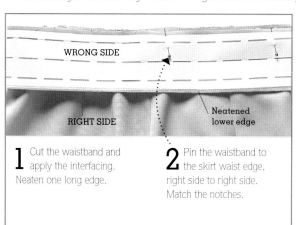

WRONG SIDE

RIGHT SIDE

Neatened lower edge

1 Cut the waistband and apply the interfacing. Neaten one long edge.

2 Pin the waistband to the skirt waist edge, right side to right side. Match the notches.

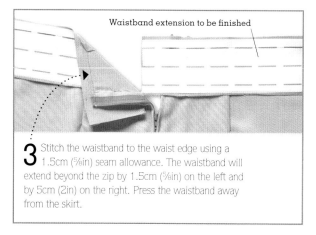

Waistband extension to be finished

3 Stitch the waistband to the waist edge using a 1.5cm (⅝in) seam allowance. The waistband will extend beyond the zip by 1.5cm (⅝in) on the left and by 5cm (2in) on the right. Press the waistband away from the skirt.

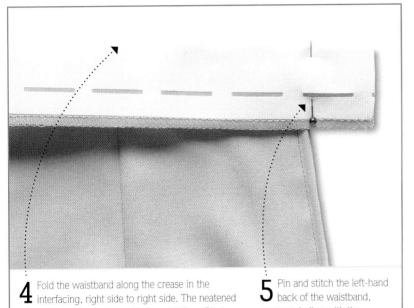

4 Fold the waistband along the crease in the interfacing, right side to right side. The neatened edge of the waistband should extend 1.5cm (⅝in) below the stitching line.

5 Pin and stitch the left-hand back of the waistband, as worn, in line with the centre back.

6 On the right-hand back, as worn, extend the waist/skirt stitching line along the waistband and pivot to stitch across the end.

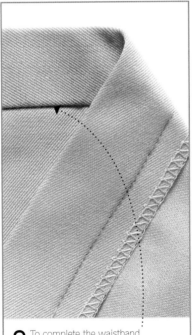

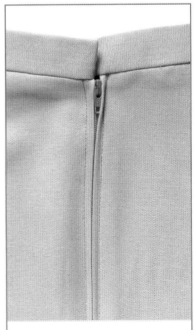

7 Turn the ends of the waistband to the right side. The extension on the waistband should be on the right-hand back. Add your chosen fasteners.

8 To complete the waistband, stitch through the band to the skirt seam. This is known as stitching in the ditch.

9 The finished straight waistband.

Sleeves

Sleeves come in all shapes and lengths, and form an important part of the design of a garment. A set-in sleeve should always hang from the end of the wearer's shoulder, without wrinkles. The lower end of the sleeve is normally finished by means of a hem, elastic, or a cuff.

Inserting a set-in sleeve

A set-in sleeve should feature a smooth sleeve head that fits on the end of your shoulder accurately. This is achieved by the use of ease stitches, which are long stitches used to tighten the fabric but not gather it.

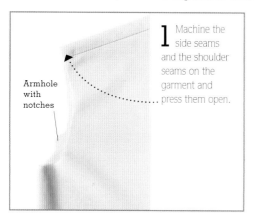

Armhole with notches

1 Machine the side seams and the shoulder seams on the garment and press them open.

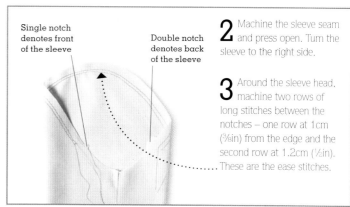

Single notch denotes front of the sleeve

Double notch denotes back of the sleeve

2 Machine the sleeve seam and press open. Turn the sleeve to the right side.

3 Around the sleeve head, machine two rows of long stitches between the notches – one row at 1cm (⅜in) from the edge and the second row at 1.2cm (½in). These are the ease stitches.

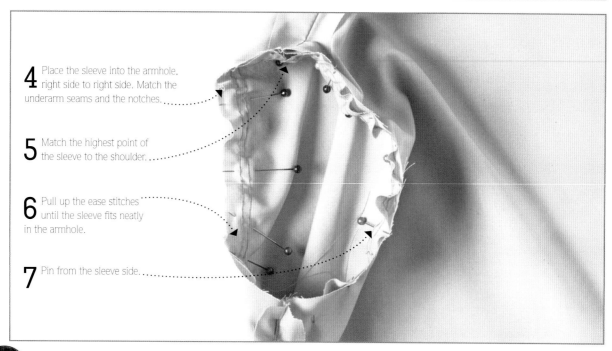

4 Place the sleeve into the armhole, right side to right side. Match the underarm seams and the notches.

5 Match the highest point of the sleeve to the shoulder.

6 Pull up the ease stitches until the sleeve fits neatly in the armhole.

7 Pin from the sleeve side.

8 Machine the sleeve in place, starting at the underarm seam and using a 1.5cm (⅝in) seam allowance. When you machine, have the sleeve on top and keep the machining straight over the shoulder.

9 Overlap the machining at the underarm to reinforce the stitching.

10 Stitch around the sleeve again inside the seam allowance.

11 Trim the raw edges of the sleeve.

Smooth sleeve head

RIGHT SIDE

12 Neaten the seam with a zigzag or overlock stitch, then turn the sleeve through the armhole. Do not press or you will flatten the sleeve head.

Sleeve hems

The simplest way to finish a sleeve is with a self hem. Here the edge of the sleeve is turned up onto itself. An alternative finish is to insert elastic into a casing.

SELF HEM

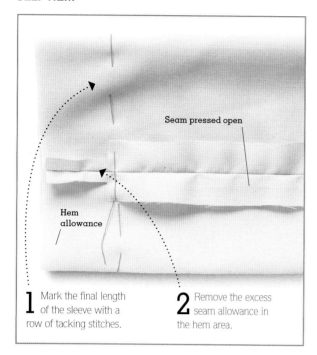

Seam pressed open

Hem allowance

1 Mark the final length of the sleeve with a row of tacking stitches.

2 Remove the excess seam allowance in the hem area.

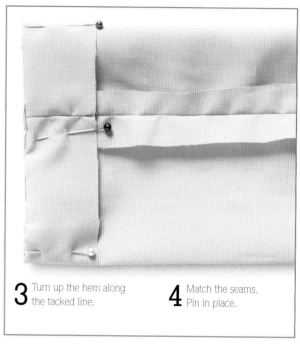

3 Turn up the hem along the tacked line.

4 Match the seams. Pin in place.

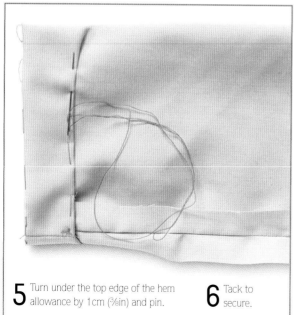

5 Turn under the top edge of the hem allowance by 1cm (⅜in) and pin.

6 Tack to secure.

Finished hem

7 Hand stitch the sleeve hem in place using a slip stitch.

ELASTICATED SLEEVE EDGE

1 Make up the sleeve and press the seam open.

2 Work a row of tacking stitches on the foldline of the hem.

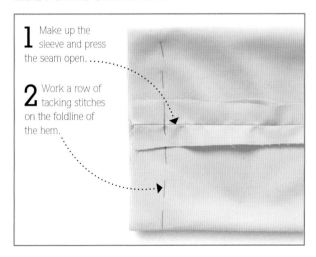

3 To make a double-turn hem, turn up 5mm (³⁄₁₆in) at the raw edge and press.

4 Turn again on to the tacking line.

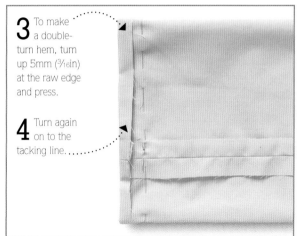

5 Machine to hold the hem in place, 2mm (¹⁄₁₆in) from the folded edge. Leave a gap either side of the seam allowance through which you will insert the elastic.

Gap to insert the elastic.

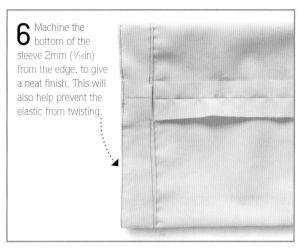

6 Machine the bottom of the sleeve 2mm (¹⁄₁₆in) from the edge, to give a neat finish. This will also help prevent the elastic from twisting.

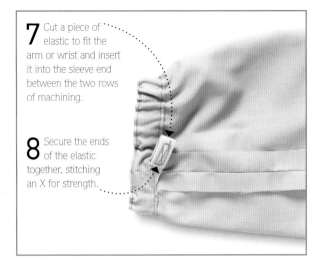

7 Cut a piece of elastic to fit the arm or wrist and insert it into the sleeve end between the two rows of machining.

8 Secure the ends of the elastic together, stitching an X for strength.

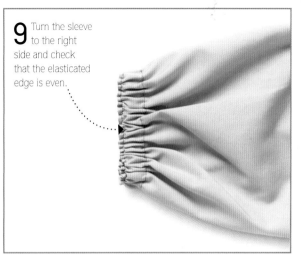

9 Turn the sleeve to the right side and check that the elasticated edge is even.

Openings

This finish uses a piece of bias strip (see p.49) to complete a cuff opening or a slashed neckline. Use it on fabrics that fray easily.

BOUND OPENING

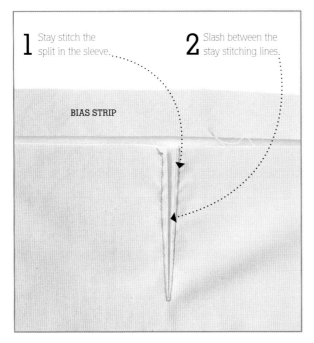

1 Stay stitch the split in the sleeve.

2 Slash between the stay stitching lines.

BIAS STRIP

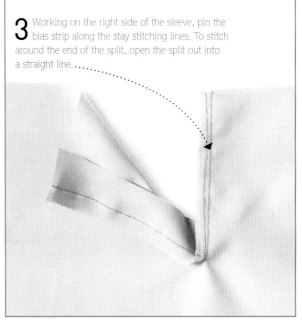

3 Working on the right side of the sleeve, pin the bias strip along the stay stitching lines. To stitch around the end of the split, open the split out into a straight line.

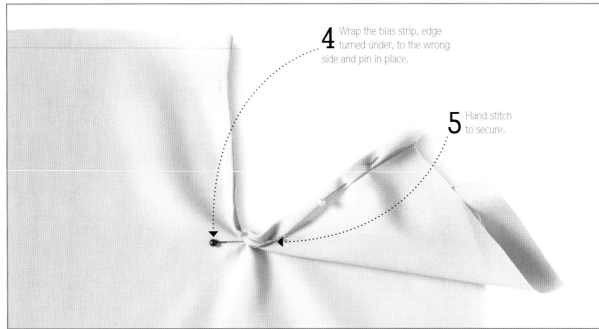

4 Wrap the bias strip, edge turned under, to the wrong side and pin in place.

5 Hand stitch to secure.

6 Allow the bias strip to close. One side of the strip will fold under and the other will extend over it.

7 Secure the top fold in the bias strip with a double stitch.

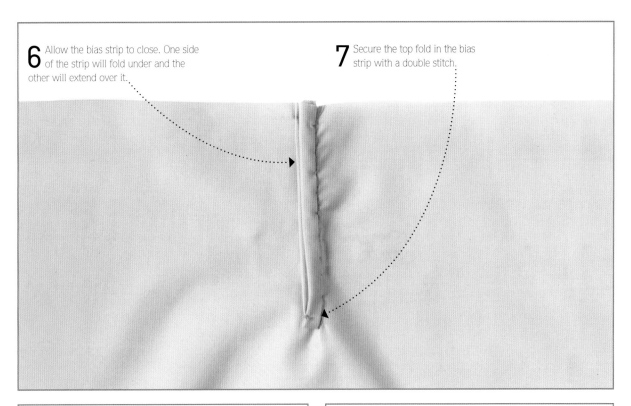

8 If adding a cuff, tailor tack the cuff end of the bias strip to aid the placement of the cuff.

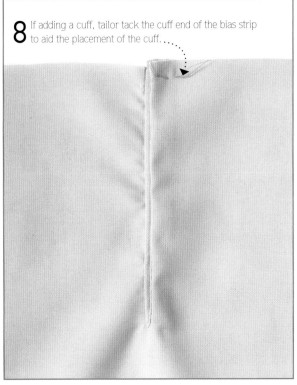

9 The finished bias-bound opening.

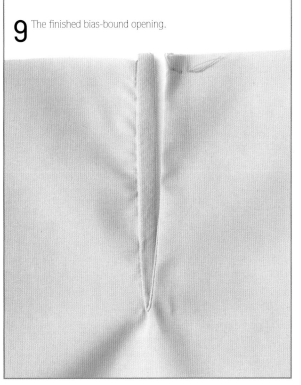

Pockets

Pockets come in lots of shapes and formats. Some, such as patch pockets, are external and can be decorative, while others, including front hip pockets, are more discreet and hidden from view. You can also have a pocket flap that is purely decorative. This can be made from the same fabric as the garment or from a contrasting fabric.

Decorative pocket flap

This pocket flap is sewn where the pocket would be, but there is no opening beneath it. This is to reduce the bulk that would arise if there was a complete pocket.

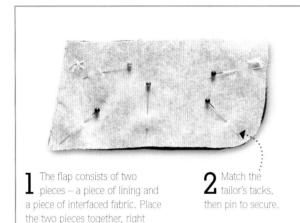

1 The flap consists of two pieces – a piece of lining and a piece of interfaced fabric. Place the two pieces together, right side to right side.

2 Match the tailor's tacks, then pin to secure.

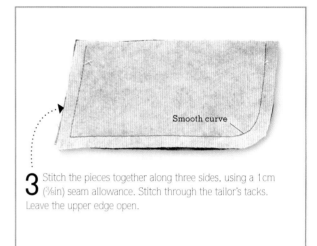

Smooth curve

3 Stitch the pieces together along three sides, using a 1cm (⅜in) seam allowance. Stitch through the tailor's tacks. Leave the upper edge open.

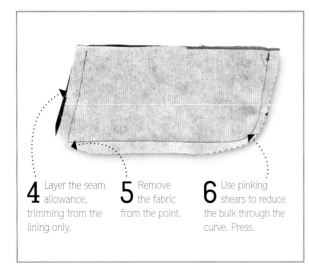

4 Layer the seam allowance, trimming from the lining only.

5 Remove the fabric from the point.

6 Use pinking shears to reduce the bulk through the curve. Press.

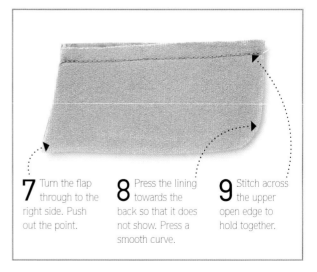

7 Turn the flap through to the right side. Push out the point.

8 Press the lining towards the back so that it does not show. Press a smooth curve.

9 Stitch across the upper open edge to hold together.

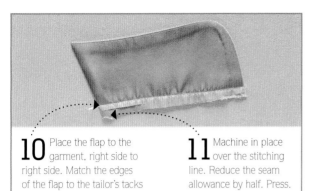

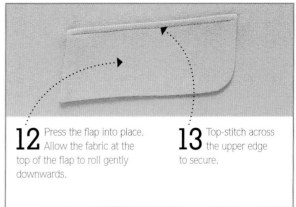

10 Place the flap to the garment, right side to right side. Match the edges of the flap to the tailor's tacks on the garment.

11 Machine in place over the stitching line. Reduce the seam allowance by half. Press.

12 Press the flap into place. Allow the fabric at the top of the flap to roll gently downwards.

13 Top-stitch across the upper edge to secure.

Lined patch pocket

If a self-lined patch pocket is likely to be too bulky, then a lined pocket is the answer. It is advisable to interface the pocket fabric.

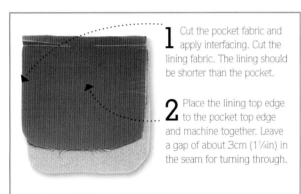

1 Cut the pocket fabric and apply interfacing. Cut the lining fabric. The lining should be shorter than the pocket.

2 Place the lining top edge to the pocket top edge and machine together. Leave a gap of about 3cm (1¼in) in the seam for turning through.

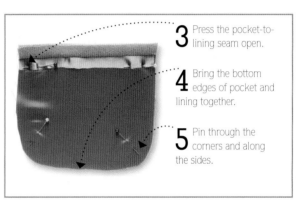

3 Press the pocket-to-lining seam open.

4 Bring the bottom edges of pocket and lining together.

5 Pin through the corners and along the sides.

6 Stitch around the three open sides of the pocket to attach the lining to the pocket fabric.

7 Trim away the corners.

8 Use pinking shears to trim the curves.

9 Turn the pocket to the right side through the gap left in the seam. Press.

10 Hand stitch the gap with a flat fell or blind hem stitch.

11 The lined patch pocket is ready to be attached.

In-seam pocket

In trousers and skirts, the pocket is sometimes disguised in the seam line. In the method below, a separate pocket is attached to the seam, but the pocket shape could also be cut as part of the main fabric.

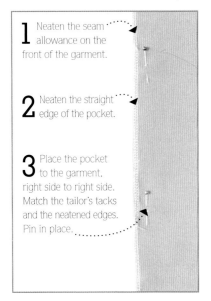

1 Neaten the seam allowance on the front of the garment.

2 Neaten the straight edge of the pocket.

3 Place the pocket to the garment, right side to right side. Match the tailor's tacks and the neatened edges. Pin in place.

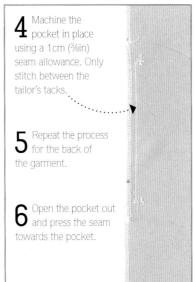

4 Machine the pocket in place using a 1cm (⅜in) seam allowance. Only stitch between the tailor's tacks.

5 Repeat the process for the back of the garment.

6 Open the pocket out and press the seam towards the pocket.

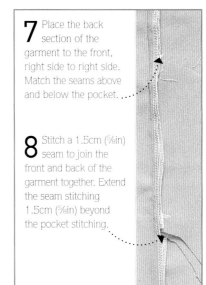

7 Place the back section of the garment to the front, right side to right side. Match the seams above and below the pocket.

8 Stitch a 1.5cm (⅝in) seam to join the front and back of the garment together. Extend the seam stitching 1.5cm (⅝in) beyond the pocket stitching.

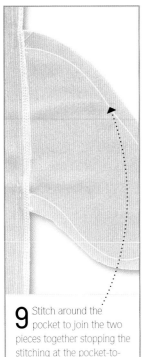

9 Stitch around the pocket to join the two pieces together stopping the stitching at the pocket-to-garment stitching line.

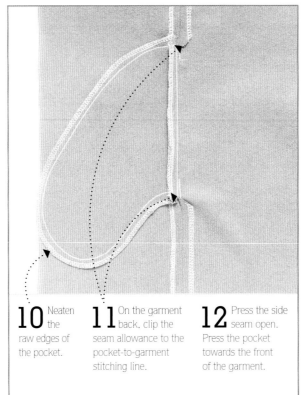

10 Neaten the raw edges of the pocket.

11 On the garment back, clip the seam allowance to the pocket-to-garment stitching line.

12 Press the side seam open. Press the pocket towards the front of the garment.

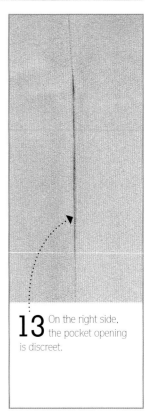

13 On the right side, the pocket opening is discreet.

Front hip pocket

On many trousers and casual skirts, the pocket is placed on the hipline. It can be low on the hipline or cut quite high, as on jeans. The construction is the same for all types of hip pockets. When inserted at an angle, hip pockets can slim the figure.

1 Apply a piece of fusible tape on the garment along the line of the pocket.

WRONG SIDE

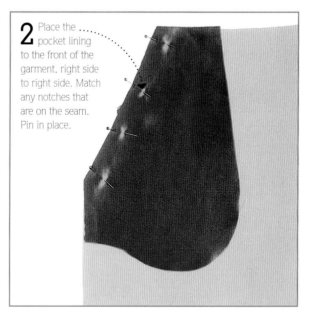

2 Place the pocket lining to the front of the garment, right side to right side. Match any notches that are on the seam. Pin in place.

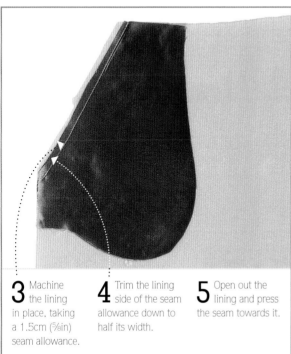

3 Machine the lining in place, taking a 1.5cm (⅝in) seam allowance.

4 Trim the lining side of the seam allowance down to half its width.

5 Open out the lining and press the seam towards it.

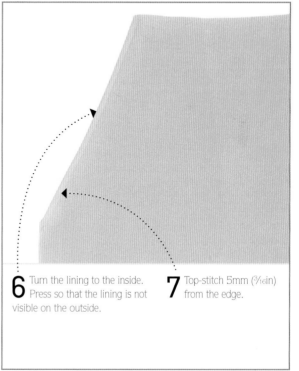

6 Turn the lining to the inside. Press so that the lining is not visible on the outside.

7 Top-stitch 5mm (³⁄₁₆in) from the edge.

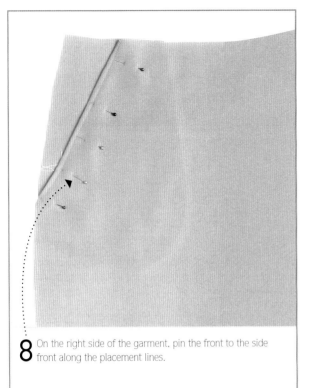

8 On the right side of the garment, pin the front to the side front along the placement lines.

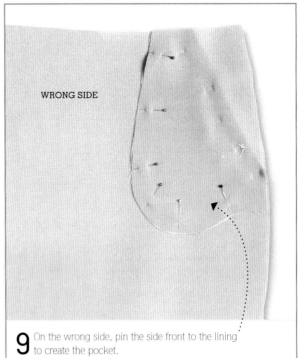

WRONG SIDE

9 On the wrong side, pin the side front to the lining to create the pocket.

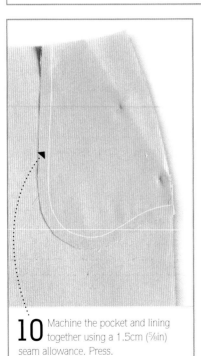

10 Machine the pocket and lining together using a 1.5cm (⅝in) seam allowance. Press.

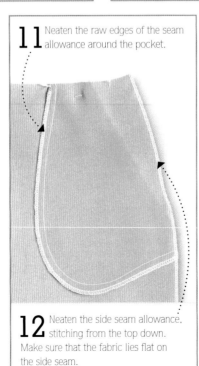

11 Neaten the raw edges of the seam allowance around the pocket.

12 Neaten the side seam allowance, stitching from the top down. Make sure that the fabric lies flat on the side seam.

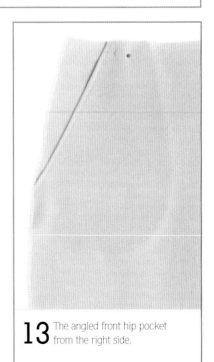

13 The angled front hip pocket from the right side.

Hemlines

The lower edge of a garment is normally finished with a hem. Sometimes the style of the garment dictates the type of hem used, and sometimes the fabric.

Marking a hemline

On a skirt or a dress the hemline should be level all around. Even if the fabric has been cut straight, the hems of A-line or circular skirts may "drop", which means that the hem edge is longer in some places. This is due to the fabric stretching where it is not on the straight of the grain. Hang the garment for 24 hours in a warm room before hemming to ensure a level hem line.

USING A RULER

1 Put on the skirt or dress but no shoes. With the end of the ruler on the floor, have a helper measure and mark.

2 Use pins to mark the crease line of the proposed hem. Ensure the measurement from floor to pin line is the same all the way round.

USING A DRESSMAKER'S DUMMY

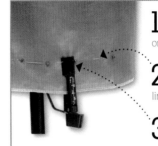

1 Adjust the dummy to your height and measurements. Place the skirt or dress on the dummy.

2 The hem marker on its stand will hold the fabric. Use the marker to mark the crease line of the proposed hem.

3 Slide a pin through the slot in the marker, then gently release the marker.

Hand-stitched hems

One of the most popular ways to secure a hem edge is by hand. Hand stitching is discreet and, if a fine hand-sewing needle is used, the stitching should not show on the right side of the work. Always finish the raw edge before stitching the hem.

TIPS FOR SEWING HEMS BY HAND

- Always use a single thread in the needle – a polyester all-purpose thread is ideal for hemming.
- Once the raw edge of the hem allowance has been neatened (see right), secure it using a hem stitch (see p.31). Take half of the stitch into the neatened edge and the other half into the wrong side of the garment fabric.
- Start and finish the hand stitching with a double stitch, not a knot, because knots will catch and pull the hem down.
- It is a good idea to take a small back stitch every 10cm (4in) or so to make sure that if the hem does come loose in one place it will not all unravel.

OVERLOCKED FINISH

1 Using a 3-thread overlock stitch, stitch along the raw edge of the hem allowance.

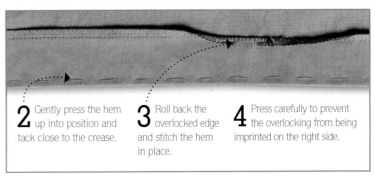

2 Gently press the hem up into position and tack close to the crease.

3 Roll back the overlocked edge and stitch the hem in place.

4 Press carefully to prevent the overlocking from being imprinted on the right side.

CURVED HEM FINISH

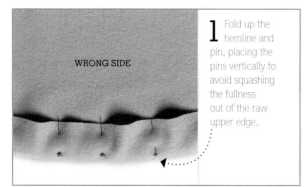

1 Fold up the hemline and pin, placing the pins vertically to avoid squashing the fullness out of the raw upper edge.

WRONG SIDE

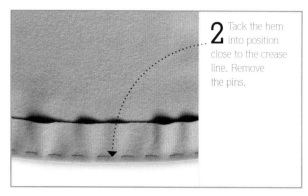

2 Tack the hem into position close to the crease line. Remove the pins.

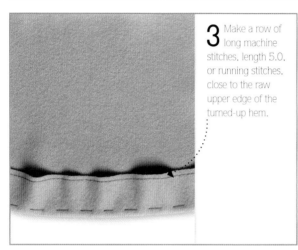

3 Make a row of long machine stitches, length 5.0, or running stitches, close to the raw upper edge of the turned-up hem.

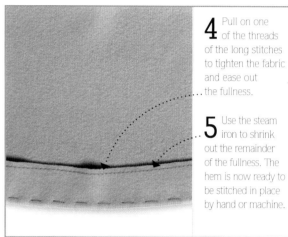

4 Pull on one of the threads of the long stitches to tighten the fabric and ease out the fullness.

5 Use the steam iron to shrink out the remainder of the fullness. The hem is now ready to be stitched in place by hand or machine.

Machined hems

On some occasions, the hem or edge of a garment or other item is turned up and secured using the sewing machine. It can be stitched with a straight stitch, a zigzag stitch, or a blind hem stitch if you have the appropriate machine foot. Hems can also be made on the overlocker (see p.16).

DOUBLE-TURN HEM

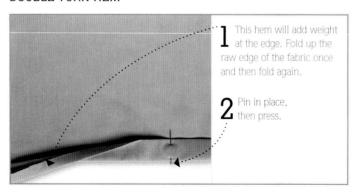

1 This hem will add weight at the edge. Fold up the raw edge of the fabric once and then fold again.

2 Pin in place, then press.

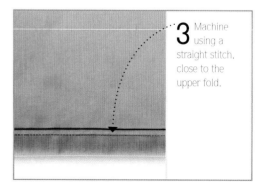

3 Machine using a straight stitch, close to the upper fold.

Zips

The zip is probably the most used of all fastenings. There are a great many types available, in a variety of lengths, colours, and materials, but they all fall into one of five categories: skirt or trouser zips, metal or jeans zips, concealed zips, open-ended zips, and decorative zips.

Lapped zip

A skirt zip in a skirt or a dress is usually put in by means of a lapped technique or a centred zip technique (see p.68). For both of these techniques you will require the zip foot on the sewing machine. A lapped zip features one side of the seam – the left-hand side – lapping over the teeth of the zip to conceal them.

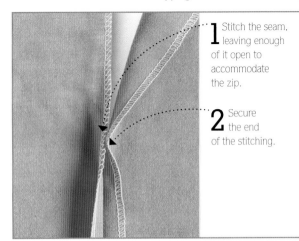

1 Stitch the seam, leaving enough of it open to accommodate the zip.

2 Secure the end of the stitching.

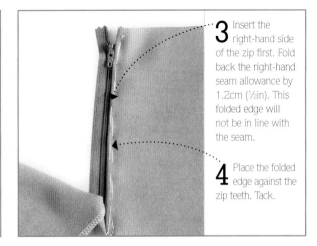

3 Insert the right-hand side of the zip first. Fold back the right-hand seam allowance by 1.2cm (½in). This folded edge will not be in line with the seam.

4 Place the folded edge against the zip teeth. Tack.

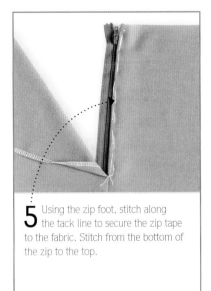

5 Using the zip foot, stitch along the tack line to secure the zip tape to the fabric. Stitch from the bottom of the zip to the top.

6 Fold back the left-hand seam allowance by 1.5cm (⅝in). Place the folded edge over the machine line of the other side. Pin and then tack.

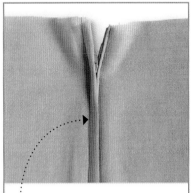

7 Starting at the bottom of the zip, stitch across from the centre seamline and then up the left side of the zip. The finished zip should have its teeth covered by the fabric.

Centred zip

With a centred zip, the two folded edges of the seam allowances meet over the centre of the teeth, to conceal the zip completely.

1 Stitch the seam, leaving a gap for the zip.

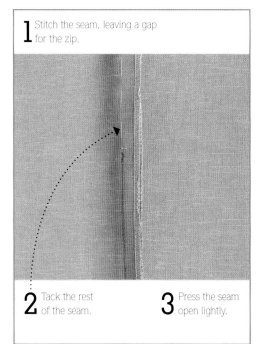

2 Tack the rest of the seam.

3 Press the seam open lightly.

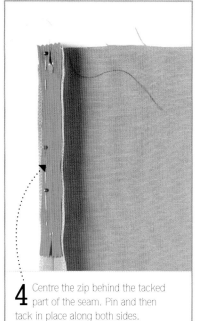

4 Centre the zip behind the tacked part of the seam. Pin and then tack in place along both sides.

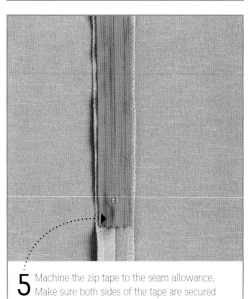

5 Machine the zip tape to the seam allowance. Make sure both sides of the tape are secured to the seam allowances. Stitch right to the end of the zip tape.

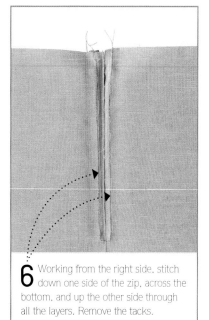

6 Working from the right side, stitch down one side of the zip, across the bottom, and up the other side through all the layers. Remove the tacks.

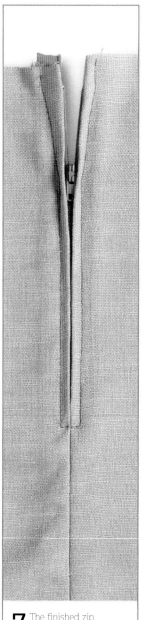

7 The finished zip from the right side.

Faced fly-front zip

Whether it be for a classic pair of trousers or a pair of jeans, a fly front is the most common technique for inserting a trouser zip. The zip usually has a facing behind it to prevent the zip teeth from catching.

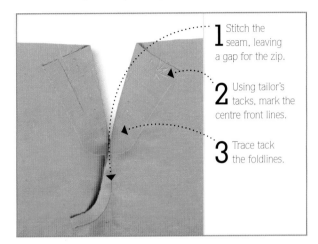

1 Stitch the seam, leaving a gap for the zip.

2 Using tailor's tacks, mark the centre front lines.

3 Trace tack the foldlines.

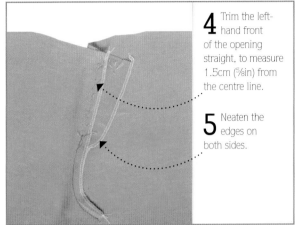

4 Trim the left-hand front of the opening straight, to measure 1.5cm (⅝in) from the centre line.

5 Neaten the edges on both sides.

6 Fold the left-hand front along the foldline.

7 Place the fold adjacent to the zip teeth and pin in place. The zip may be too long; if so, it will extend beyond the top of the fabric.

8 Machine along the foldline using the zip foot. Extend the machining past the seam stitching line.

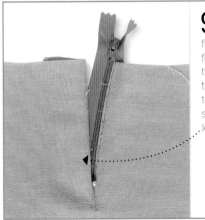

9 Fold the right-hand front along the foldline. Place the foldline over the zip and pin to the machine stitching on the left-hand side.

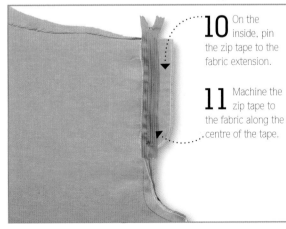

10 On the inside, pin the zip tape to the fabric extension.

11 Machine the zip tape to the fabric along the centre of the tape.

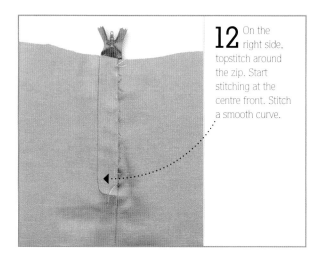

12 On the right side, topstitch around the zip. Start stitching at the centre front. Stitch a smooth curve.

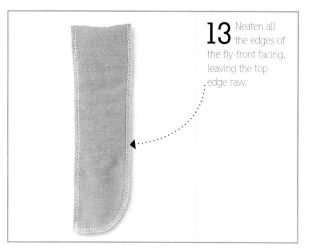

13 Neaten all the edges of the fly-front facing, leaving the top edge raw.

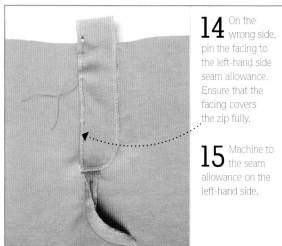

14 On the wrong side, pin the facing to the left-hand side seam allowance. Ensure that the facing covers the zip fully.

15 Machine to the seam allowance on the left-hand side.

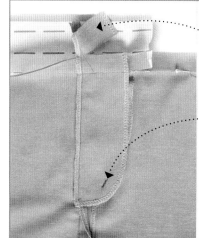

16 Attach the waistband over the zip and the facings. Trim facing and zip.

17 Secure the lower edge of the facing on the right-hand side to the right-hand seam allowance.

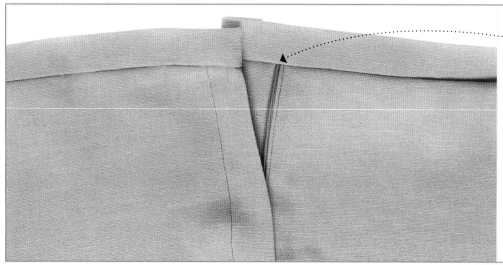

18 The waistband goes over the zip and acts as the zip stop. Attach a trouser hook and eye.

Buttons

Buttons are one of the oldest forms of fastening. They come in many shapes and sizes, and can be made from a variety of materials including shell, bone, plastic, nylon, and metal. Buttons are normally sewn on by hand, although a two-hole button can be sewn on by machine.

Sewing on a two-hole button

This is the most popular type of button and requires a thread shank to be made when sewing in place. A cocktail stick on top of the button will help you to make the shank.

1 Position the button on the fabric. Start with a double stitch and double thread in the needle. Place a cocktail stick on top of the button. Stitch up and down through the holes, going over the stick.

2 Remove the cocktail stick.

3 Wrap the thread around the thread loops under the button to make a shank.

4 Take the thread through to the back of the fabric.

5 Buttonhole stitch over the loop of threads on the back of the work.

Sewing on a four-hole button

This is stitched in the same way as a two-hole button except that the threads make an X over the top of the button.

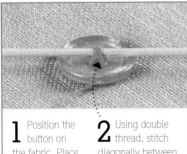

1 Position the button on the fabric. Place a cocktail stick on the button.

2 Using double thread, stitch diagonally between the holes to make an X on top of the cocktail stick.

3 Remove the cocktail stick.

4 Wrap the thread around the thread loops under the button to make the shank.

5 On the reverse of the fabric, buttonhole stitch over the X-shaped thread loops.

Buttonholes

Adding buttons and buttonholes is one of the last things you will do when you are making a garment. Your pattern instructions will tell you where to position the buttons and buttonholes on the garment, while the size of your button will determine the size of buttonhole.

Vertical or horizontal?

Generally, buttonholes are only placed vertically on a garment with a placket or strip to contain the buttonhole. All other buttonholes should be horizontal. Any strain on the buttonhole will then be taken by the end stop and prevent the button from coming undone.

VERTICAL BUTTONHOLES

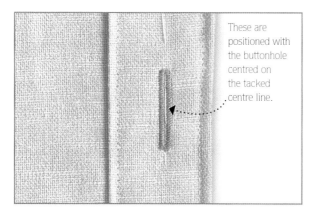

These are positioned with the buttonhole centred on the tacked centre line.

HORIZONTAL BUTTONHOLES

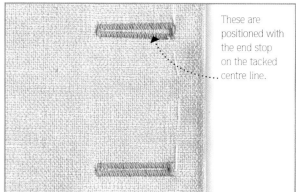

These are positioned with the end stop on the tacked centre line.

Stages of a buttonhole

A sewing machine stitches a buttonhole in three stages. The stitch can be varied slightly in width and length to suit the fabric, but the stitches need to be tight and close together.

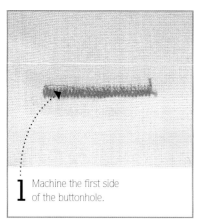

1 Machine the first side of the buttonhole.

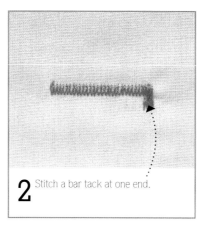

2 Stitch a bar tack at one end.

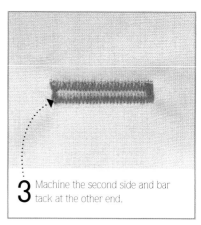

3 Machine the second side and bar tack at the other end.

Hooks and eyes

There are a multitude of different types of hook and eye fasteners. Purchased hooks and eyes are made from metal and are normally silver or black in colour. Different-shaped hooks and eyes are used on different garments – large, broad hooks and eyes can be decorative and stitched to show on the outside, while tiny fasteners are meant to be discreet.

Attaching hooks and eyes

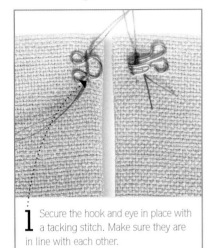

1 Secure the hook and eye in place with a tacking stitch. Make sure they are in line with each other.

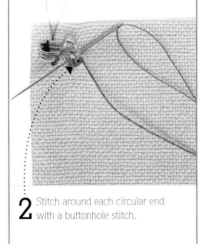

2 Stitch around each circular end with a buttonhole stitch.

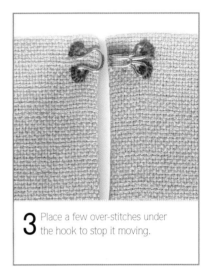

3 Place a few over-stitches under the hook to stop it moving.

Trouser hook and eye

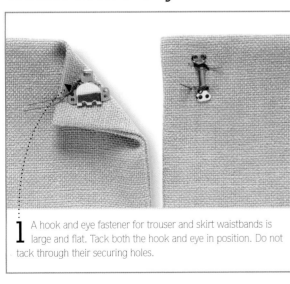

1 A hook and eye fastener for trouser and skirt waistbands is large and flat. Tack both the hook and eye in position. Do not tack through their securing holes.

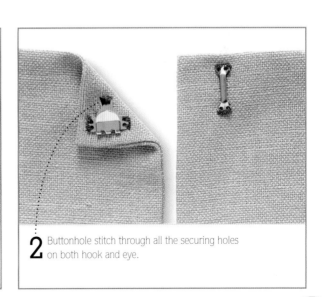

2 Buttonhole stitch through all the securing holes on both hook and eye.

Garments

Classic A-line skirt

This A-line skirt will never go out of fashion and can be worn at all times of the year and to all occasions. It is also one of the easiest garments for a beginner to make. It has only three pattern pieces – a front, a back, and a waistband. The skirt needs to fit comfortably around the waist and across the tummy, so check your measurements carefully against the pattern.

Corduroy

Linen ....

This skirt is made in a cotton print, but works well in a wide range of fabrics. For winter you could choose a cosy corduroy, while for summer, linen will keep you cool and fresh.

BEFORE YOU START

YOU WILL NEED

- 1.3m (51in) x 150cm (59in) fabric
- 1 x reel matching all-purpose sewing thread
- 1 x reel contrasting all-purpose sewing thread for pattern marking
- 1m x waistband interfacing
- 1 x 22cm (8½in) skirt zip
- 1 x button

PREPARING THE PATTERN

- This skirt is made using Skirt pattern one (see pp.168–169)
- Follow the instructions (see pp.166–167) to download or copy the pattern in your size

GARMENT CONSTRUCTION

This A-line skirt is shaped by the two darts in the front and back. There is a zip in the left-hand side. The narrow waistband is fastened with a button and buttonhole fastening. The finished skirt should sit just above the knee.

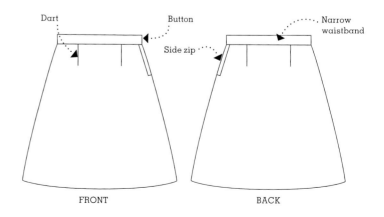

Dart

Button

Side zip

Narrow waistband

FRONT

BACK

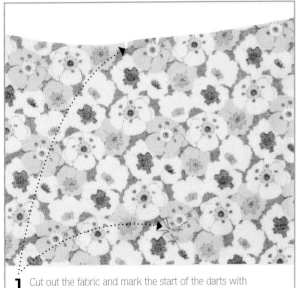

1 Cut out the fabric and mark the start of the darts with tailor's tacks (see p.27). Clip the end of the darts on the raw edge (see p.26).

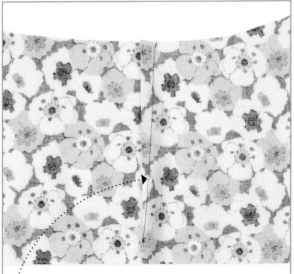

2 Make the darts (see pp.40–41) and press towards the centre of the garment.

3 Neaten the side seams on the back and the front using a 3-thread overlock stitch or a small zigzag stitch (see p.34).

4 Stitch the LH (left hand) side seam, leaving a gap for the zip. Press the seam open then insert a lapped zip (see p.67).

5 Stitch the RH (right hand) side seam and press the seam open (see p.33).

6 Attach the waistband interfacing to the waistband (see p.47).

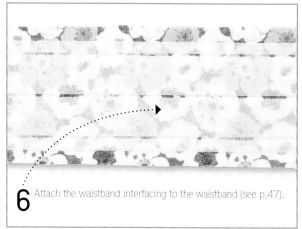

matched notches

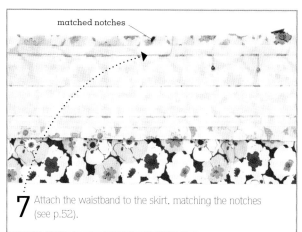

7 Attach the waistband to the skirt, matching the notches (see p.52).

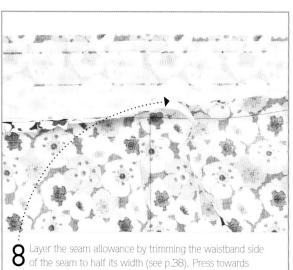

8 Layer the seam allowance by trimming the waistband side of the seam to half its width (see p.38). Press towards the waistband.

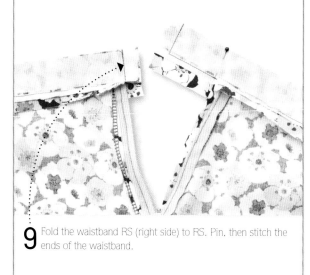

9 Fold the waistband RS (right side) to RS. Pin, then stitch the ends of the waistband.

10 Clip the ends of the waistband to reduce bulk.

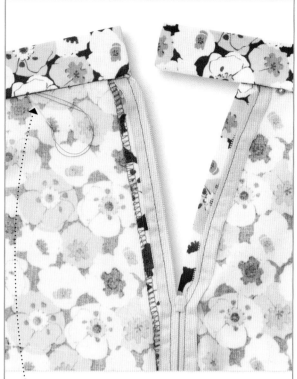

11 Turn the waistband to the RS, pushing the clipped ends out. Fold under the raw edge, then pin and handstitch in place.

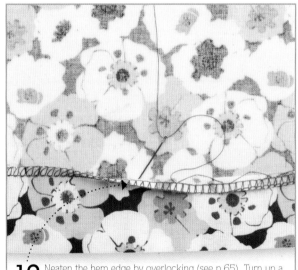

12 Neaten the hem edge by overlocking (see p.65). Turn up a 4cm (1½in) hem and handstitch in place.

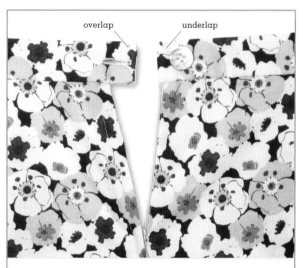

overlap   underlap

13 Make a buttonhole on the overlap of the waistband (see p.72). Sew a button on the underlap (see p.71).

Classic tailored skirt

A straight skirt is a staple garment in every woman's wardrobe. It could be the bottom half of a suit, made in a party fabric for a night out, or just be a simple, hardworking everyday skirt. The vent in the centre back hemline ensures you won't have trouble walking whatever the occasion. The skirt should be close-fitting, so choose the pattern size by your hip measurement.

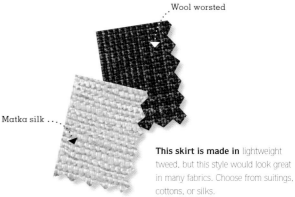

Wool worsted

Matka silk

This skirt is made in lightweight tweed, but this style would look great in many fabrics. Choose from suitings, cottons, or silks.

BEFORE YOU START

YOU WILL NEED

- 1m (39¼in) x 150cm (59in) fabric
- 1 x reel matching all-purpose sewing thread
- 1 x reel contrasting all-purpose sewing thread for pattern marking
- 50cm (19½in) lightweight fusible interfacing
- 1 x 18cm (7in) skirt zip

PREPARING THE PATTERN

- This skirt is made using Skirt pattern two (see pp.170–171)
- Follow the instructions (see pp.166–167) to download or copy the pattern in your size

GARMENT CONSTRUCTION

This close-fitting skirt narrows slightly towards the hem and has a centre back vent. One dart in the front and two in the back shape the skirt to the waist and there is a zip in the centre back. The waistline is finished with a facing.

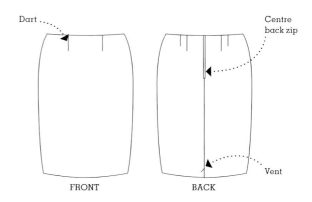

Dart

Centre back zip

Vent

FRONT   BACK

HOW TO MAKE THE CLASSIC TAILORED SKIRT

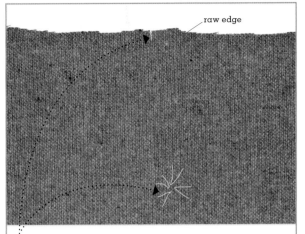

raw edge

1 Cut out the fabric and mark the darts using tailor's tacks (see p.27). Clip the end of the darts on the raw edge (see p.26).

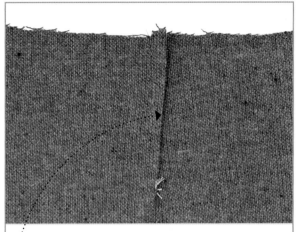

2 Make the darts (see pp.40–41) and press towards the centre of the garment.

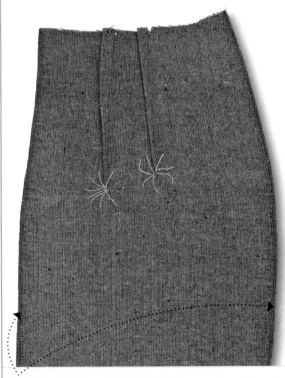

3 Neaten the side and CB (centre back) seams using a 3-thread overlock stitch or a small zigzag stitch (see p.34).

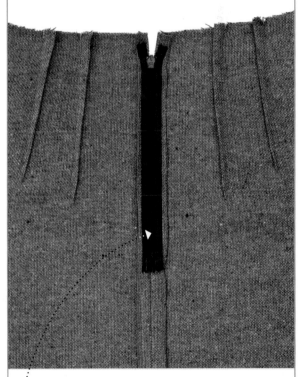

4 Insert a centred zip at the CB (see p.68).

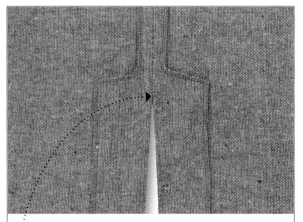

5 Stitch the remainder of the CB seam, stopping at the dot marking the top of the vent. Press the seam open.

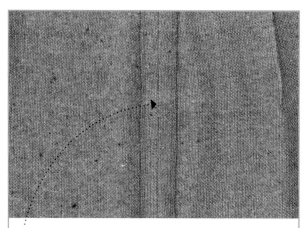

6 Join the front to the back at the side seams and press the seams open.

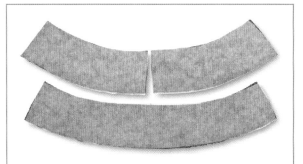

7 Attach a lightweight fusible interfacing to the waist facing pieces (see p.47).

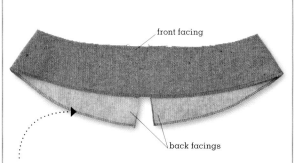

front facing

back facings

8 Join the front and back facings and press the seams open. Neaten the lower edge of the facing using a 3-thread overlock stitch or a small zigzag stitch.

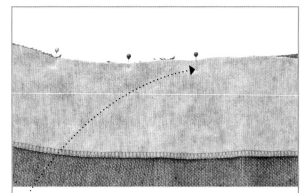

9 Place the facing to the skirt at the waist edge RS (right side) to RS, matching the side seams and matching at the top of the zip. Pin and machine.

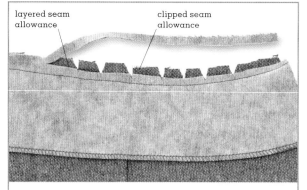

layered seam allowance

clipped seam allowance

10 Layer the seam allowance by trimming the facing side of the seam to half its width. Clip the seam allowance to reduce bulk (see p.38).

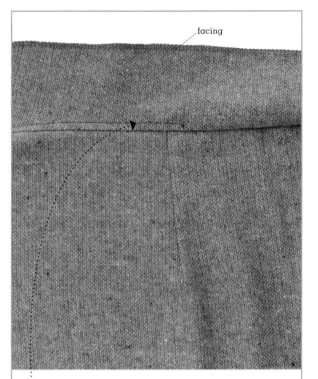

facing

11 Press the seam towards the facing and understitch (see p.39).

12 Turn the facing to the inside then, at the CB, fold the edge of the facing in to meet the zip tape. Pin and handstitch in place.

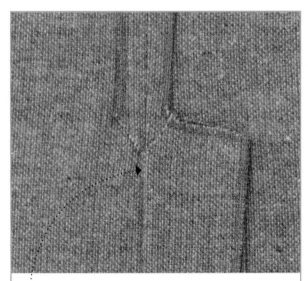

13 At the vent, snip through the seam allowance on the LH (left hand) side and press the seam extension to the RH (right hand) side.

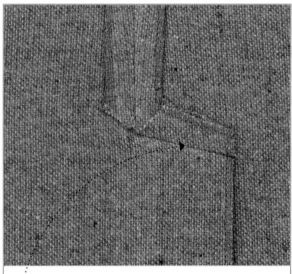

14 Machine the extension in place.

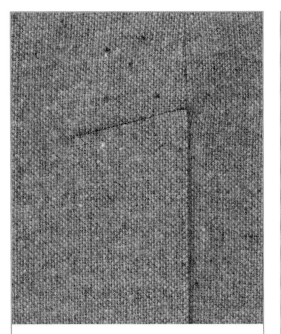

15 From the RS, the top of the vent can be seen as a line of stitching.

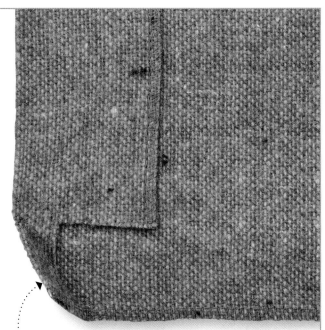

16 Neaten the hem edge (see p.65). On each side of the vent, remove the surplus fabric in the hem allowance.

17 Mitre the hem at the bottom of the vent. Pin.

18 Turn up the remainder of the hem, pin and handstitch in place.

Tailored evening skirt

For this version of the skirt you will add a lining for a more luxurious finish. You will also shorten the skirt, which means you no longer need a centre back vent to make walking easier. This skirt has been made in silk for an evening out, but would also work well in a heavier fabric worn with thick tights.

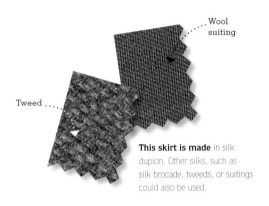

Wool suiting

Tweed

This skirt is made in silk dupion. Other silks, such as silk brocade, tweeds, or suitings could also be used.

BEFORE YOU START

YOU WILL NEED

- 90cm (36in) x 150cm (59in) fabric
- 90cm (36in) x 150cm (59in) lining fabric
- 1 x reel matching all-purpose sewing thread
- 1 x reel contrasting all-purpose sewing thread for pattern marking
- 50cm (20in) lightweight fusible interfacing
- 1 x 18cm (7in) skirt zip

PREPARING THE PATTERN

- This skirt is made using Skirt pattern two (see pp.170–171)
- Follow the instructions (see pp.166–167) to download or copy the pattern in your size

GARMENT CONSTRUCTION

This lined variation of the Classic tailored skirt is shorter without a back vent. There is a zip in the centre back. The waistline is finished with a facing. The lining is cut from the same pattern pieces as the skirt.

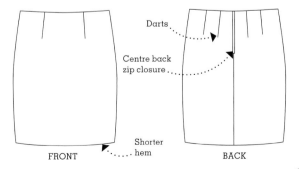

Darts

Centre back zip closure

Shorter hem

FRONT

BACK

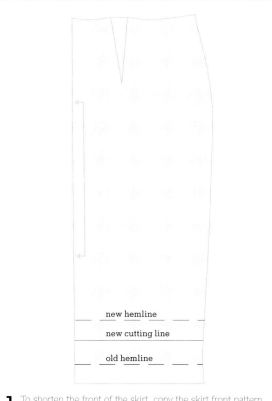

1 To shorten the front of the skirt, copy the skirt front pattern piece. Mark the hemline. Mark the new hemline 8cm (3¼in) above the old hemline. Draw a new cutting line 4cm (1½in) below the new hemline.

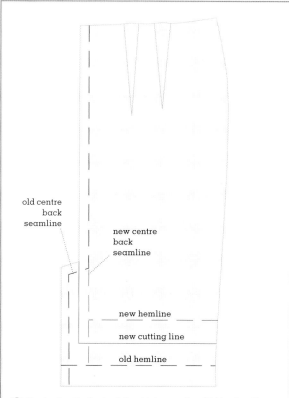

old centre back seamline

new centre back seamline

new hemline

new cutting line

old hemline

2 To shorten the back of the skirt, copy the skirt back pattern piece. Shorten the skirt as for step 1. To remove the vent, extend the CB (centre back) seamline to the hemline.

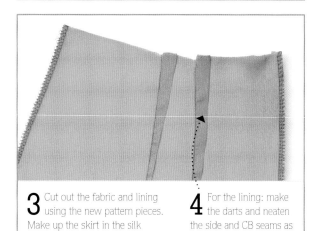

3 Cut out the fabric and lining using the new pattern pieces. Make up the skirt in the silk fabric as for the Classic Tailored Skirt steps 1–6.

4 For the lining: make the darts and neaten the side and CB seams as for the skirt.

5 Stitch the CB (centre back) seam in the lining between the marked dots, leaving the seam above open for the zip. Press open.

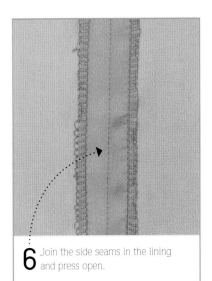

6 Join the side seams in the lining and press open.

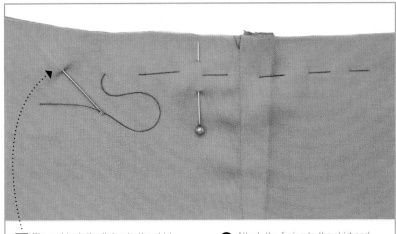

7 Pin and tack the lining to the skirt at the waist edge WS (wrong side) to WS, matching the darts and seams.

8 Attach the facing to the skirt and lining as for the Classic tailored skirt steps 7–11.

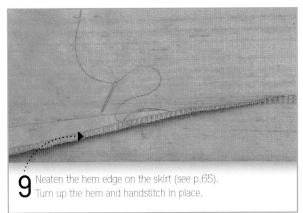

9 Neaten the hem edge on the skirt (see p.65). Turn up the hem and handstitch in place.

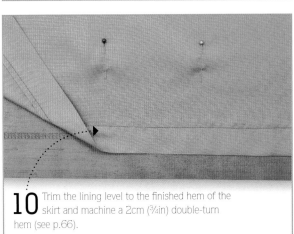

10 Trim the lining level to the finished hem of the skirt and machine a 2cm (¾in) double-turn hem (see p.66).

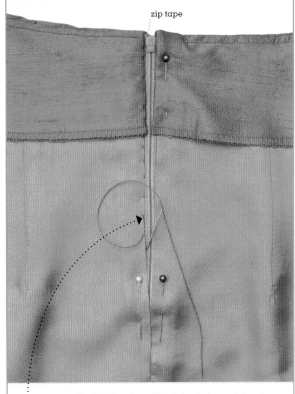

zip tape

11 At the CB, fold the edge of the lining in to meet the zip tape. Pin and handstitch in place.

Classic pleated skirt

In this skirt you'll be introduced to making box pleats and adding a yoke. You should take care and work accurately as you'll have to transfer all the marks for the folds from the pattern to your fabric. The flattering yoke over the tummy avoids any bulk. Choose your size by your hip measurement to make sure the pleats hang straight and be sure you know the width of your belt before you construct the carriers. Once you've finished, you'll have a timeless pleated skirt to add to your wardrobe.

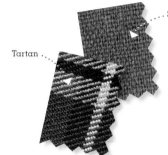

Suiting linen

Tartan

For a winter or autumn skirt, choose a fabric that presses well but isn't too heavy. Here a wool with a twill weave has been used but you could try a lightweight suiting, tweed, or tartan. For summer, a crisp linen print is a good option.

BEFORE YOU START

YOU WILL NEED

- 1.5m (59in) x 150cm (59in) fabric
- 2 x reels matching all-purpose polyester sewing thread
- 2 x reels contrasting all-purpose sewing thread in two different colours for pattern marking
- 1 x 18cm (7in) skirt zip
- 50cm (20in) medium-weight interfacing
- 50cm (20in) lightweight interfacing

PREPARING THE PATTERN

- This skirt is made using Skirt pattern three (see pp.172–175)
- Follow the instructions (see pp.166–167) to download or copy the pattern in your size

GARMENT CONSTRUCTION

This classic pleated unlined skirt has three box pleats at the back and front. The skirt has a self-lined yoke that sits just below the natural waistline, with two belt carriers at the front and back. There is a zip in the left-hand side.

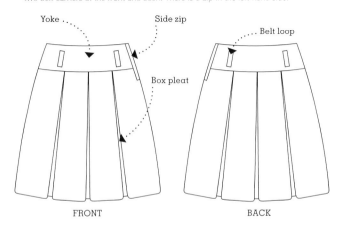

Yoke

Side zip

Belt loop

Box pleat

FRONT

BACK

HOW TO MAKE THE CLASSIC PLEATED SKIRT

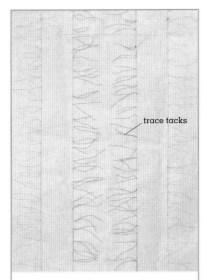

trace tacks

1 Cut out the fabric and mark the fold lines and crease lines with trace tacks (see p.27), each type of line in a different coloured thread. Cut through the loops in the trace tacks.

2 Remove the pattern carefully so as not to pull the trace tacks out.

3 Fold the fabric RS (right side) to RS and match tacks of the same colour to each other. Pin along the line of tacks that is farther from the fold. Tack through the pins then remove the pins.

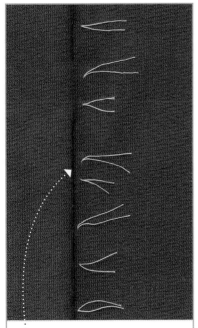

4 From the RS, the tacked pleat can be seen with its trace tacks.

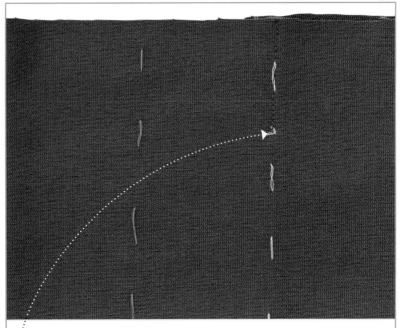

5 On the WS (wrong side), machine along this tack line to the dot marking on the pattern.

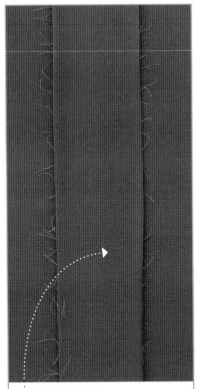

6 Press gently on the WS to make the pleat. Repeat for each pleat. For sharp pleats, press more heavily, placing a pressing cloth over the fabric.

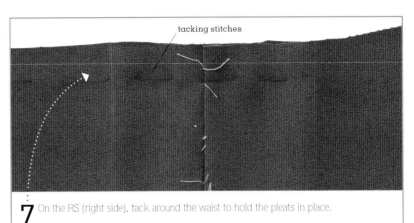

tacking stitches

7 On the RS (right side), tack around the waist to hold the pleats in place.

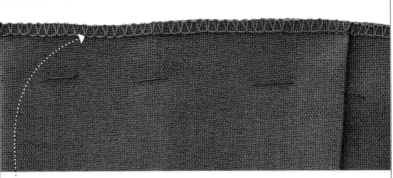

8 Neaten the waist edge, including the top edge of the pleats, using a 3-thread overlock stitch or a small zigzag stitch (see p.34)

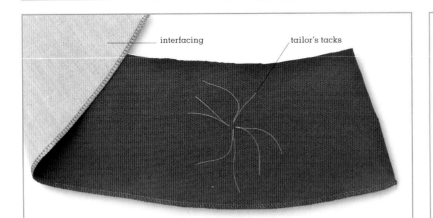

interfacing   tailor's tacks

9 Attach a medium-weight fusible interfacing to one front and one back yoke (see p.47), join the yoke pieces together at the RH (right hand) side, press the seams open, and neaten the lower edge using a 3-thread overlock stitch or a small zigzag stitch. Mark the position of the belt carriers with tailor's tacks (see p.27).

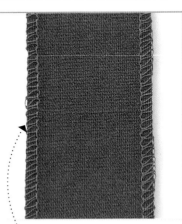

10 For the belt carriers: Neaten the edges of the belt carriers using a 3-thread overlock stitch or a small zigzag stitch.

11 Fold the edges of the belt carriers to the centre WS to WS and press....

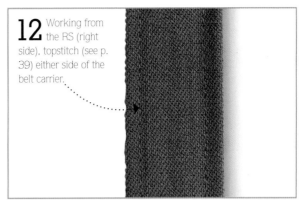

12 Working from the RS (right side), topstitch (see p. 39) either side of the belt carrier.

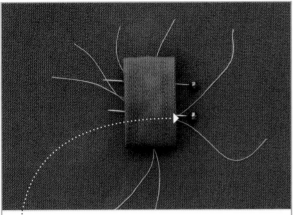

13 Cut the belt carriers to the length required to hold your belt. Fold the carriers into a loop and pin at the marked positions.

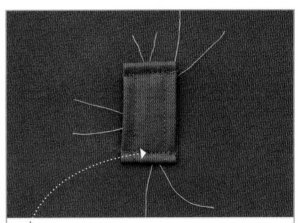

14 Topstitch the top and bottom of the belt carriers to secure. Remove the tailor's tacks.

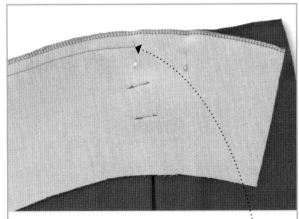

15 Place the yoke to the skirt front and back. Pin and machine. Press the seam open.

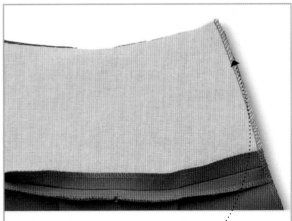

16 Press the skirt-to-yoke seam open, then neaten the side seams using a 3-thread overlock stitch or a small zigzag stitch.

17 Insert a zip of your choice on the LH (left hand) side (see pp.67–68). Stitch the remainder of the side seam and press open.

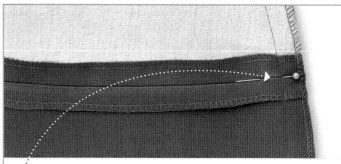

18 Join the RH side seam, matching at the skirt-to-yoke seam. Press open.

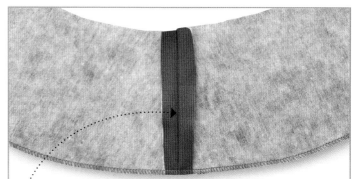

19 Attach a lightweight interfacing to the remaining set of yokes to make the yoke facings. Join the facings at the RH side and press the seam open. Neaten the lower edge using either a 3-thread overlock stitch or a small zigzag stitch.

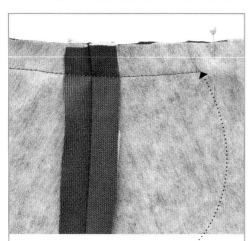

20 Place the yoke facing to the yoke RS (right side) to RS, matching at the side seam. Pin and machine.

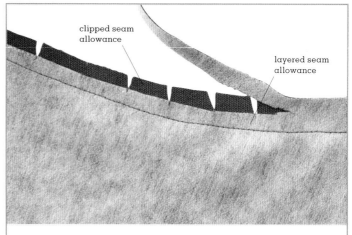

clipped seam allowance

layered seam allowance

21 Layer the seam allowance by trimming the facing side of the seam to half its width. Clip the seam allowance to reduce bulk (see p.38).

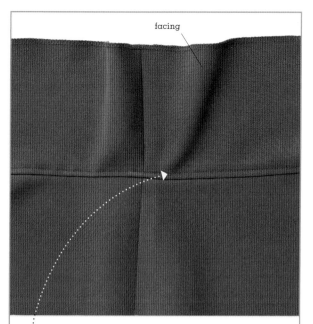

facing

22 Press the seam towards the facing and understitch (see p.39).

23 Turn the facing to the inside then fold the edge of the facing in to meet the zip tape. Pin, then pin the facing to the skirt-to-yoke seam.

24 Working from the RS (right side) of the skirt stitch in the ditch – the line produced by the skirt-to-yoke seam – through all layers. This will secure the facing on the inside.

25 Neaten the hem edge (see p.65). Turn up and handstitch in place. Remove the tacks in the pleats.

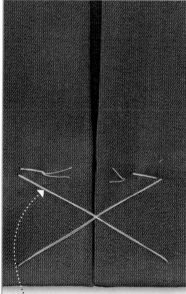

26 Fold the pleats at the hem edge back into place and tack together with a large X. Press. Remove any remaining tacks and trace tacks.

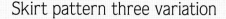

Topstitched pleated skirt

With its contrast topstitching and shorter length, this skirt is rather youthful. The pleats swing out from the thigh and the deep, topstitched hem gives the skirt a casual feel. Try this version in a chunky winter tweed worn with thick tights or leggings; for the summer, a crisp linen would be ideal.

Linen · · · · · · ·   · · · · · · · Tweed

For winter, choose heavy fabrics such as chunky tweed or a wool blend (used here); for summer, light crisp linens.

BEFORE YOU START

YOU WILL NEED

- 1.2m (47¼in) x 150cm (59in) fabric
- 1 x reel matching all-purpose sewing thread
- 2 x reels contrasting all-purpose sewing thread in two different colours for pattern marking
- 1 x reel contrasting all-purpose sewing thread for topstitching
- 50cm (20in) medium-weight interfacing
- 1 x 18cm (7in) skirt zip

PREPARING THE PATTERN

- This skirt is made using Skirt pattern three (see pp.172–175)
- Follow the instructions (see pp.166–167) to download or copy the pattern in your size

GARMENT CONSTRUCTION

This variation of the Classic pleated skirt is shorter. The pleats start lower and they are topstitched below the yoke in a contrast colour. The yoke and the deep hem are also topstitched.

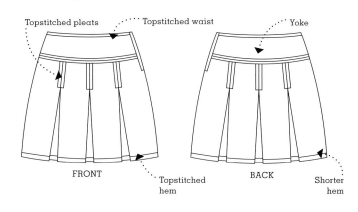

Topstitched pleats   Topstitched waist   Yoke

FRONT   Topstitched hem   BACK   Shorter hem

HOW TO MAKE THE TOPSTITCHED PLEATED SKIRT

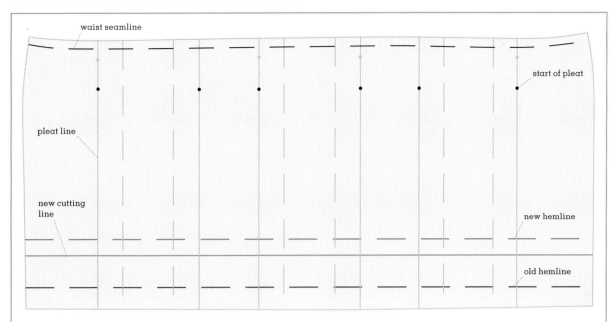

waist seamline

start of pleat

pleat line

new cutting line

new hemline

old hemline

1 Copy the front and back pattern pieces and mark the waist seamline, the hemline, and the pleat lines. Mark the new hemline 9cm (3½in) above the old hemline. Draw a new cutting line 4cm (1½in) below the new hemline. Mark the start of the pleats on the pleat line and 8cm (3¼in) below the waist seamline.

2 Cut out the fabric and make up as for the Classic pleated skirt steps 1–6.

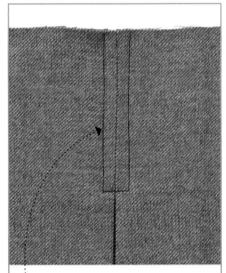

3 Working from the RS (right side) of the skirt, topstitch (see p.39) around the pleats in a contrasting thread using the edge of the presser foot as a guide.

4 Continue as for the Classic pleated skirt steps 7, 8, 9, and 15 (i.e. omitting the belt carriers).

5 Topstitch the skirt-to-yoke seam in a contrasting thread.

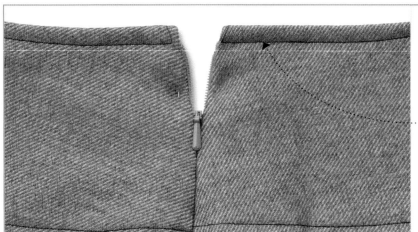

6 Continue as for the Classic pleated skirt steps 16–21 to make and attach the yoke facing.

7 Fold the facing to the inside of the skirt and topstitch around the waist. Fold the edge of the facing in to meet the zip tape and handstitch in place.

8 Pin the facing to the skirt-to-yoke seam as in step 23 of the Classic pleated skirt. Working from the RS of the skirt stitch in the ditch through all layers to secure the facing on the inside.

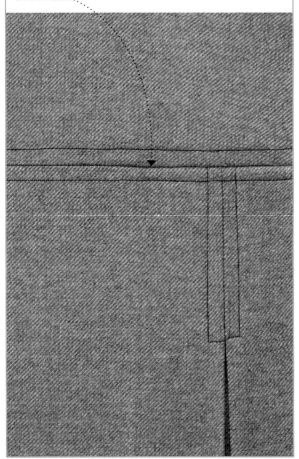

9 Neaten the hem edge (see p.65) and topstitch in place using contrasting thread 3cm (1¼in) from the fold.

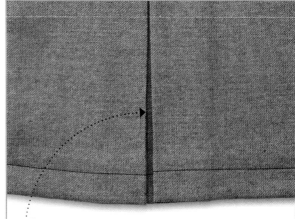

10 Press the pleats from the top to the hem.

Classic shift dress

A classic fitted dress like this never goes out of fashion and you can make it in almost any fabric. The dress must fit well across the bust and in the hip area, so choose your pattern by your bust measurement and alter the waist and hip as required. As with any fitted style, it's best to make the pattern up in calico first and try it out.

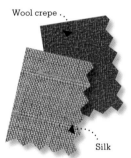

Wool crepe

Silk

This dress is made in wool crepe but tweed, silk, or cotton could also be used. Fine suiting works well for the office and printed stretch cotton makes a great summer outfit.

BEFORE YOU START

YOU WILL NEED

- 1.7m (67in) x 150cm (59in) fabric
- 1 x reel matching all-purpose sewing thread
- 1 x reel contrasting all-purpose sewing thread for pattern marking
- 50cm (20in) lightweight interfacing
- 1 x 56cm (22in) zip

PREPARING THE PATTERN

- This dress is made using Dress pattern one (see pp.176–180)
- Follow the instructions (see pp.166–167) to download or copy the pattern in your size

GARMENT CONSTRUCTION

This unlined one-piece fitted dress has darts at the bust and waist to ensure a fitted silhouette. It also has a zip in the centre back and a centre-back vent. It features a high round neck and long set-in sleeves. The hemline just brushes the knee.

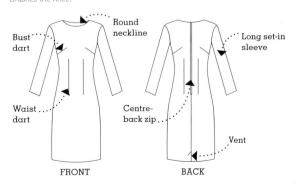

Round neckline

Bust dart

Long set-in sleeve

Waist dart

Centre-back zip

Vent

FRONT

BACK

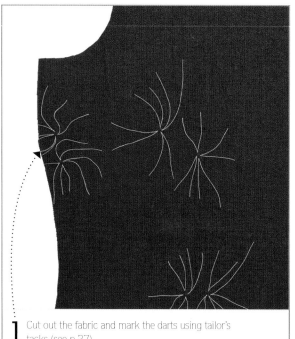

1 Cut out the fabric and mark the darts using tailor's tacks (see p.27).

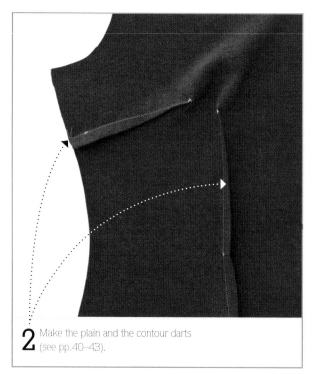

2 Make the plain and the contour darts (see pp.40–43).

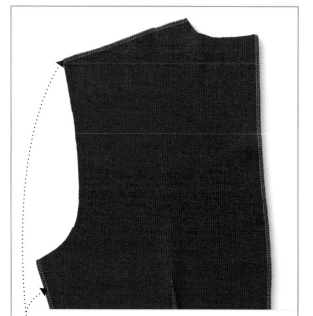

3 Neaten the shoulder seam, side seams on the front and back, and the CB (centre back) seams, using a 3-thread overlock stitch or a small zigzag stitch (see p.34).

4 Insert a zip of your choice in the CB. A centred zip is used here (see p.68).

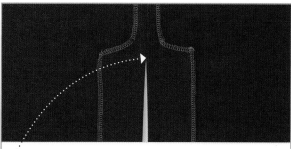

5 Stitch the remainder of the CB seam, stopping at the dot marking the top of the vent. Press the seam open.

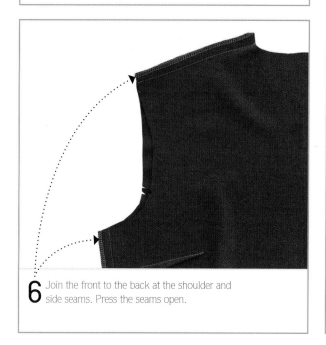

6 Join the front to the back at the shoulder and side seams. Press the seams open.

7 Neaten the sides and lower edge of both sleeves using either a 3-thread overlock stitch or a small zigzag stitch.

8 Machine the sleeve seam and press it open.

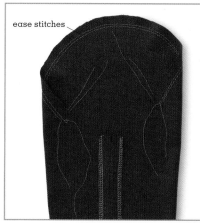

ease stitches

9 Using the longest stitch available, machine two rows of ease stitches through the sleeve head (see p.54).

10 Insert the sleeve into the armhole, RS (right side) to RS, remembering to pin and stitch from the sleeve side (see pp.54–55).

11 Attach a lightweight fusible interfacing to the neck facing pieces (see p.47).

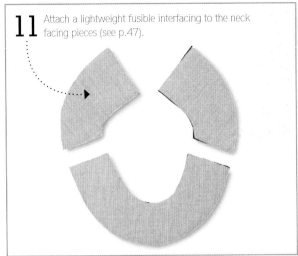

12 Join the facings at the shoulder seams and press the seams open. Neaten the lower edge (see pp.48–49).

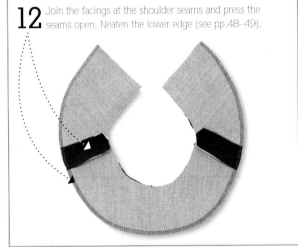

13 Place the facings to the neck edge of the dress RS to RS, matching the seams. Pin and machine.

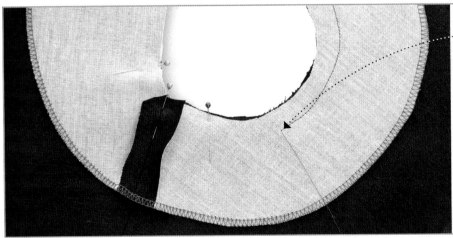

14 Layer the seam allowance by trimming the facing side of the seam to half its width. Clip the seam allowance to reduce bulk (see p.38).

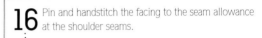
clipped seam allowance

layered seam allowance

15 Press the seam towards the facing and understitch (see p.39).

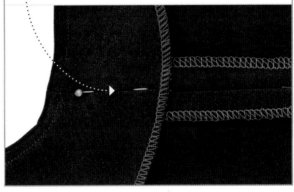

16 Pin and handstitch the facing to the seam allowance at the shoulder seams.

17 At the CB, fold the edge of the facing in to meet the zip tape. Pin and handstitch in place.

18 From the RS, the back neck edge should now look neatly finished.

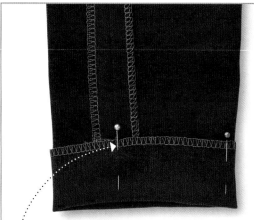

19 Turn up a 4cm (1½in) hem at the bottom of each sleeve. Pin and handstitch in place.

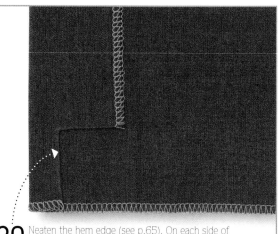

20 Neaten the hem edge (see p.65). On each side of the vent, remove a square of surplus fabric in the hem allowance.

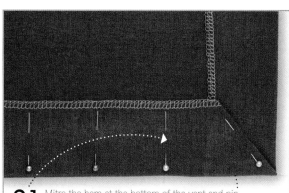

21 Mitre the hem at the bottom of the vent and pin. Turn up the remainder of the hem and pin.

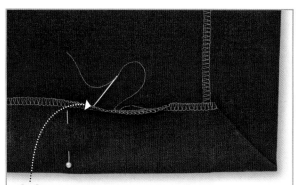

22 Handstitch the mitre and hem in place.

23 Machine through all layers at the top of the vent to secure.

Classic waisted dress

This dress has a darted bodice fitted into the waist for a smooth, flattering line at the waist and hips. Choose your pattern by your bust measurement and adjust at the waist and hips if necessary.

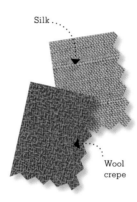

Silk

Wool crepe

This dress is made in polyester brocade, but this style of dress could be made in a variety of fabrics from cotton prints to lightweight wools, or silk.

BEFORE YOU START

YOU WILL NEED
- 2.5m (98in) x 150cm (59in) fabric
- 1 x reel matching all-purpose sewing thread
- 1 x reel contrasting all-purpose sewing thread for pattern marking
- 50cm (20in) lightweight interfacing
- 1 x 56cm (22in) zip

PREPARING THE PATTERN
- This dress is made using Dress pattern two (see pp.181–184)
- Follow the instructions (see pp.166–167) to download or copy the pattern in your size

GARMENT CONSTRUCTION

This unlined two-piece dress has waist darts in the bodice and in the skirt. It has long, fitted set-in sleeves and a lower neckline finished with a facing. There is a zip in the centre back and the A-line skirt sits just on the knee.

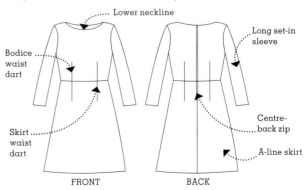

Lower neckline

Bodice waist dart

Skirt waist dart

Long set-in sleeve

Centre-back zip

A-line skirt

FRONT   BACK

HOW TO MAKE THE CLASSIC WAISTED DRESS

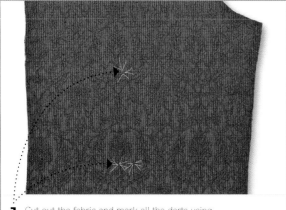

1 Cut out the fabric and mark all the darts using tailor's tacks (see p.27).

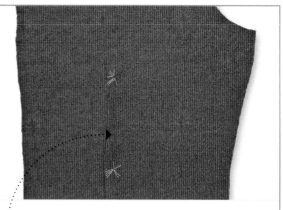

2 Make all the darts (see pp.40–41) and press towards the centre of the garment.

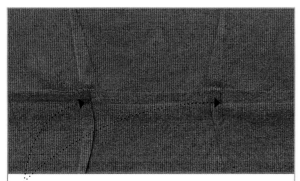

3 Join the front and back skirts to the front and back bodices, matching the darts. To ensure they match, you may have to ease the skirt to the bodice by stretching the bodice slightly. Press the seam allowances together.

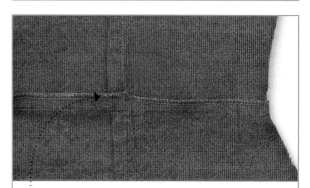

4 Neaten the seam allowances together using either a 3-thread overlock stitch or a small zigzag stitch (see p.34). Press up towards the bodice.

5 Using either a 3-thread overlock stitch or a small zigzag stitch, neaten the CB (centre back) seam, the side seams, and the shoulder seams on both the front and the back.

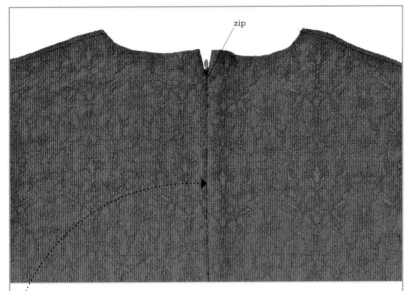

zip

6 Making sure the waist seams match on either side, insert a zip of your choice in the CB (see pp.67–68). Stitch the remainder of the CB seam and press open.

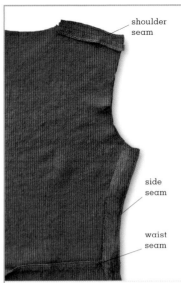

shoulder seam

side seam

waist seam

7 Join the front to the back at the shoulder and side seams, matching at the waist seam. Press the seams open.

8 Neaten the sides and lower edge of both sleeves using either a 3-thread overlock stitch or a small zigzag stitch.

ease stitches

9 Machine the sleeve seam and press open. Using stitch length 5, machine two rows of ease stitches through the sleeve head (see p.54).

10 Insert the sleeve (see pp.54–55) and neaten the raw edges using either a 3-thread overlock stitch or a small zigzag stitch.

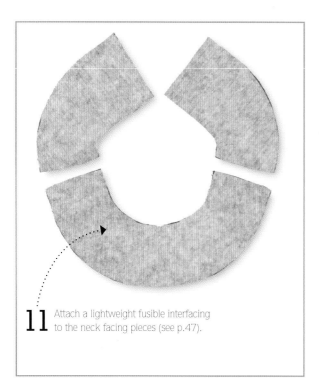

11 Attach a lightweight fusible interfacing to the neck facing pieces (see p.47).

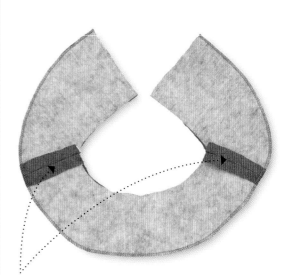

12 Join the facings at the shoulder seams and press the seams open (see p.48). Neaten the lower edge using either a 3-thread overlock stitch or a small zigzag stitch (see p.49).

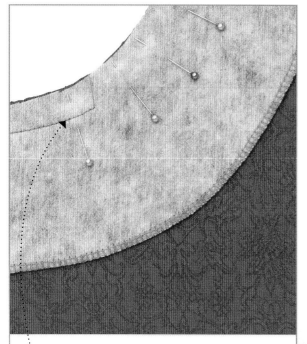

13 Place the facings to the neck edge of the dress RS (right side) to RS, matching the seams. Pin and machine.

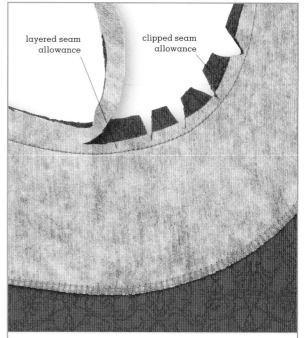

layered seam allowance

clipped seam allowance

14 Layer the seam allowance by trimming the facing side of the seam to half its width. Clip the seam allowance to reduce bulk (see p.38).

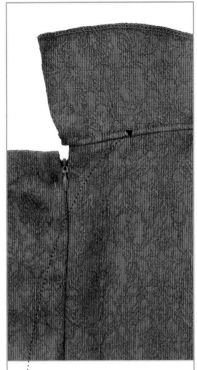

15 Underststitch the seam allowances to the facing (see p.39).

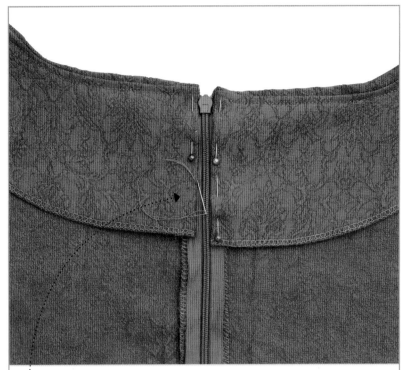

16 Turn the facing to the inside then, at the CB, fold the edge of the facing in to meet the zip tape. Pin and handstitch in place.

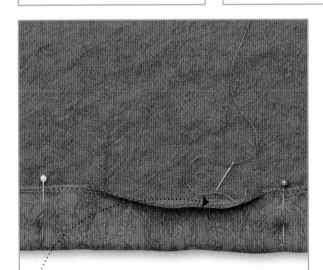

17 Neaten the hem edge (see p.65) and turn up by 4cm (1½in). To ease the fullness out of the hem, make a row of running stitches close to the neatened edge (see p.66). Pull the thread to tighten the fabric. Handstitch, then remove the tacking stitches.

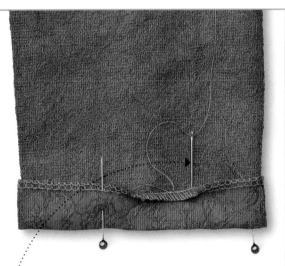

18 Turn up a 2.5cm (1in) hem at the bottom of each sleeve. Pin and handstitch in place.

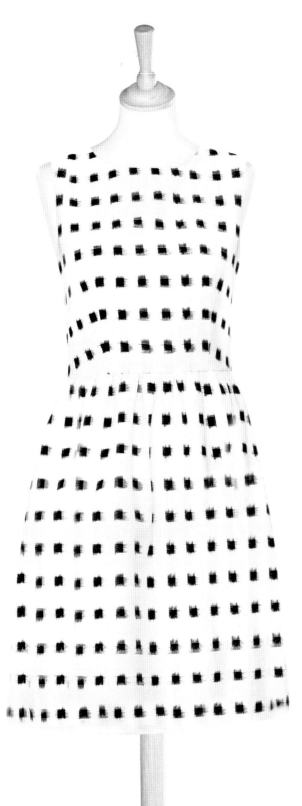

Sleeveless waisted dress

In this version of the Classic waisted dress the sleeves have been removed and a lining added. The dress has a gathered skirt. In a patterned fabric, it would be lovely for a summer wedding or even an evening function; in a plain fabric, it would be ideal for office wear.

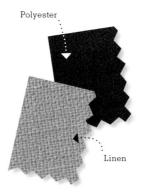

Polyester

Linen

This dress is made in a linen ikat weave, but heavy cotton, linen, polyester, and poly-viscose fabrics are all suitable.

BEFORE YOU START

YOU WILL NEED
- 2.2m (87in) x 150cm (59in) fabric
- 2.2m (87in) x 150cm (59in) lining fabric
- 1 x reel matching all-purpose sewing thread
- 1 x reel contrasting all-purpose sewing thread for pattern marking
- 1 x 56cm (22in) zip

PREPARING THE PATTERN
- This dress is made using Dress pattern two (see pp.181–184)
- Follow the instructions (see pp.166–167) to download or copy the pattern in your size

GARMENT CONSTRUCTION

This lined dress has a gathered A-line skirt and a fitted bodice with waist darts. The dress is sleeveless and has a scoop neck. There is a CB (centre back) zip.

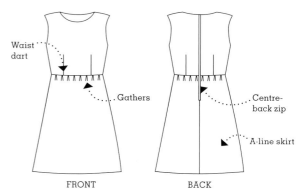

Waist dart

Gathers

FRONT

Centre-back zip

A-line skirt

BACK

HOW TO MAKE THE SLEEVELESS WAISTED DRESS

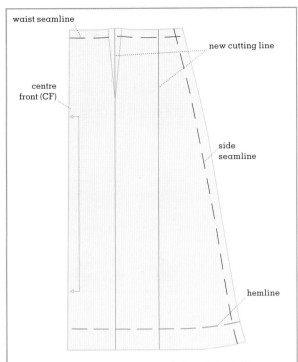

1 Copy the front skirt piece and mark the waist and side seamlines. Draw a vertical line parallel to the CF (centre front) through the dart from waist to hem. Draw a second line 9cm (3½in) away from this line (solid red lines). Repeat on the back skirt piece, drawing the vertical line parallel to the CB (centre back) seam.

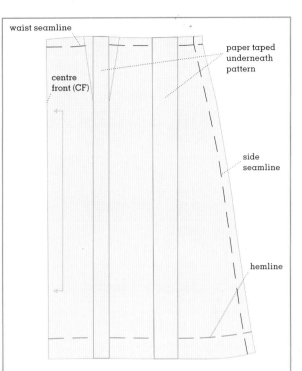

2 Cut through the vertical lines. Spread the cut pattern pieces apart through the dart by 3cm (1½in) at the waist and 2cm (¾in) at the hem, and at the second cut by 5cm (2in) at the waist and 4cm (1½in) at the hem. Place paper behind the pattern pieces and tape them down. (For sizes over a size 14 or for more fullness, double these measurements.) Repeat on the back.

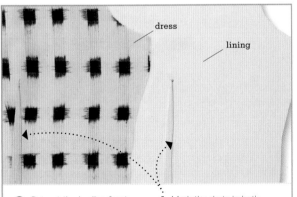

3 Cut out the bodice front, bodice back, skirt front, and skirt back from both the dress fabric and the lining.

4 Mark the darts in both fabrics with tailor's tacks (see p.27). Make the darts (see pp.40–41) and press towards the centre of the garment.

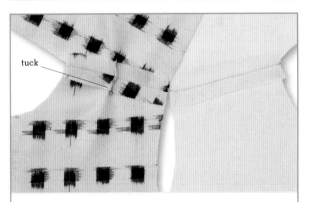

5 Join the front bodice to the back bodice RS (right side) to RS at the shoulder seam in both the dress fabric and the lining. Press the seams open. On the shoulder seam of the dress fabric make a 2mm (¹⁄₁₆in) tuck and pin in place.

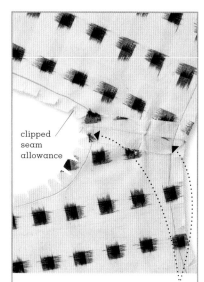

6 Place the dress fabric bodice to the lining bodice RS to RS matching at the shoulder seams. Pin and machine around the armholes and the neck. Clip the seam allowance to reduce bulk (see p.38).

clipped seam allowance

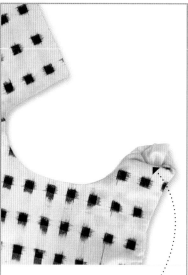

7 Remove the pin in each shoulder. To turn through to the right side, pull the back of the dress through the shoulders to the front. Roll the lining to the inside and press.

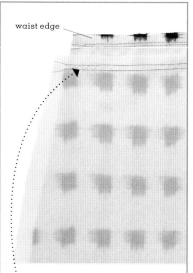

waist edge

8 Stitch two rows of long machine stitches, length 5, at the waist edge of the front and back skirt pieces in both the dress fabric and the lining (see p.44). Start and finish the stitching 2.5cm (1in) from the CB and side seams.

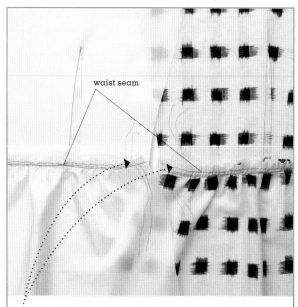

waist seam

9 In both the dress fabric and the lining place the front skirt to the front bodice RS to RS, and the back bodice pieces to the back skirts, RS to RS. Match the notches, pull up the two rows of stitches, and pin (see pp.44–45). Machine the waist seam.

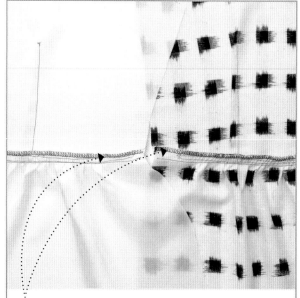

10 Neaten the seam allowances together using either a 3-thread overlock stitch or a small zigzag stitch (see p.34). Press the seam towards the bodice.

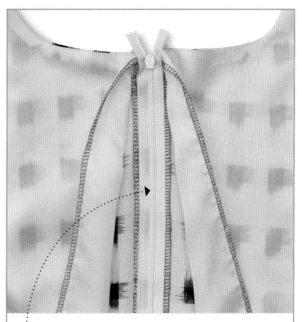

11 Using either a 3-thread overlock stitch or a small zigzag stitch, neaten the CB seam and the side seam allowances in both the dress fabric and the lining.

12 Insert a zip of your choice in the CB of just the dress fabric (see pp.67–68). Stitch the remainder of the CB seam in the dress fabric.

13 Stitch the CB seam in the lining leaving a gap for the zip.

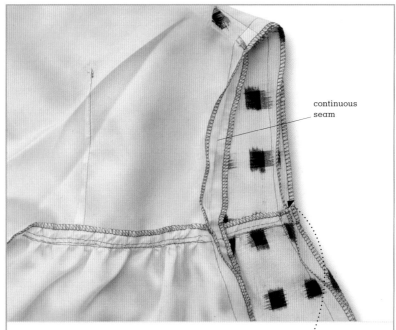

continuous seam

14 With RS to RS place the front to the back. Join the side seams by stitching through the fabric and lining in one continuous seam. Match the seams at the waist and armholes.

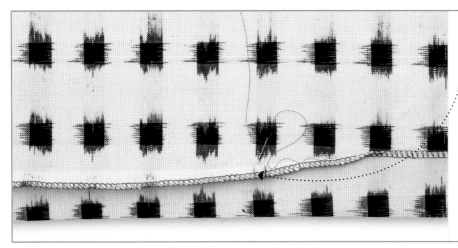

15 Neaten the hem edge of the dress (see p.65). Turn up a 4cm (1½in) hem and handstitch in place.

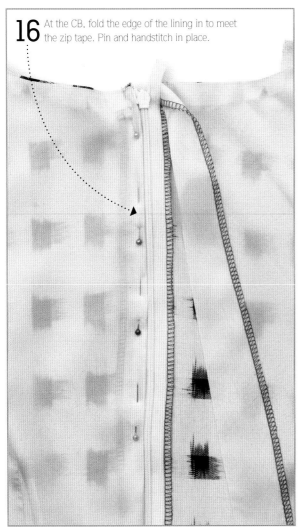

16 At the CB, fold the edge of the lining in to meet the zip tape. Pin and handstitch in place.

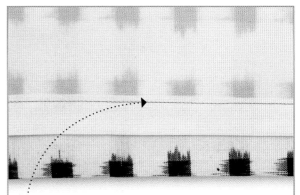

17 Trim the lining level to the finished hem of the dress and machine a 1.5cm (⅝in) double-turn hem (see p.66).

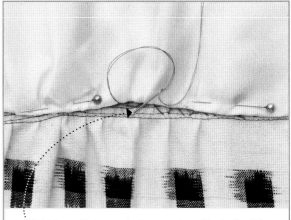

18 At the waist, turn under the raw edge of the bodice lining. Pin and handstitch to the waist seam.

Classic empire line dress

Those ladies of The First French Empire certainly knew how to flatter the figure. The high waist conceals a fuller waistline and the low neck sets off the face and neck. Choose your pattern size by your bust measurement and check for fit in the hip and waist areas. This is an easy-to-wear day dress that can take you from work to dinner.

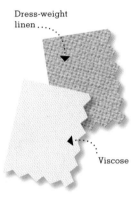

Dress-weight linen

Viscose

This dress has been made in cotton, but many fabrics suit this style including lightweight tweeds, wool suiting, silks, linens, viscose, or polyester.

BEFORE YOU START

YOU WILL NEED

- 2.50m (98½in) x 150cm (59in) fabric
- 1 x reel matching all-purpose sewing thread
- 1 x reel contrasting all-purpose sewing thread for pattern marking
- 50cm (20in) lightweight interfacing
- 1 x 56cm (22in) zip

PREPARING THE PATTERN

- This dress is made using Dress pattern three (see pp.185–189)
- Follow the instructions (see pp.166–167) to download or copy the pattern in your size

GARMENT CONSTRUCTION

This unlined dress has wrist-length sleeves and a wide, low neckline finished with a facing. The waist darts of the bodice meet the skirt darts at an under-bust seamline. There is a centre back (CB) zip and a vent in the gently shaped A-line skirt.

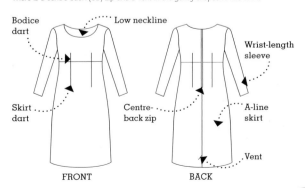

Bodice dart

Low neckline

Skirt dart

Centre-back zip

Wrist-length sleeve

A-line skirt

Vent

FRONT

BACK

HOW TO MAKE THE CLASSIC EMPIRE LINE DRESS

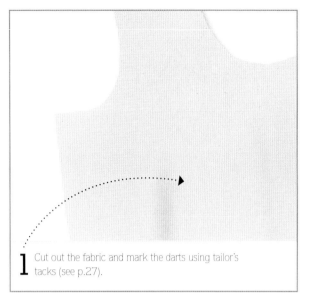

1 Cut out the fabric and mark the darts using tailor's tacks (see p.27).

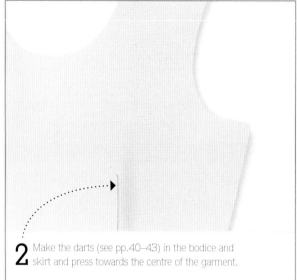

2 Make the darts (see pp.40–43) in the bodice and skirt and press towards the centre of the garment.

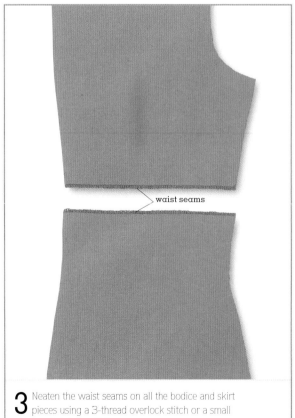

waist seams

3 Neaten the waist seams on all the bodice and skirt pieces using a 3-thread overlock stitch or a small zigzag stitch (see p.34).

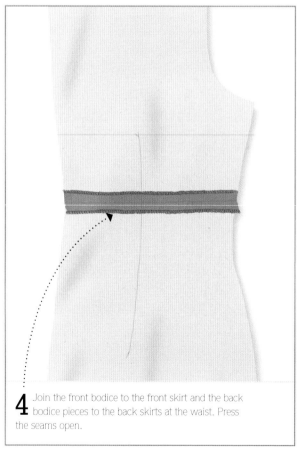

4 Join the front bodice to the front skirt and the back bodice pieces to the back skirts at the waist. Press the seams open.

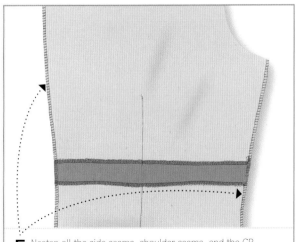

5 Neaten all the side seams, shoulder seams, and the CB (centre back) seam using a 3-thread overlock stitch or a small zigzag stitch.

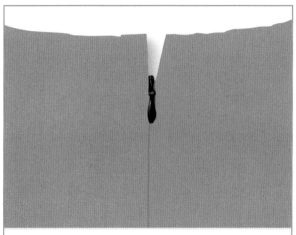

6 Insert a zip of your choice in the CB (see pp.67–68). Stitch the remainder of the CB seam, stopping at the dot marking the top of the vent.

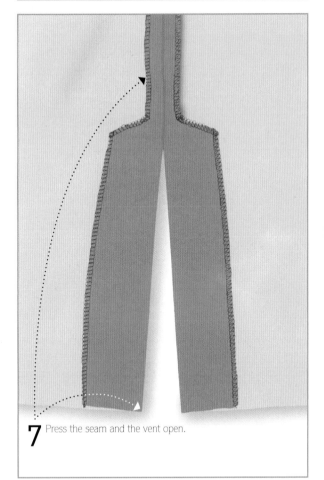

7 Press the seam and the vent open.

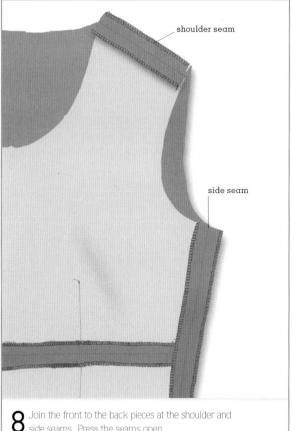

shoulder seam

side seam

8 Join the front to the back pieces at the shoulder and side seams. Press the seams open.

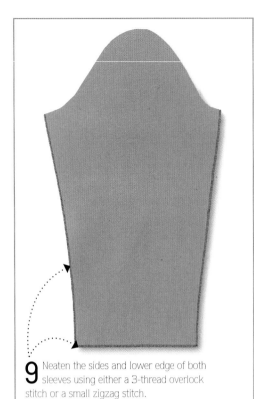

9 Neaten the sides and lower edge of both sleeves using either a 3-thread overlock stitch or a small zigzag stitch.

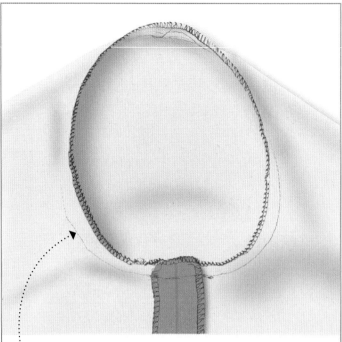

10 Machine the sleeve side seam and press it open. Using the longest stitch available, machine two rows of ease stitches through the sleeve head (see p.54). Fit the sleeve into the armhole, RS (right side) to RS. Pin, then stitch the sleeve into place from the sleeve side (see pp.54–55).

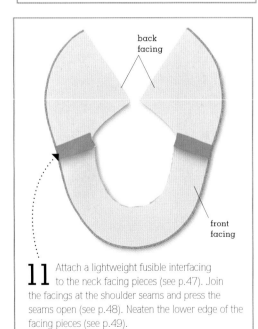

back facing

front facing

11 Attach a lightweight fusible interfacing to the neck facing pieces (see p.47). Join the facings at the shoulder seams and press the seams open (see p.48). Neaten the lower edge of the facing pieces (see p.49).

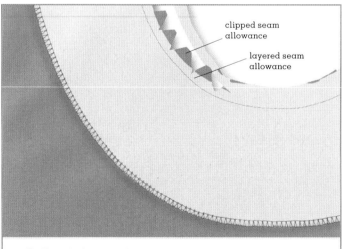

clipped seam allowance

layered seam allowance

12 Place the facings to the neck edge of the dress RS to RS, matching the seams. Pin and machine. Layer the seam allowance by trimming the facing side of the seam to half its width. Clip the seam allowance to reduce bulk (see p.38).

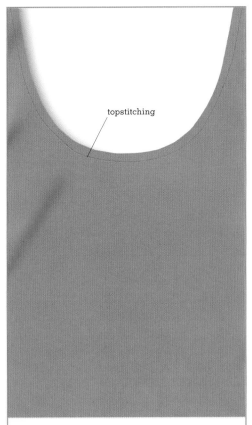

13 Turn the facing to the WS (wrong side), press and topstitch (see p.39) to hold in place.

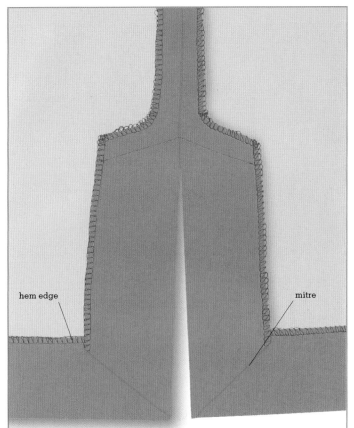

14 Neaten the hem edge (see p.65). On each side of the vent, remove the surplus fabric in the hem allowance. Mitre the hem at the bottom of the vent and pin. Turn up the remainder of the hem and pin. Handstitch the mitre and hem in place.

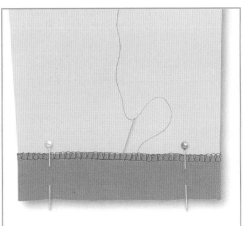

15 Turn up the sleeve hem by 3cm (1½in), pin and handstitch in place.

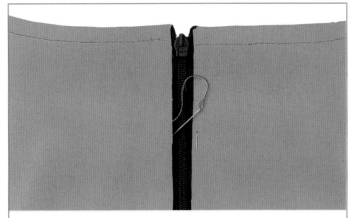

16 At the CB, fold the edge of the facing in to meet the zip tape. Pin and handstitch in place.

Sleeveless empire line dress

This dress features tucks in the skirt, which give a full yet sleek, smooth line. It is lined but also has facings to show an alternative way of inserting a lining into a sleeveless dress. Made in silk, this is ideal for a party; try a poly-cotton mix for daywear.

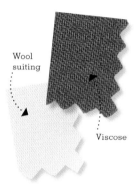

Wool suiting

Viscose

This dress is silk dupion but it could also be made in poly-cotton, viscose, or wool suiting.

BEFORE YOU START

YOU WILL NEED

- 1.75m (69in) x 150cm (59in) fabric
- 1.75m (69in) x 150cm (59in) lining fabric
- 1 x reel matching all-purpose sewing thread
- 1 x reel contrasting all-purpose sewing thread for pattern marking
- 50cm (20in) x lightweight fusible interfacing
- 1 x 56cm (22in) zip

PREPARING THE PATTERN

- This dress is made using Dress pattern three (see pp.185–189)
- Follow the instructions (see pp.166–167) to download or copy the pattern in your size

GARMENT CONSTRUCTION

This sleeveless empire line dress has front and back bodice darts at the waist that line up with tucks in the skirt. The tucks give a fuller skirt. The dress is lined and the neckline is faced.

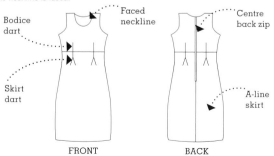

Bodice dart

Faced neckline

Centre back zip

Skirt dart

A-line skirt

FRONT

BACK

HOW TO MAKE THE SLEEVELESS EMPIRE LINE DRESS

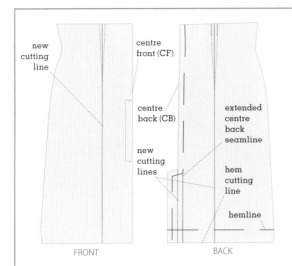

FRONT   BACK

1 Copy the skirt front and back and mark the seamlines and hemlines. On the front, draw a vertical line parallel to the CF (centre front). On the back, draw a vertical line parallel to the CB (centre back) seam through the dart to the hem cutting line. To remove the vent, extend the CB seamline to the hemline. Draw a new cutting line 1.5cm (⅝in) to the left of it.

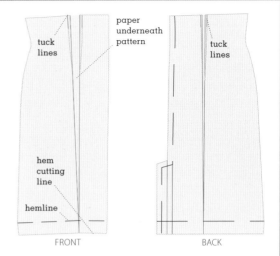

FRONT   BACK

2 Cut through the vertical lines to within 3mm (⅛in) of the hem cutting line. Place paper underneath, and spread the cut pattern pieces apart through the front waist by 3cm (1½in) and through the back waist by 1.5cm (⅝in). Tape the pattern pieces to the paper. Mark the tuck lines at points 4cm (1½in) below the waist, following the original dart seamlines.

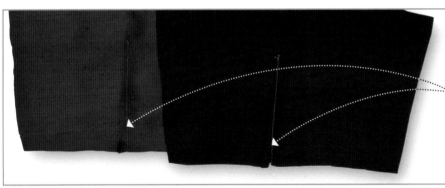

3 Cut out the fabric and the lining using the new skirt pieces and the bodice pieces.

4 Mark the darts in both the fabric and the lining bodices with tailor's tacks (see p.27). Make the darts (see pp.40–41) and press towards the centre of the body.

5 Make the tucks in both the fabric and lining skirt front and skirt backs by bringing the tuck lines at the waist edge together RS (right side) to RS. Stitch along the tuck lines 4cm (1½in). Press towards the side seamlines.

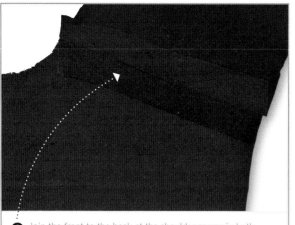

6 Join the front to the back at the shoulder seams in both the fabric and the lining bodices. Press the seams open.

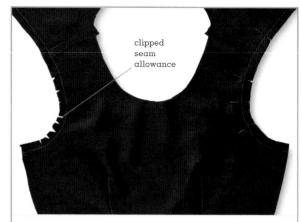

clipped seam allowance

7 Place the fabric bodice to the lining bodice RS to RS and matching at the shoulder seams. Pin and machine just around the armholes. Clip the seam allowance (see p.38).

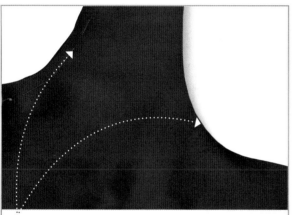

8 Turn through to the right side, roll the lining to the inside and press. Tack the raw edges together around the neck.

9 Working separately on the fabric and the lining, follow steps 3–7 of the Classic empire line dress, leaving a gap corresponding to the zip in the lining. Do not neaten the bodice seams and ignore the reference to the CB vent.

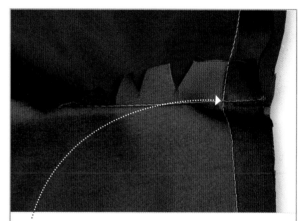

10 With RS to RS place the front to the back. Join the side seams by stitching through the fabric and lining in one continuous seam. Press the seams open.

11 Make and attach the neck facing to the tacked raw neck edge as for the Classic empire line dress steps 11–12.

12 Neaten the hem edge of the dress (see p.65). Turn up a 4cm (1½in) hem and handstitch in place. Trim the lining level to the finished hem of the dress and machine a 2cm (¾in) double-turn hem (see p.66).

Classic tailored trousers

These trousers with their slanted hip pockets and shaped waistband have a timeless appeal. Choose your pattern according to your full hip measurement. To ensure a good fit, check your crotch measurements against the pattern and make the trousers in calico first. If necessary, alter the pattern before cutting out your fabric.

Gabardine

Stretch cotton

We made our trousers in a wool flannel but you can also try them in a gabardine or a polyester and wool mix. They would also work well in a fabric with a 2 or 3 per cent stretch.

BEFORE YOU START

YOU WILL NEED

- 2.5m (98½in) x 150cm (59in) fabric
- 30cm (12in) x 150cm lining fabric
- 1 x reel matching all-purpose sewing thread
- 1 x reel contrasting all-purpose sewing thread for pattern marking
- 50cm (20in) x medium-weight fusible interfacing
- 1 x 18cm (7¼in) trouser zip
- 1 x trouser hook and eye

PREPARING THE PATTERN

- These trousers are made using Trouser pattern one (see pp.190–193)
- Follow the instructions (see pp.166–167) to download or copy the pattern in your size

GARMENT CONSTRUCTION

The trousers feature a flat front with a fly-front zip opening and a slightly tapered leg. They have slanted pockets on the hip and a shaped waistband that sits just below the natural waistline.

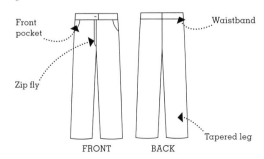

Front pocket

Zip fly

Waistband

Tapered leg

FRONT   BACK

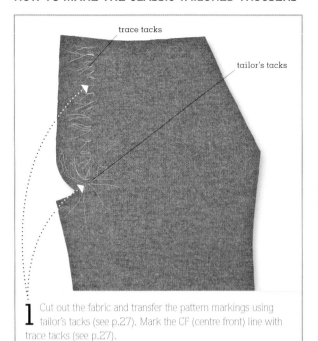

trace tacks

tailor's tacks

1 Cut out the fabric and transfer the pattern markings using tailor's tacks (see p.27). Mark the CF (centre front) line with trace tacks (see p.27).

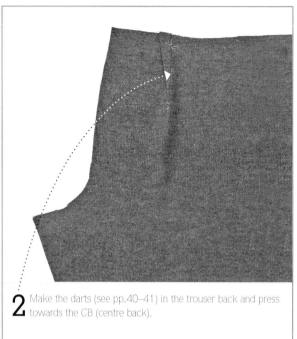

2 Make the darts (see pp.40–41) in the trouser back and press towards the CB (centre back).

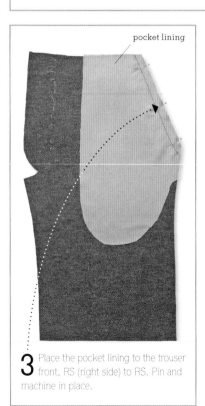

pocket lining

3 Place the pocket lining to the trouser front. RS (right side) to RS. Pin and machine in place.

topstitching

4 Clip the seam allowance. Turn the pocket lining to the inside and press. Topstitch (see p.39) to secure.

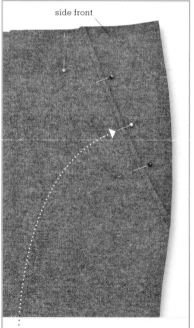

side front

5 On the RS, pin the trouser front to the side front, matching the markings. Pin securely.

6 On the WS (wrong side), pin and stitch around the pocket bag. Neaten using a 3-thread overlock stitch or a small zigzag stitch (see p.34). Be careful not to sew through the trouser front.

7 Neaten the side, crotch, and inside leg seams of the front and back trouser legs using a 3-thread overlock stitch or a small zigzag stitch.

8 Join a front leg to a back leg at the outside and inside leg seams to make each leg. Press the seams open.

9 Join the crotch seams, RS to RS, stopping at the tailor's tack at the CF.

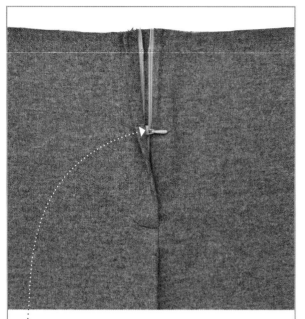

10 Insert a faced fly-front zip (see pp.69–70) at the CF.

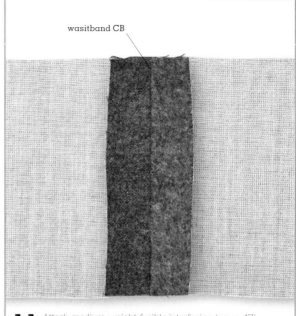

wasitband CB

11 Attach medium-weight fusible interfacing (see p.47) to one set of waistbands. Join each set of waistbands at the CB and press the seams open.

layered seam allowance

12 Attach the waistband to the trousers, matching at the CB seams (see p.52). Layer the seam allowance by trimming the trouser side of the seam to half its width (see p.38). Press towards the waistband.

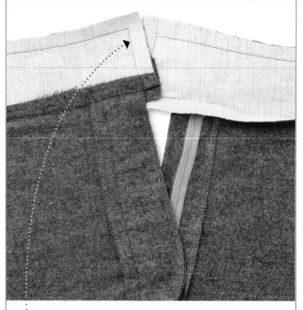

13 Place the remaining waistband to the interfaced waistband RS to RS and stitch around the waistband.

clipped end

14 Clip the ends of the waistband to reduce bulk. Turn the waistband to the RS, fold under the raw edge, pin and handstitch in place to the trouser-to-waistband seamline.

15 The finished waist at the CF from the RS.

16 Neaten the hem edge of the trouser legs by overlocking (see p.65). Turn up a 4cm (1½in) hem and handstitch in place.

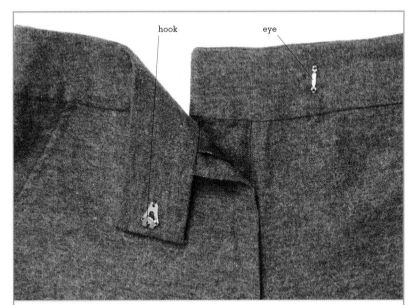

hook   eye

17 Attach a trouser hook to the waistband extension and an eye to the other end of the waistband (see p.73).

Classic palazzo trousers

Wide-leg, or palazzo, trousers are very flattering especially if worn with a high heel. They retain their smooth silhouette by having discreet in-seam pockets.

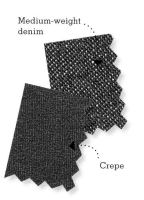

Medium-weight denim

Crepe

We made our trousers in linen, but you could try a crepe for evening, or a medium-weight denim or printed linen for daywear. Medium-weight fabrics give maximum impact for this style.

BEFORE YOU START

YOU WILL NEED

- 2.7m (106¼in) x 150cm (59in) fabric
- 30cm (12in) x 150cm (59in) lining fabric
- 1 x reel matching all-purpose sewing thread
- 1 x reel contrasting all-purpose sewing thread for pattern marking
- 1m (39¼in) x fusible waistband interfacing
- 1 x trouser hook and eye
- 1 x 18cm (7in) trouser zip

PREPARING THE PATTERN

- These are made using Trouser pattern two (see pp.194–197)
- Follow the instructions (see pp.166–167) to download or copy the pattern in your size

GARMENT CONSTRUCTION

These wide-leg trousers have a fly-front zip opening and a fitted waistband. Belt loops on the waistband take a narrow belt. The trousers feature in-seam pockets and front and back tucks at the waist.

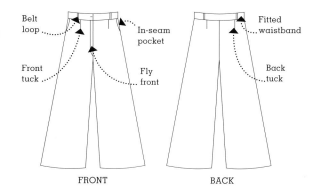

Belt loop

In-seam pocket

Front tuck

Fly front

FRONT

Fitted waistband

Back tuck

BACK

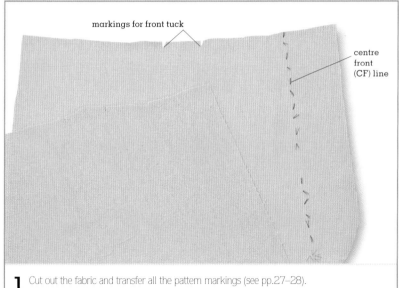

markings for front tuck

centre front (CF) line

1 Cut out the fabric and transfer all the pattern markings (see pp.27–28). Mark the CF (centre front) line, the front tuck, and the pocket opening with trace tacks (see p.27).

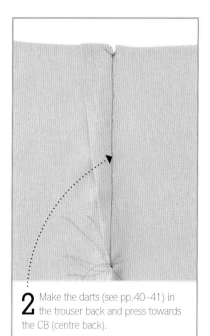

2 Make the darts (see pp.40–41) in the trouser back and press towards the CB (centre back).

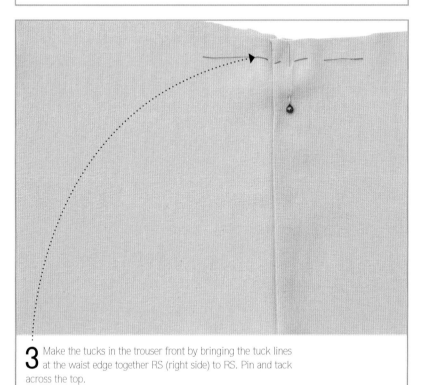

3 Make the tucks in the trouser front by bringing the tuck lines at the waist edge together RS (right side) to RS. Pin and tack across the top.

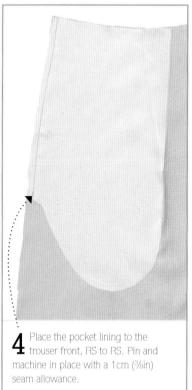

4 Place the pocket lining to the trouser front, RS to RS. Pin and machine in place with a 1cm (⅜in) seam allowance.

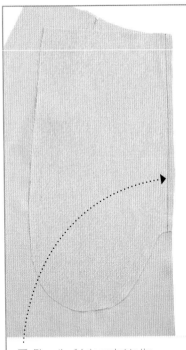

5 Place the fabric pocket to the trouser back, RS to RS. Pin and machine in place with a 1cm (⅜in) seam allowance.

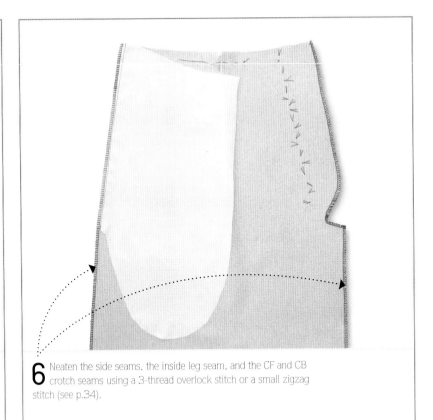

6 Neaten the side seams, the inside leg seam, and the CF and CB crotch seams using a 3-thread overlock stitch or a small zigzag stitch (see p.34).

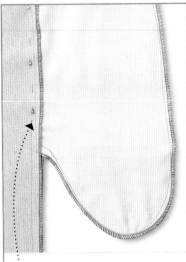

7 Join the trouser front to the trouser back at the side seams, leaving open above the point marked for the pocket opening. Stitch around the edges of the pocket bag and neaten.

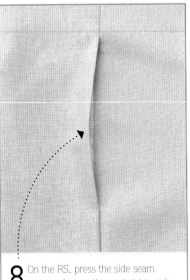

8 On the RS, press the side seam open and press the pocket towards the trouser front.

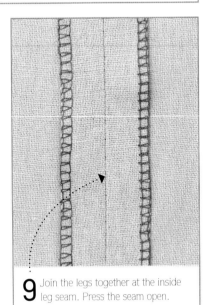

9 Join the legs together at the inside leg seam. Press the seam open.

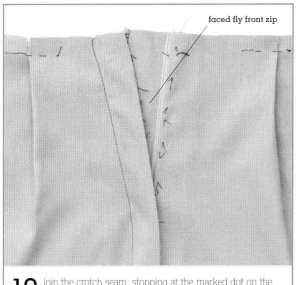

faced fly front zip

10 Join the crotch seam, stopping at the marked dot on the CF. Insert a faced fly-front zip (see pp.69–70).

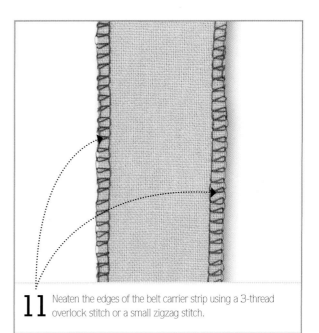

11 Neaten the edges of the belt carrier strip using a 3-thread overlock stitch or a small zigzag stitch.

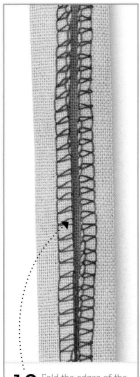

12 Fold the edges of the belt carrier strip to the centre, WS (wrong side) to WS, and press.

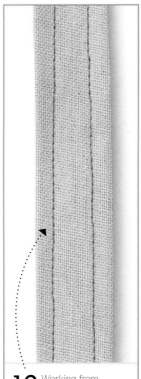

13 Working from the RS, topstitch (see p.39) either side of the belt carrier strip.

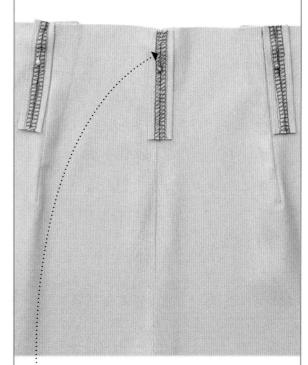

14 Cut the belt carrier strip into five pieces as indicated on the pattern. Pin, then stitch a belt carrier to each tuck, to each back dart, and to the CB seam.

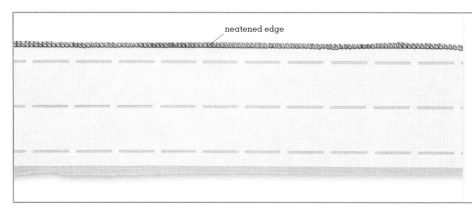

15 Attach fusible interfacing to the waistband (see p.47). Neaten one long edge using a 3-thread overlock stitch or a small zigzag stitch.

neatened edge

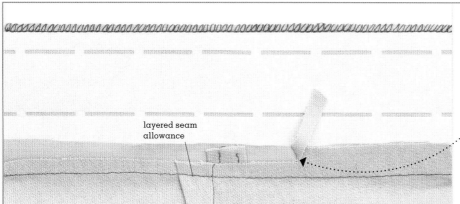

16 Attach the other edge of the waistband to the trousers, RS to RS (see p.52), stitching over the ends of the belt carriers. Layer the seam allowance by trimming the waistband side of the seam to half its width (see p.38). Press towards the waistband.

layered seam allowance

17 Fold the waistband along the crease in the interfacing RS to RS. At the CF, stitch along the ends of the waistband.

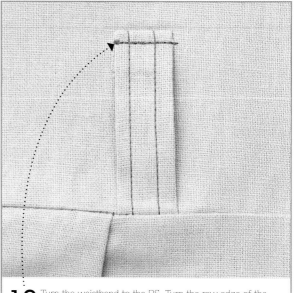

18 Turn the waistband to the RS. Turn the raw edge of the free ends of the belt carriers under and topstitch in place.

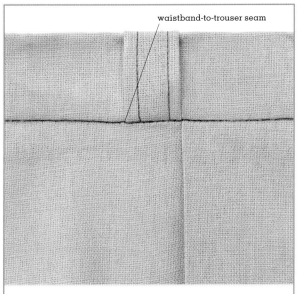

waistband-to-trouser seam

19 Fold the waistband WS to WS. Pin the free edge of the waistband to the waistband-to-trouser seam. Working from the RS of the trousers, stitch in the ditch – the line produced by the waistband-to-trouser seam – through all layers to secure the waistband in place.

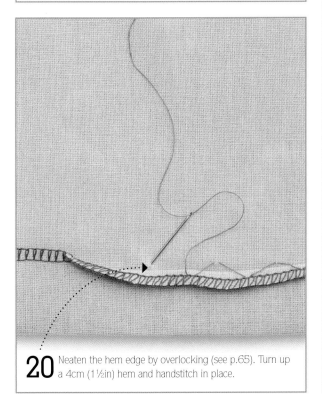

20 Neaten the hem edge by overlocking (see p.65). Turn up a 4cm (1½in) hem and handstitch in place.

hook

eye

21 Attach a trouser hook and eye to the waistband (see p.73).

Wide-leg shorts

Here the palazzo trousers have been shortened and their front tucks widened to give more fullness. The result? A pair of shorts that are super-comfortable to wear. We made ours in cotton with a small spot print, but almost any lightweight fabric would work for this summery style.

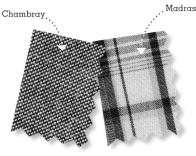

Chambray · · · · · ·   · · · · · · Madras

Cotton, linen, polyester, chambray, and madras all work well for these shorts.

BEFORE YOU START

YOU WILL NEED
- 1.20m (47¼in) x 150cm (59in) fabric
- 30cm (12in) x lining fabric
- 1 x reel matching all-purpose sewing thread
- 1 x reel contrasting all-purpose sewing thread for pattern marking
- 1m (39¼in) x fusible waistband interfacing
- 1 x 18cm (7¼in) trouser zip
- 1 x button

PREPARING THE PATTERN
- These shorts are made using Trouser pattern two (see pp.194–197)
- Follow the instructions (see pp.166–167) to download or copy the pattern in your size

GARMENT CONSTRUCTION

The wide-leg shorts have a fly-front zip opening and a fitted waistband, and feature in-seam pockets. There are generous front and back tucks at the waist for comfort.

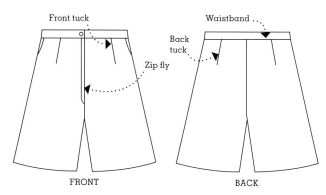

Front tuck

Zip fly

Waistband · · · ·

Back tuck · · · · · ·

FRONT   BACK

HOW TO MAKE THE WIDE-LEG SHORTS

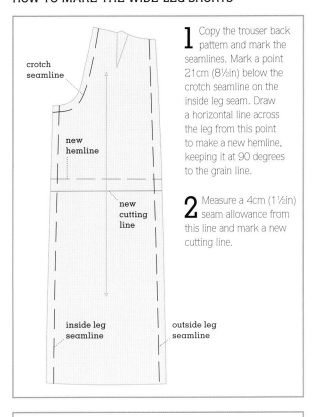

1 Copy the trouser back pattern and mark the seamlines. Mark a point 21cm (8½in) below the crotch seamline on the inside leg seam. Draw a horizontal line across the leg from this point to make a new hemline, keeping it at 90 degrees to the grain line.

2 Measure a 4cm (1½in) seam allowance from this line and mark a new cutting line.

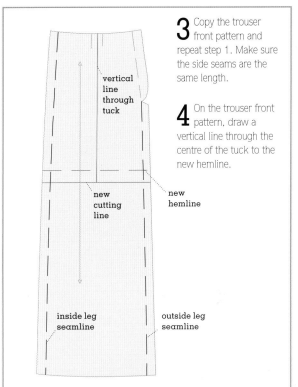

3 Copy the trouser front pattern and repeat step 1. Make sure the side seams are the same length.

4 On the trouser front pattern, draw a vertical line through the centre of the tuck to the new hemline.

5 Cut through the vertical line, place paper underneath, and spread the cut pattern pieces apart by 2cm (¾in) at the waist and 3cm (1¼in) at the hem to make the shorts fuller at the front. Tape the pattern pieces to the paper. (For sizes over a size 14 or for fuller thighs, you may need to increase this measurement by 50 per cent.)

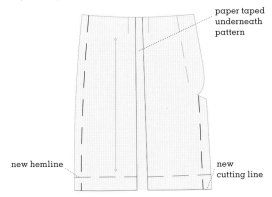

6 Cut out and make the shorts as for the Classic palazzo trousers, steps 1–18. You can add belt carriers if you wish.

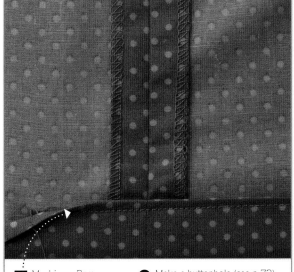

7 Machine a 2cm (¾in) double-turn hem (see p.66). Press.

8 Make a buttonhole (see p.72) on the waistband overlap and attach a corresponding button (see p.71) to the underlap.

Classic shell top

The ultimate in simplicity, this style of top is known as a shell top as it fits the upper body like a shell fits an oyster. The centre-back zip helps ensure a smooth line for a top that is easy office wear, whether under a jacket or on its own. It would comfortably tuck into a skirt or trousers, or could be worn untucked. Choose the pattern by your bust measurement and, if necessary, widen at the hip.

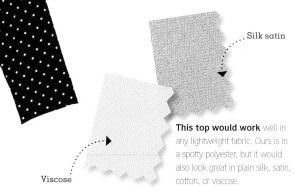

Silk satin

Viscose

This top would work well in any lightweight fabric. Ours is in a spotty polyester, but it would also look great in plain silk, satin, cotton, or viscose.

BEFORE YOU START

YOU WILL NEED

- 1.75m (68¾in) x 150cm (59in) fabric
- 1 x reel matching all-purpose sewing thread
- 1 x reel contrasting all-purpose sewing thread for pattern marking
- 50cm (20in) lightweight fusible interfacing
- 1 x 40cm (16in) zip

PREPARING THE PATTERN

- This top is made using Top pattern one (see pp.198–200)
- Follow the instructions (see pp.166–167) to download or copy the pattern in your size

GARMENT CONSTRUCTION

The top is shaped with bust darts and has a round neckline finished with a facing. It has wrist-length, set-in sleeves that should sit comfortably at the end of the shoulder. There is a CB (centre-back) zip for ease of wear.

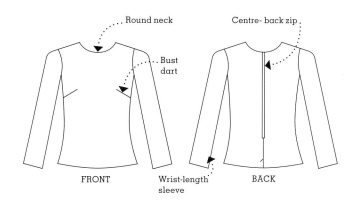

Round neck

Bust dart

Centre- back zip

FRONT

Wrist-length sleeve

BACK

HOW TO MAKE THE CLASSIC SHELL TOP

1 Cut out the fabric and mark the darts using tailor's tacks (see p.27).

2 Make the darts in the front (see pp.40–41) and press towards the waist.

3 Neaten the CB (centre back) seam, using either a 3-thread overlock stitch or a small zigzag stitch (see p.34).

4 Insert a 40cm (16in) zip of your choice in the CB (see pp.67–68). Stitch the remainder of the CB seam.

5 Join the front to the back at the shoulder and side seams, RS (right side) to RS. Neaten the seam allowances together using either a 3-thread overlock stitch or a small zigzag stitch.

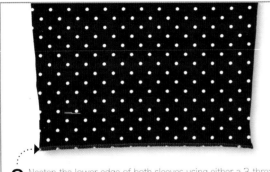

6 Neaten the lower edge of both sleeves using either a 3-thread overlock stitch or a small zigzag stitch.

ease stitches

7 Machine the sleeve seam. Neaten the seam allowances together using either a 3-thread overlock stitch or a small zigzag stitch. Using the longest stitch available, machine two rows of ease stitches through the sleeve head (see p.54).

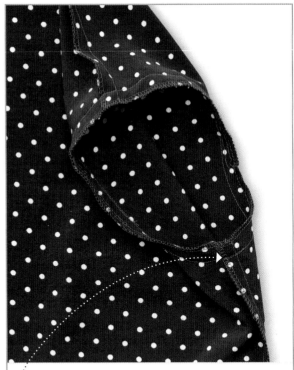

8 Fit the sleeve into the armhole, RS (right side) to RS, remembering to pin and stitch from the sleeve side (see pp.54–55). Neaten the seam allowances together using either a 3-thread overlock stitch or a small zigzag stitch.

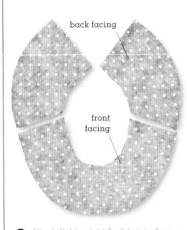

back facing

front facing

9 Attach lightweight fusible interfacing to the neck facing pieces (see p.47).

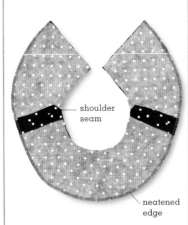

shoulder seam

neatened edge

10 Join the facings at the shoulder seams and press the seams open (see p.48). Neaten the lower edge (see p.49).

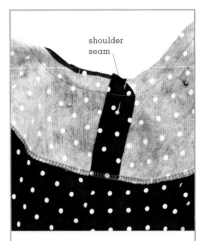

shoulder seam

11 Place the facings to the neck edge of the top RS to RS, matching the shoulder seams. Pin and machine.

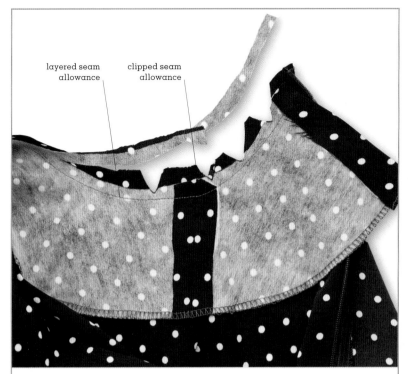

layered seam allowance

clipped seam allowance

12 Layer the seam allowance by trimming the facing side of the seam to half its width. Clip the seam allowance to reduce bulk (see p.38).

13 Turn the facing to the WS (wrong side) and press.

14 At the CB, fold the edge of the facing in to meet the zip tape. Pin and handstitch in place.

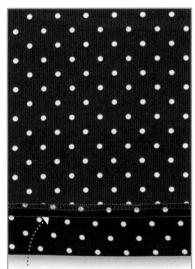

15 Neaten the lower edge of the top. Pin up 4cm (1½in) on the top and 3cm (1¼in) on the sleeves. Press and machine in place.

16 Topstitch around the neck (see p.39), using stitch length 3.5.

Tie-neck top

The shell top has now become a top with a slightly lower neckline, a tie neck, and a gathered sleeve. The back no longer features a zip but is cut in one piece. This neckline flatters the face and is easy to wear with a skirt, trousers, or jeans.

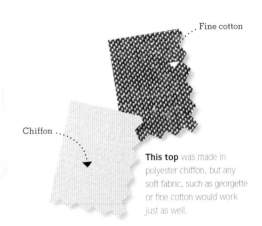

Fine cotton

Chiffon

This top was made in polyester chiffon, but any soft fabric, such as georgette or fine cotton would work just as well.

BEFORE YOU START

YOU WILL NEED

- 2m (79in) x 150cm (59in) fabric
- 1 x reel matching all-purpose sewing thread
- 1 x reel contrasting all-purpose sewing thread for pattern marking
- 50cm (20in) x 2cm (¾in) wide elastic

PREPARING THE PATTERN

- This top is made using Top pattern one (see pp.198–200)
- Follow the instructions (see pp.166–167) to download or copy the pattern in your size

GARMENT CONSTRUCTION

This blouse has bust darts, a self-bound neck opening, a tie neck, and sleeves that are elasticated to fit the wrist.

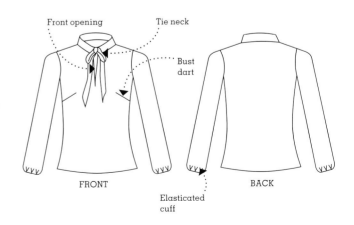

Front opening

Tie neck

Bust dart

FRONT

BACK

Elasticated cuff

HOW TO MAKE THE TIE-NECK TOP

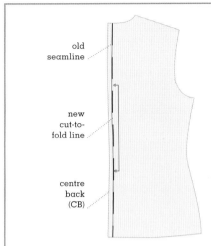

old seamline

new cut-to-fold line

centre back (CB)

1 To cut the back as one piece, copy the pattern back and mark the CB (centre back) seamline. Put a ruler along the seamline and rule a new straight line in its place. This line will be placed to a fold for cutting.

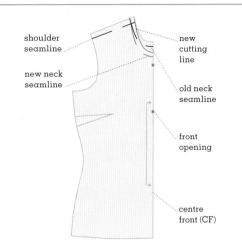

shoulder seamline

new neck seamline

new cutting line

old neck seamline

front opening

centre front (CF)

2 Copy the pattern front and mark the seamlines. Mark a point on the CF (centre front) 3.5cm (1⅜in) below the neck seamline. From here, draw a new neck seamline to the point where the neck and shoulder seamlines meet. Measure a 1.5cm (⅝in) seam allowance from the new neck seamline and mark a new cutting line. On the CF, mark a point 16cm (6⅓in) below the new neck seamline.

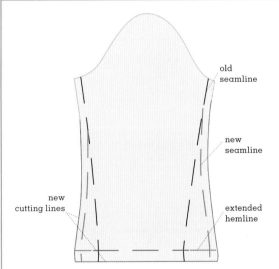

old seamline

new seamline

new cutting lines

extended hemline

3 To widen the sleeve, copy the sleeve pattern and mark the seamlines. Extend the hemline by 6cm (2⅜in) on each side. Draw a slightly curving line from these two points to join them to the sleeve seamlines in the upper arm area. Draw new cutting lines 1.5cm (⅝in) below the new hemline and at either side of the new sleeve seamlines.

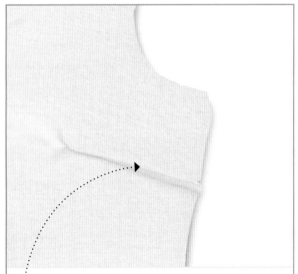

4 Cut out the fabric using the new pattern pieces. Mark the darts using tailor's tacks (see p.27). Make the darts (see pp.40–41) and press towards the waist.

5 Make up as for the Classic shell top steps 5–8, using the seam for sheer fabrics method (see p.36).

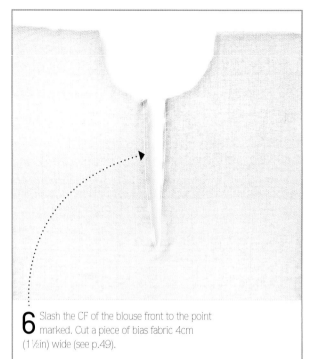

6 Slash the CF of the blouse front to the point marked. Cut a piece of bias fabric 4cm (1½in) wide (see p.49).

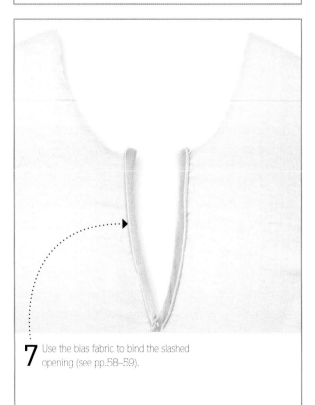

7 Use the bias fabric to bind the slashed opening (see pp.58–59).

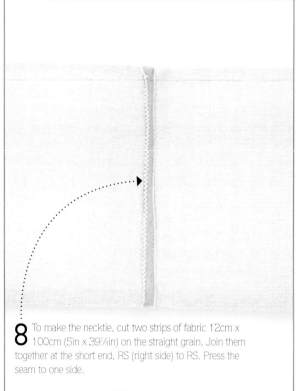

8 To make the necktie, cut two strips of fabric 12cm x 100cm (5in x 39¼in) on the straight grain. Join them together at the short end, RS (right side) to RS. Press the seam to one side.

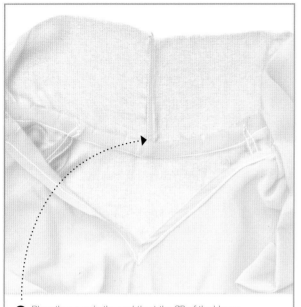

9 Place the seam in the necktie at the CB of the blouse, RS to RS. Machine around the neck edge. Clip the seam allowance and press towards the necktie.

10 Fold the necktie, RS to RS. Starting at the slash in the neck, stitch the sides of the necktie together, pivoting at the corners (see p.37). Clip the corners.

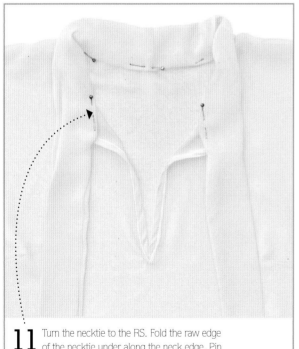

11 Turn the necktie to the RS. Fold the raw edge of the necktie under along the neck edge. Pin and handstitch in place.

12 Machine a 3cm (1¼in) double-turn hem (see p.57) in the ends of the sleeve. Press. Insert elastic to fit the wrist (see p.57).

13 Complete as for the Classic shell top step 15.

Classic princess-line blouse

This stylish blouse is very versatile. It will look efficient at the office in a plain fabric or a stripe, or is perfect for a country weekend in a cotton check. The princess lines at the front have a slimming effect that many women will appreciate. Choose the pattern by your bust measurement; you should also check your neck measurement to make sure the blouse is comfortable. Making this blouse will teach you some advanced sewing techniques, such as how to apply a yoke, collar, and cuffs.

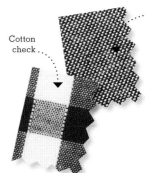

Cotton check

Chambray

Made in striped cotton shirting, this blouse is very suitable for office wear, but in printed viscose, cotton check, or a chambray it will happily accompany you on a weekend in the country.

BEFORE YOU START

YOU WILL NEED

- 2.4m (94in) x 150cm (59in) fabric
- 1 x reel matching all purpose sewing thread
- 1 x reel contrasting all-purpose sewing thread for pattern marking
- 75cm (30in) x lightweight fusible interfacing
- 9 x 7mm (11⁄40in) diameter buttons

PREPARING THE PATTERN

- This blouse is made using Top pattern two (see pp.201–205)
- Follow the instructions (see pp.166–167) to download or copy the pattern in your size

GARMENT CONSTRUCTION

The long-sleeved, button-through blouse has princess-line seams at the front, deep darts at the back, and a one-piece collar. It also features a shoulder yoke which is topstitched to match the topstitched collar and buttoned cuffs.

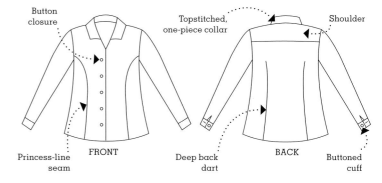

Button closure

Topstitched, one-piece collar

Shoulder

Princess-line seam

FRONT

Deep back dart

BACK

Buttoned cuff

HOW TO MAKE THE CLASSIC PRINCESS-LINE BLOUSE

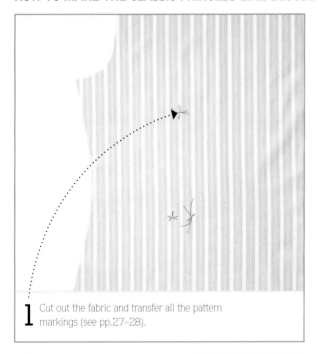

1 Cut out the fabric and transfer all the pattern markings (see pp.27–28).

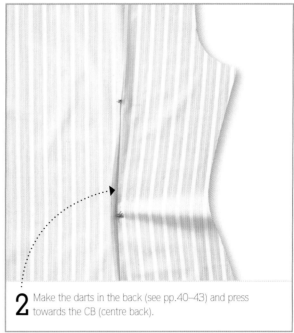

2 Make the darts in the back (see pp.40–43) and press towards the CB (centre back).

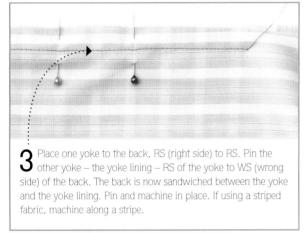

3 Place one yoke to the back. RS (right side) to RS. Pin the other yoke – the yoke lining – RS of the yoke to WS (wrong side) of the back. The back is now sandwiched between the yoke and the yoke lining. Pin and machine in place. If using a striped fabric, machine along a stripe.

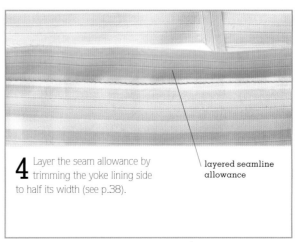

4 Layer the seam allowance by trimming the yoke lining side to half its width (see p.38).

layered seamline allowance

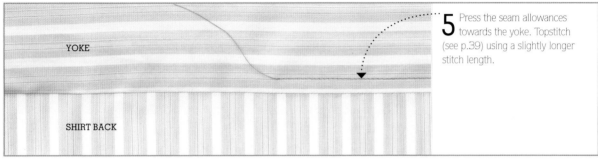

YOKE

SHIRT BACK

5 Press the seam allowances towards the yoke. Topstitch (see p.39) using a slightly longer stitch length.

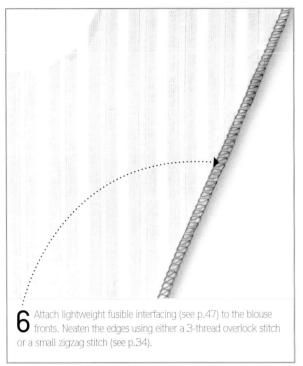

6 Attach lightweight fusible interfacing (see p.47) to the blouse fronts. Neaten the edges using either a 3-thread overlock stitch or a small zigzag stitch (see p.34).

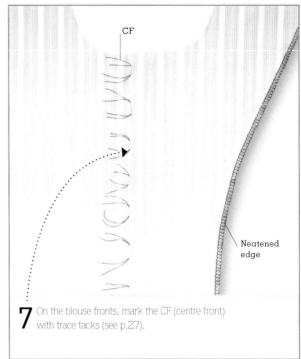

CF

Neatened edge

7 On the blouse fronts, mark the CF (centre front) with trace tacks (see p.27).

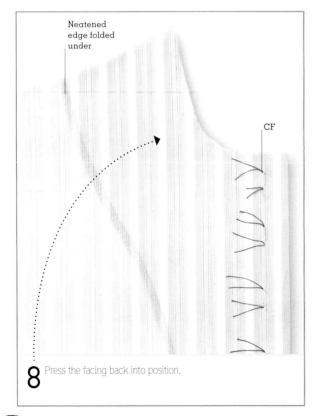

Neatened edge folded under

CF

8 Press the facing back into position.

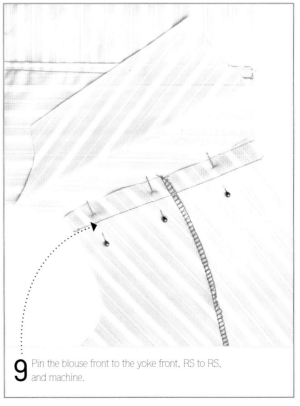

9 Pin the blouse front to the yoke front, RS to RS, and machine.

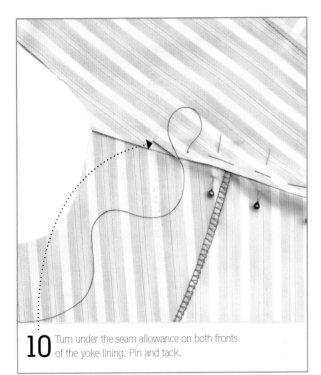

10 Turn under the seam allowance on both fronts of the yoke lining. Pin and tack.

11 Topstitch to match the yoke back (see step 5).

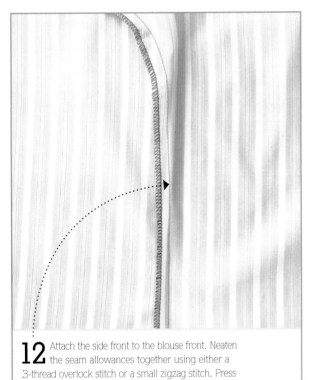

12 Attach the side front to the blouse front. Neaten the seam allowances together using either a 3-thread overlock stitch or a small zigzag stitch. Press towards the side.

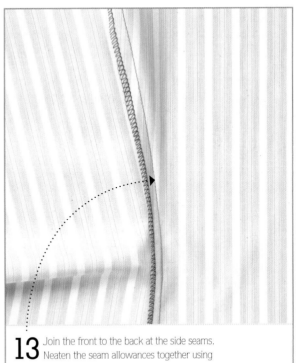

13 Join the front to the back at the side seams. Neaten the seam allowances together using either a 3-thread overlock stitch or a small zigzag stitch. Press towards the back.

14 Attach lightweight fusible interfacing to both collar pieces and mark the location of the button and the buttonhole with tailor's tacks.

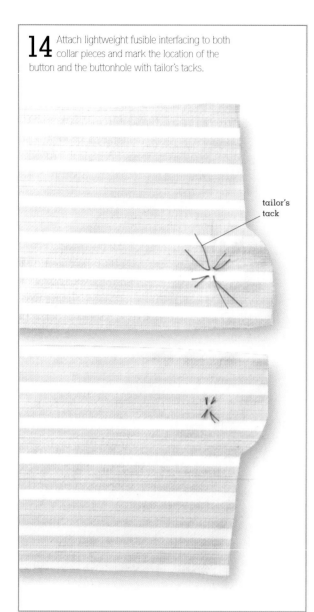

tailor's tack

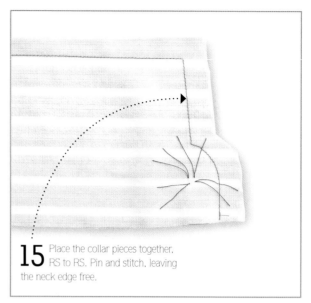

15 Place the collar pieces together, RS to RS. Pin and stitch, leaving the neck edge free.

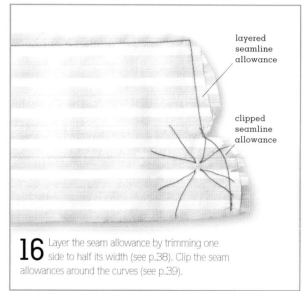

layered seamline allowance

clipped seamline allowance

16 Layer the seam allowance by trimming one side to half its width (see p.38). Clip the seam allowances around the curves (see p.39).

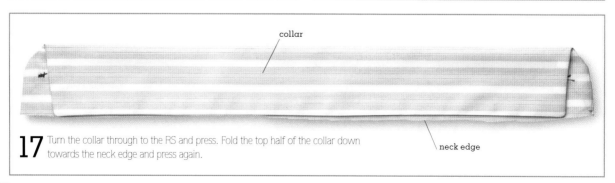

collar

17 Turn the collar through to the RS and press. Fold the top half of the collar down towards the neck edge and press again.

neck edge

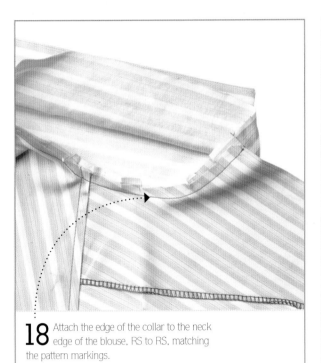

18 Attach the edge of the collar to the neck edge of the blouse, RS to RS, matching the pattern markings.

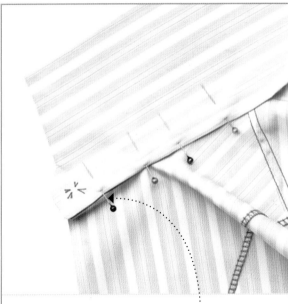

19 On the inside, turn under the raw edge of the collar, pin and handstitch in place to the collar-to-neck seam.

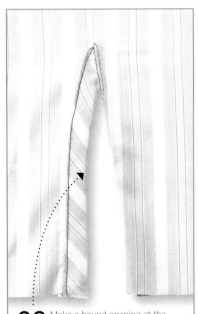

20 Make a bound opening at the wrist of the sleeve as marked (see pp.58–59).

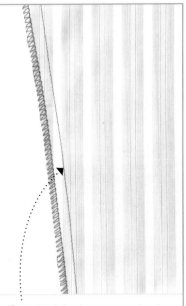

21 Stitch the sleeve seam and neaten the seam allowances together using either a 3-thread overlock stitch or a small zigzag stitch.

clipped end

22 Attach lightweight interfacing to the whole cuff. Pin and machine one edge of the cuff to the sleeve end, RS to RS. Turn the cuff RS to RS and stitch the short ends. Clip and turn.

23 Turn under the raw edge of the cuff and pin. Handstitch in place to the sleeve-to-cuff seamline.

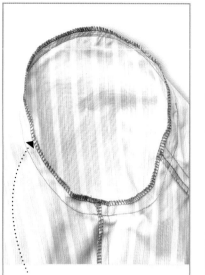

24 Using the longest stitch available, machine two rows of ease stitches through the sleeve head (see p.54). Insert the sleeve into the armhole, RS to RS (see pp.54–55), pin and stitch. Neaten the seam allowances together.

25 Topstitch the collar to match the yoke back (see step 5).

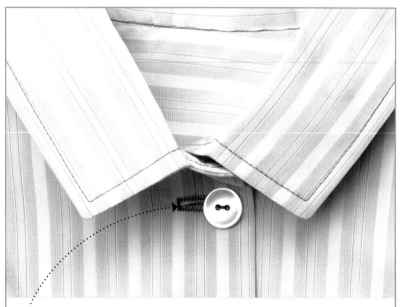

26 Make six evenly spaced horizontal buttonholes on the CF of the right side as worn, as marked on the pattern, plus one on the collar, and one on each of the cuffs (see p.72). Attach buttons to correspond (see p.71).

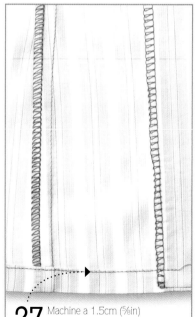

27 Machine a 1.5cm (⅝in) double-turn hem along the bottom of the blouse (see p.66). Press.

Classic boxy jacket

This simple boxy jacket looks good with trousers or a skirt, or even over a dress. Choose your pattern by your bust measurement but note that, if you have a fuller bust, you may need to make a bust adjustment to ensure the jacket meets at the front edges. This unlined jacket looks as good inside as out. The jacket and pocket flaps have been trimmed with grosgrain ribbon, while inside all the seams have been finished with bias binding.

Linen

Silk

This jacket has been made in a medium-weight, firmly woven modern tweed. Other good choices include wool mixes, boiled wool, or linen. To wear as part of a wedding outfit, make it in silk.

BEFORE YOU START

YOU WILL NEED

- 1.75m (69in) x 150cm (59in) fabric
- 2 x reels matching all-purpose sewing thread
- 1 x reel contrasting all-purpose sewing thread for pattern marking
- 1m (39in) x medium-weight fusible interfacing
- 5m (197in) x 5mm (³⁄₁₆in) grosgrain ribbon
- 15m (580in) x 2cm (³⁄₄in) bias binding

PREPARING THE PATTERN

- This jacket is made using Jacket pattern one (see pp.206–209)
- Follow the instructions (see pp.166–167) to download or copy the pattern in your size

GARMENT CONSTRUCTION

The jacket features princess lines at the front and back. It has set-in wrist-length sleeves, a round neck, and decorative pocket flaps.

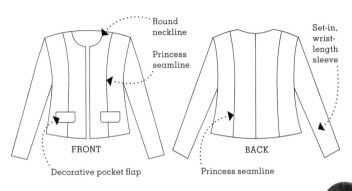

Round neckline

Princess seamline

FRONT

Decorative pocket flap

Set-in, wrist-length sleeve

BACK

Princess seamline

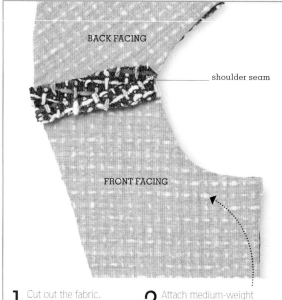

BACK FACING

shoulder seam

FRONT FACING

1 Cut out the fabric. If working with a check fabric see pp.23–25.

2 Attach medium-weight fusible interfacing to the front and back facings (see p.47). Join the facings together at the shoulder seam and press.

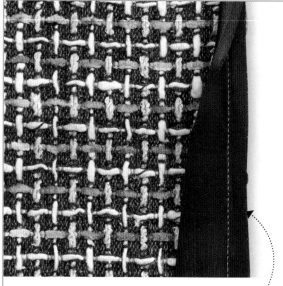

3 Bind the long edge of the facing using a Hong Kong finish (see p.35) and 2cm (¾in) bias binding. Place the binding to the facing, RS (right side) to RS, and machine stitch in the creaseline of the binding.

4 Wrap the binding round the raw edge of the fabric and secure by machining from the RS through the edge of the binding. Press.

side seam with Hong Kong finish

5 Join the back jacket to the side back, the side back to the side front, and the side front to the front. Neaten the seams with a Hong Kong finish. Press the seams open.

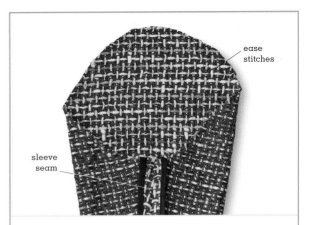

shoulder seam with
Hong Kong finish

ease
stitches

sleeve
seam

6 Join the front to the back at the shoulders and neaten the seams with a Hong Kong finish.

7 Machine the sleeve seams, neaten with a Hong Kong finish, and press the seams open. Using stitch length 5, machine two rows of ease stitches through the sleeve head (see p.54)

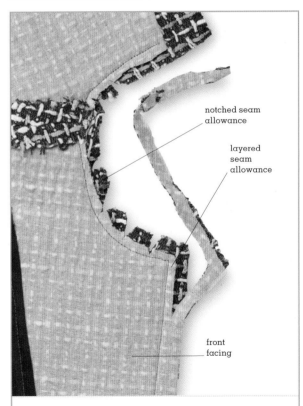

notched seam
allowance

layered
seam
allowance

front
facing

8 Fit the sleeve into the armhole, RS to RS (see pp.54–55). Join the armhole seam allowances together, wrapping them in bias binding and handstitching the long free edge of the binding to secure.

9 Attach the facing to the edge of the jacket, RS to RS. Pin and stitch. Layer the seam allowance by trimming the facing side of the seam to half its width (see p.38). Clip the seam allowance (see p.38). Turn the facing to the WS (wrong side) and press.

10 Understitch the seam allowances to the facing (see p.39).

bound edge

11 Bind the bottom edge of the sleeve using a Hong Kong finish. Pin up a 2cm (¾in) hem and handstitch in place. Press.

12 Bind the bottom edge of the jacket but not of the facing, using a Hong Kong finish. Turn up a 4cm (1½in) hem on the jacket, pin, and handstitch in place. At each CF (centre front), turn under the lower edge of the facing, pin, and handstitch in place. Press.

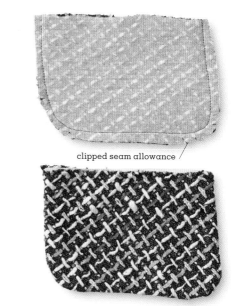

clipped seam allowance

13 Attach medium-weight fusible interfacing to one half of a pocket flap and place one interfaced flap and one non-interfaced flap together, RS to RS (see p.60). Stitch together around the lower edges using a ½cm (¼in) seam allowance. Clip, turn the flap to the right side, and press.

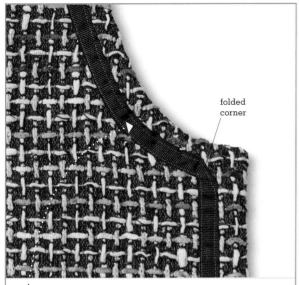

folded
corner

14 Pin decorative ribbon trim to the CF,
around the neck. Fold or mitre the trim
at the corners. Topstitch in place (see p.39) close
to each edge of the trim. Press.

15 Trim flap to match. Press.

16 Pin the jacket flap to the jacket front, RS
to RS, in a position of your choosing.
Machine along the raw edge of the flap.

17 Press the flap into place and handstitch
at each side to secure.

Classic shawl collar jacket

This waist-length, unlined jacket with a simple shawl collar has a relaxed feel; it is almost like wearing a cardigan. The jacket is secured at the centre front with just a single button, but if you prefer, you could have two or three. Choose your pattern according to your full bust measurement. The shoulder pads make the jacket slightly more structured, helping to balance the width of the shoulders to the hips. A wide choice of fabrics underlines this jacket's versatility.

Silk suiting

Flannel

We made our jacket in a chunky wool bouclé fabric, but it would also look good in a flannel or a silk suiting.

BEFORE YOU START

YOU WILL NEED

- 2m (79in) x 150cm (59in) fabric
- 1 x reel matching all-purpose sewing thread
- 1 x reel contrasting all-purpose sewing thread for pattern marking
- 1m (39in) x lightweight fusible interfacing
- 1 x pair shoulder pads
- 1 x 2.5cm (1in) button

PREPARING THE PATTERN

- This jacket is made using Jacket pattern two (see pp.210–217)
- Follow the instructions (see pp.166–167) to download or copy the pattern in your size

GARMENT CONSTRUCTION

The unlined, waist-length shawl collar jacket features front and back darts to fit it to the waist. There is a CB (centre-back) seam and the wrist-length, set-in sleeve has a shoulder pad. The jacket has a single-button closure.

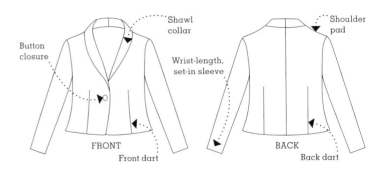

Button closure

Shawl collar

Shoulder pad

Wrist-length, set-in sleeve

FRONT

Front dart

BACK

Back dart

tailor's tack

1 Cut out the fabric and mark the pattern markings using tailor's tacks (see p.27).

2 Make all the darts (see pp.40–41). Press open the slashed dart on the front and press its point to the CF (centre front). Stitch the front shoulder dart only as far as the shoulder seamline.

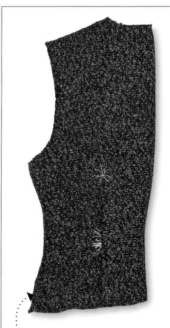

3 Neaten the seam allowances on the CB (centre-back) seams and on the back shoulder and side seams, using either a 3-thread overlock stitch or a small zigzag stitch (see p.34). On a chunky bouclé fabric, overlock stitches may look uneven; this is not a problem.

neatened front shoulder seam

4 Clip the fabric at the end of the front shoulder dart as shown. Neaten the front shoulder seam using either a 3-thread overlock stitch or a small zigzag stitch.

shoulder seam

side seam

5 Join the CB seam and join the front to the back at the side seams and the shoulder seams. Press the seams open.

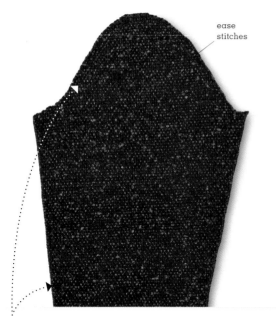

ease
stitches

6 Neaten the sleeve seam and lower edge of both sleeves using either a 3-thread overlock stitch or a small zigzag stitch. Machine the sleeve seam and press it open. Using the longest stitch available, machine two rows of ease stitches through the sleeve head (see p.54).

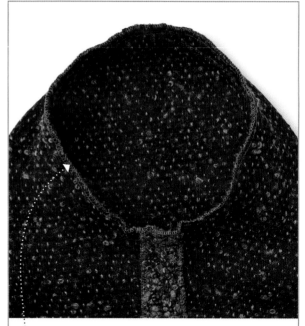

7 Insert the sleeve into the armhole, RS (right side) to RS (see pp.54–55). Neaten the seam allowances together using either a 3-thread overlock stitch or a small zigzag stitch. Turn up a 2cm (¾in) hem and stitch in place.

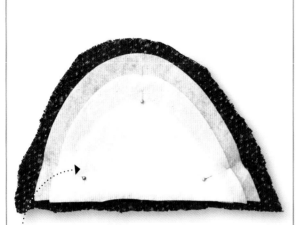

8 As this jacket is unlined, the outside of each shoulder pad needs to be covered. Cut a piece of fabric larger than the pad on the bias (see p.20). Pin to the pad.

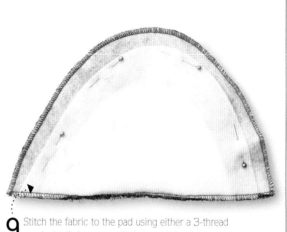

9 Stitch the fabric to the pad using either a 3-thread overlock stitch or a small zigzag stitch.

10 Place the covered shoulder pad to the sleeve-to-shoulder seam. Pin and handstitch in place along the armhole seam.

jacket collar CB seam

11 Join the jacket collar pieces at the CB. Press the seam open.

12 Place the collar to the jacket, RS to RS, matching the CB seams. Pin and stitch. Press the seam open.

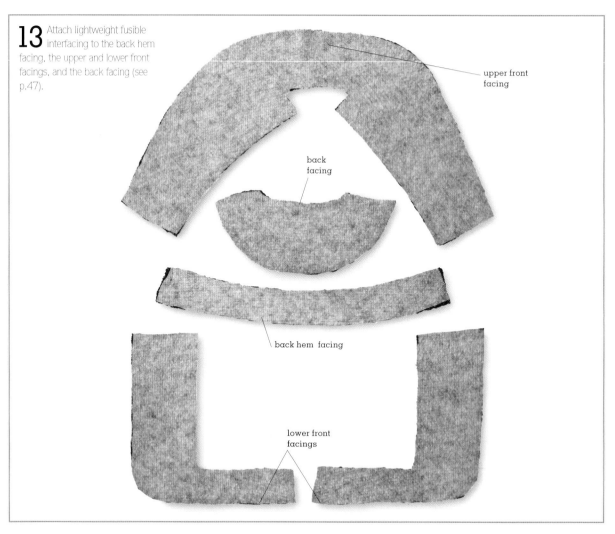

13 Attach lightweight fusible interfacing to the back hem facing, the upper and lower front facings, and the back facing (see p.47).

upper front facing

back facing

back hem facing

lower front facings

14 Clip the upper front facing at the marked dots. Join the back facing to the upper front facing, RS to RS, and stretch to fit. Stitch, pivoting (see p.37) at the clips.

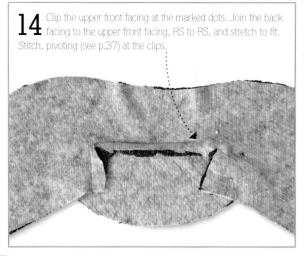

15 Join the lower front facings to each side of the upper front facing and to the back hem facing. Neaten the outer edge using an overlock stitch or a zigzag stitch.

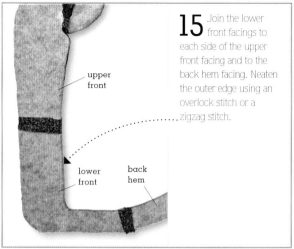

upper front

lower front

back hem

16 Join the completed facing to the edge of the jacket, RS to RS. Pin and stitch.

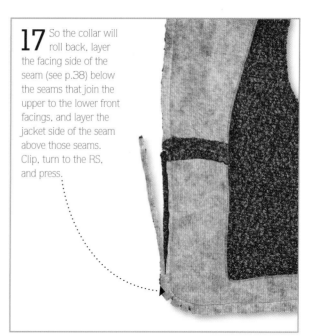

17 So the collar will roll back, layer the facing side of the seam (see p.38) below the seams that join the upper to the lower front facings, and layer the jacket side of the seam above those seams. Clip, turn to the RS, and press.

18 Topstitch (see p.39) around the outer edges of the jacket.

19 On the RH (right hand) side of the jacket (as worn), make a horizontal buttonhole as marked (see p.72). Attach a corresponding button (see p.71). Turn up the sleeve hems by 3cm (1¼in) and handstitch in place.

20 On the inside of the jacket, handstitch the seams on the facings to the jacket seams and secure the end of each shoulder pad to the shoulder seam.

Lined shawl collar jacket

This version of the jacket in a fine, boiled wool has been lined, patch pockets have been added, and these and the collar edge have been trimmed with braid. The result is a more formal jacket that would look good with a matching skirt.

Linen

Wool suiting

We made our jacket in a very fine boiled wool, but you could try a linen for the summer or a wool suiting for the office.

BEFORE YOU START

YOU WILL NEED
- 2m (79in) x 150cm (59in) fabric
- 1.5m (59in) x 150cm (59in) lining fabric
- 1m (39in) x medium-weight fusible interfacing
- 2 x reels matching all-purpose sewing thread
- 1 x reel contrasting all-purpose thread for pattern marking
- 1 x pair shoulder pads
- 5m (197in) x decorative braid
- 1 x 2½cm (1in) button

PREPARING THE PATTERN
- This jacket is made using Jacket pattern two (see pp.210–217)
- Follow the instructions (see pp.166–167) to download or copy the pattern in your size

GARMENT CONSTRUCTION

This lined, waist-length, shawl collar jacket has front and back darts. There is a CB (centre-back) seam and the wrist-length, set-in sleeve has a shoulder pad. The jacket has a single-button closure and patch pockets trimmed with braid to match the collar.

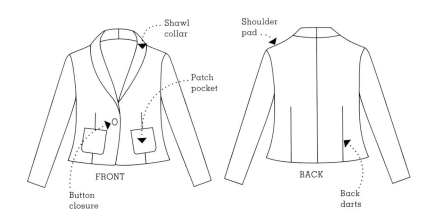

Shawl collar

Patch pocket

FRONT

Button closure

Shoulder pad

BACK

Back darts

HOW TO MAKE THE LINED SHAWL COLLAR JACKET

1 Cut out the pattern pieces from both the fabric and the lining.

2 Mark the pattern markings on both the lining and the fabric using tailor's tacks (see p.27). Make all the darts in both fabrics (see pp.40–41) as for the Classic shawl collar jacket step 2.

3 Make up the fabric as for the Classic shawl collar jacket steps 5–7 and 11–15, omitting the seam neatening.

4 Pin a shoulder pad to the sleeve-to-shoulder seam and attach with a large running stitch.

5 Make the lined patch pockets (see p.61).

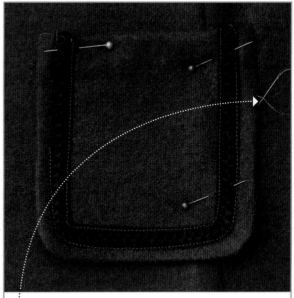

6 Pin and topstitch (see p.39) the decorative trim to the front of the pockets. Pin and handstitch the pockets to the jacket front in the marked positions.

7 Make the darts in the back lining and pin the tuck in the front lining. Join the lining at the side and shoulder seams and press the seams open.

shoulder seam

side seam

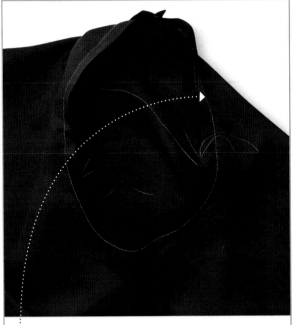

8 Make up the lining sleeve and insert it into the lining jacket in the same way as for the Classic shawl collar jacket steps 6–7.

9 Attach the interfaced facing to the lining jacket, RS (right side) to RS, matching at the shoulder seams. Do not attach the hem facing to the lining. Remove the pins in the tucks. Press the seams towards the lining.

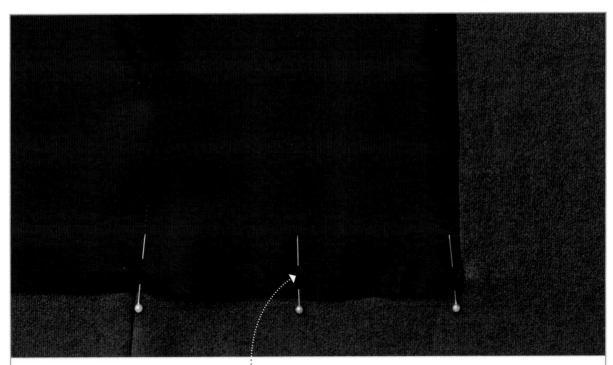

10 Continue as for the Classic shawl collar jacket steps 16–17.

11 Turn up the raw edge of the lining 1.5cm (⅝in) and pin it to overlap the jacket facing. Allow a tiny pleat to form at the CB (centre back) of the lining to ensure the lining does not pull on the jacket. Handstitch in place. Turn up the sleeve lining and the sleeve hem to match.

12 Add a decorative trim to the collar, as you did on the pocket. Topstitch the front and bottom edges of the jacket and the end of the sleeves.

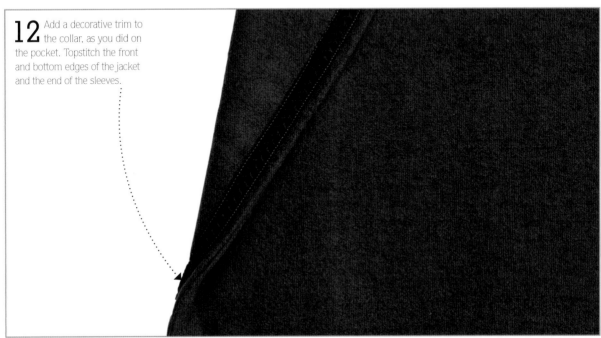

Patterns

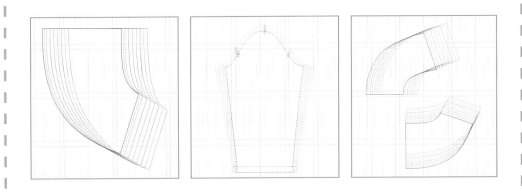

Using the pattern section

To create any of the garments in this book, you will first need to transfer the pattern to paper. You can do this in one of three ways: download it from our website, draw the pattern by hand onto pattern paper, or enlarge it on a photocopier. Before you begin, you will also need to find the correct size for you.

Find your size

Find your size by taking your bust, waist, and hip measurements and finding the closest set of measurements in the table below. If you are between sizes, choose the larger of the two.

SIZE	6–8	8–10	10–12	12–14	14–16	16–18	18–20	20–22	22–24
BUST	82cm (32¼in)	84.5cm (33¼in)	87cm (34¼in)	92cm (36¼in)	97cm (38in)	102cm (40in)	107cm (42in)	112cm (44in)	117cm (46in)
WAIST	62cm (24½in)	64.5cm (25¼in)	67cm (26¼in)	72cm (28¼in)	77cm (30¼in)	82cm (32¼in)	87cm (34¼in)	92cm (36¼in)	97cm (38 in)
HIP	87cm (34¼in)	89.5cm (35¼in)	92cm (36¼in)	97cm (38in)	102cm (40in)	107cm (42in)	112cm (44in)	117cm (46in)	122cm (48in)

VARIED SIZES
You may have noticed that your size in the table differs from what you would buy in a store. In general, dressmaking sizes tend to be smaller than store sizes.

Seam allowance

Seam allowance is the amount of fabric that is taken up by the seam. It is usually given as the distance between the cutting line and the stitching line.

The patterns in this section include a 1.5cm (⅝in) seam allowance. This means that to make a garment that is the correct size and shape, you will need to cut along the line on the pattern, and stitch 1.5cm (⅝in) inside the cutting line. An easy way to remember to do this is to mark a stitching line (seamline) onto the pattern pieces before you begin.

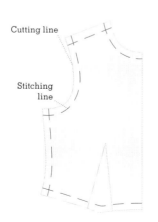

Cutting line

Stitching line

Pattern markings

The following markings are used on the patterns in this section.

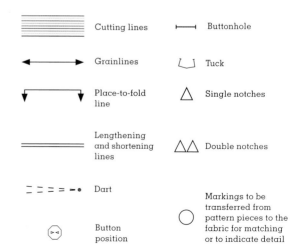

Cutting lines

Grainlines

Place-to-fold line

Lengthening and shortening lines

Dart

Button position

Buttonhole

Tuck

Single notches

Double notches

Markings to be transferred from pattern pieces to the fabric for matching or to indicate detail

Download or copy your pattern

METHOD 1: DOWNLOADING FROM THE INTERNET

 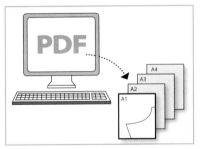 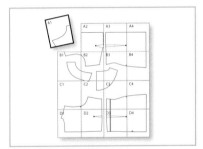

1 Start by checking which pattern is needed to make the garment or variation. This is listed on the first page of the instructions. Then go to www.dk.co.uk/dressmaking-step-by-step.

2 Find the correct PDF for your garment and your size. Download the PDF to your computer, and print it out. The pages will be labelled in the order that they fit together.

3 Trim the white margins from the printed pages, and tape the pages together, using the letters and gridlines as a guide. Cut out the pattern pieces.

METHOD 2: DRAWING THE PATTERN BY HAND

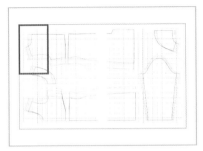 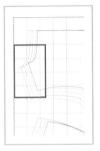 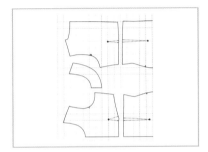

1 Each grid square in the patterns represents a 5cm square at full size. To enlarge the patterns by hand, you will need pattern paper with either a 1cm or 5cm grid.

2 Begin by finding the coloured line for your size in the pattern. Enlarge the pattern onto your paper, mapping each square of the pattern onto a 5cm square on the pattern paper.

3 Depending on the size of your pattern paper, you may need to stick together several sheets to fit all the pieces for a single pattern. Once you have copied all the pieces, cut them out.

METHOD 3: PHOTOCOPYING

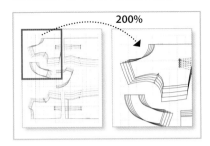 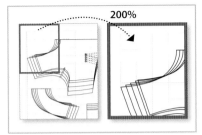 

1 To enlarge the pattern on a photocopier, begin by copying it at 100%. Find your size in the table, and draw along the line for your size in marker or pen. Enlarge the pattern by 200%.

2 Enlarge the pattern pieces again by 200% to reach full size. If you are using a photocopier that has a 400% setting, you can use this setting to enlarge the pieces in one step.

3 Once you have enlarged all parts of the original page, piece them together using the gridlines as a guide, and tape them down. Cut around your size.

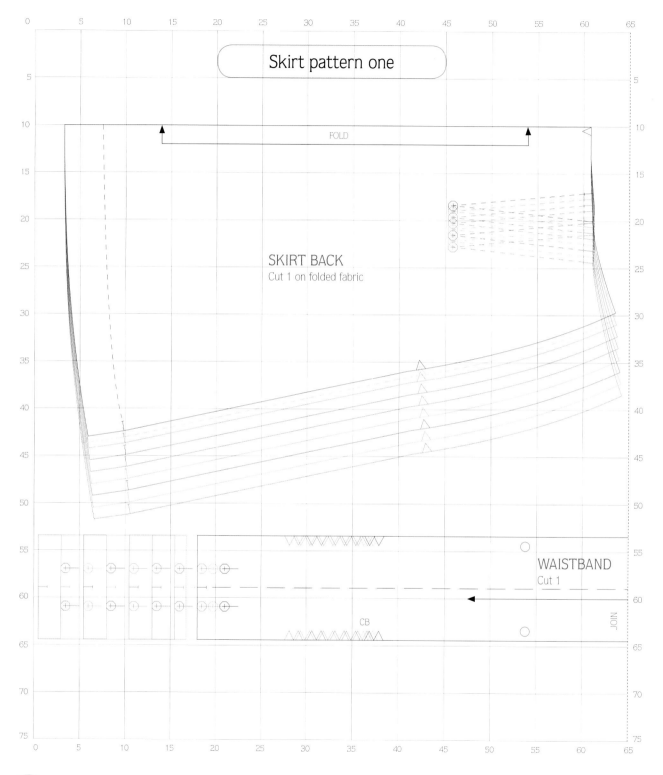

Skirt pattern one

FOLD

SKIRT BACK
Cut 1 on folded fabric

WAISTBAND
Cut 1

CB

JOIN

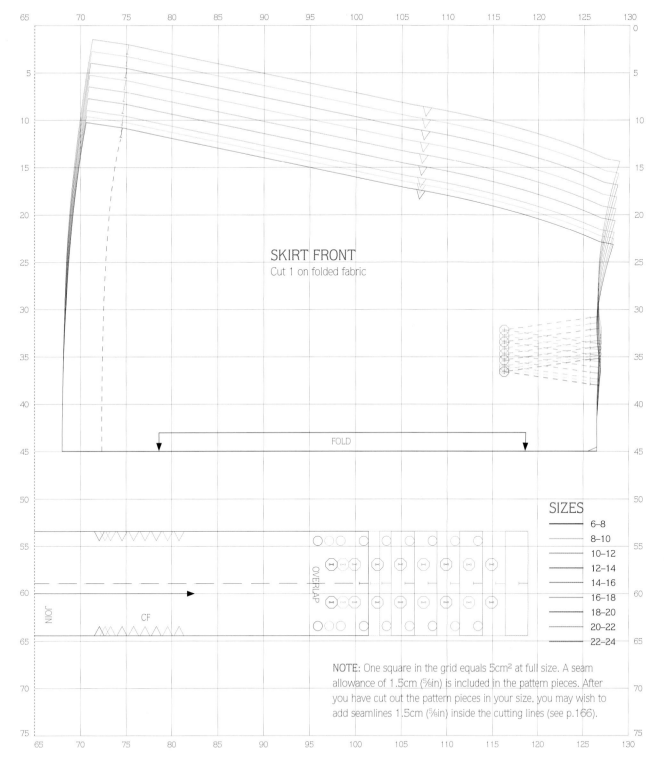

SKIRT FRONT
Cut 1 on folded fabric

FOLD

JOIN

CF

OVERLAP

SIZES

——	6–8
——	8–10
——	10–12
——	12–14
——	14–16
——	16–18
——	18–20
——	20–22
——	22–24

NOTE: One square in the grid equals 5cm² at full size. A seam allowance of 1.5cm (⅝in) is included in the pattern pieces. After you have cut out the pattern pieces in your size, you may wish to add seamlines 1.5cm (⅝in) inside the cutting lines (see p.166).

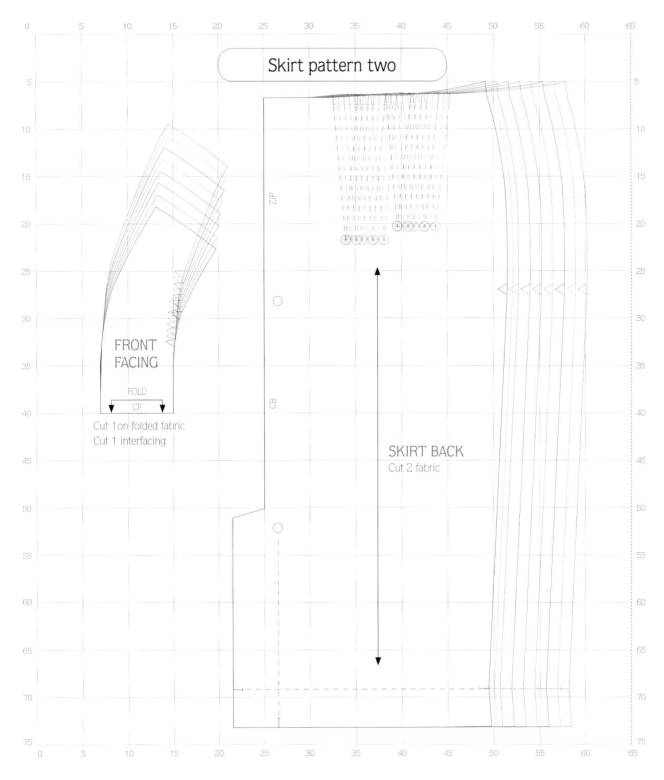

Skirt pattern two

ZIP

CB

FRONT
FACING

FOLD
CF

Cut 1 on folded fabric
Cut 1 interfacing

SKIRT BACK
Cut 2 fabric

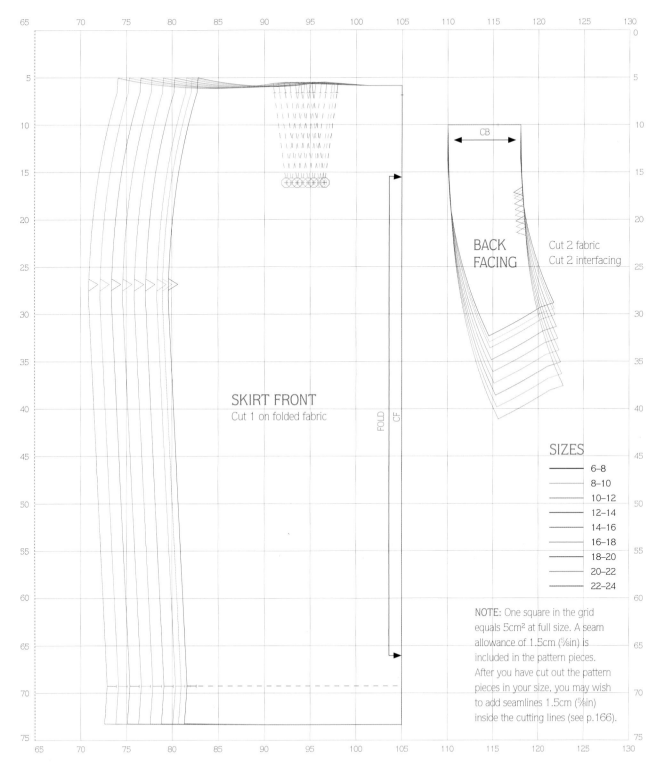

BACK
FACING

Cut 2 fabric
Cut 2 interfacing

CB

SKIRT FRONT
Cut 1 on folded fabric

FOLD

CF

SIZES

———	6–8
———	8–10
———	10–12
———	12–14
———	14–16
———	16–18
———	18–20
———	20–22
———	22–24

NOTE: One square in the grid
equals 5cm² at full size. A seam
allowance of 1.5cm (⅝in) is
included in the pattern pieces.
After you have cut out the pattern
pieces in your size, you may wish
to add seamlines 1.5cm (⅝in)
inside the cutting lines (see p.166).

Skirt pattern two **171**

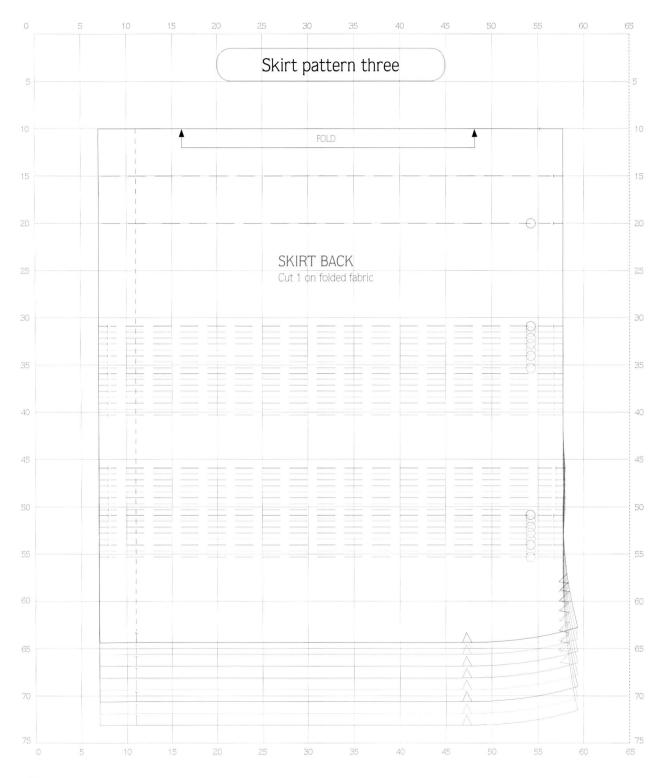

Skirt pattern three

FOLD

SKIRT BACK
Cut 1 on folded fabric

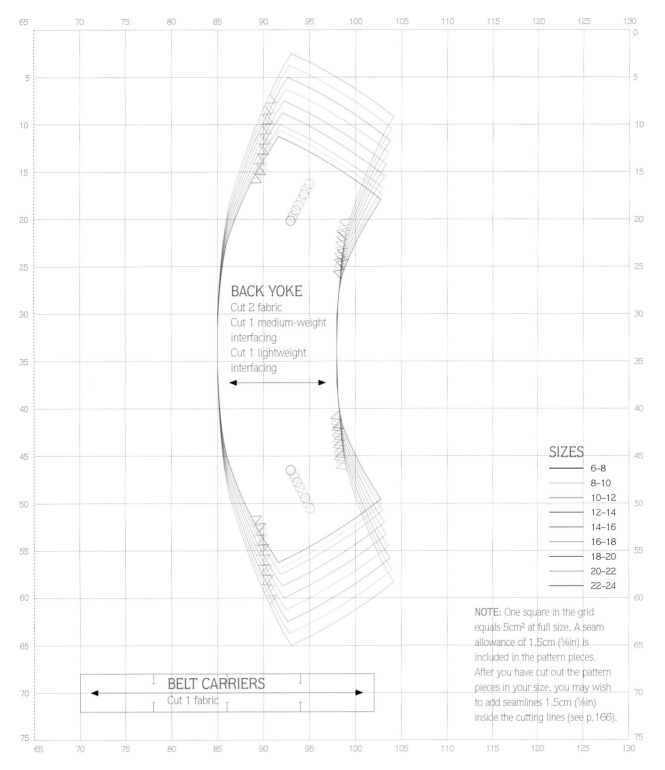

BACK YOKE
Cut 2 fabric
Cut 1 medium-weight
interfacing
Cut 1 lightweight
interfacing

SIZES
———	6–8
———	8–10
———	10–12
———	12–14
———	14–16
———	16–18
———	18–20
———	20–22
———	22–24

NOTE: One square in the grid
equals 5cm² at full size. A seam
allowance of 1.5cm (⅝in) is
included in the pattern pieces.
After you have cut out the pattern
pieces in your size, you may wish
to add seamlines 1.5cm (⅝in)
inside the cutting lines (see p.166).

BELT CARRIERS
Cut 1 fabric

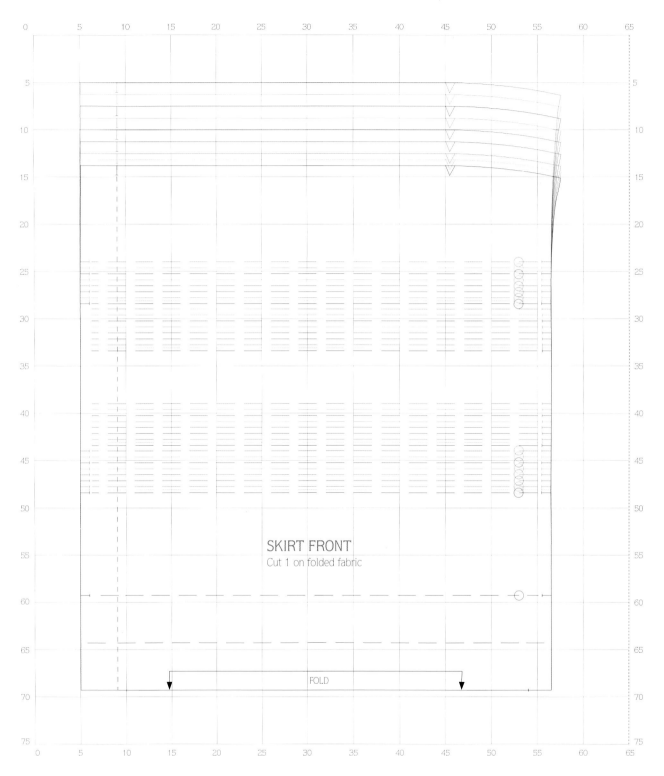

SKIRT FRONT
Cut 1 on folded fabric

FOLD

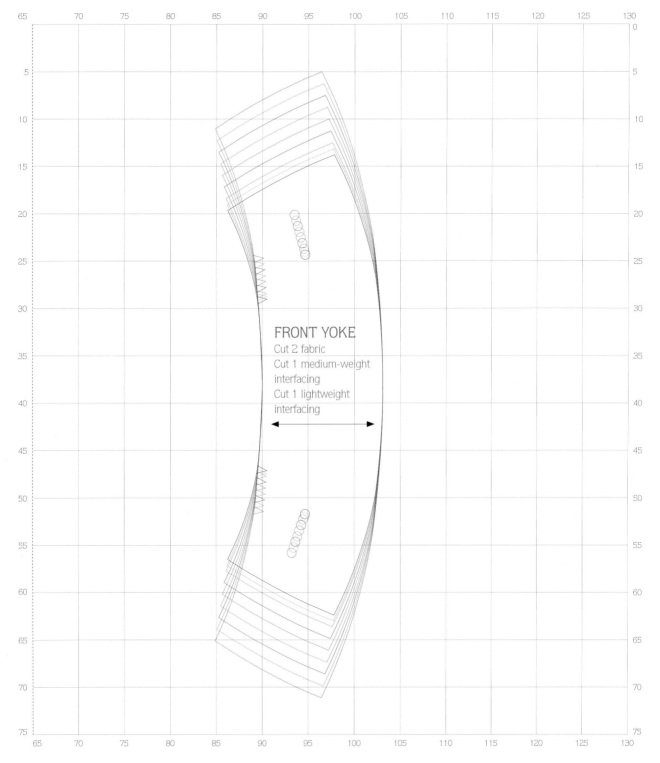

FRONT YOKE
Cut 2 fabric
Cut 1 medium-weight
interfacing
Cut 1 lightweight
interfacing

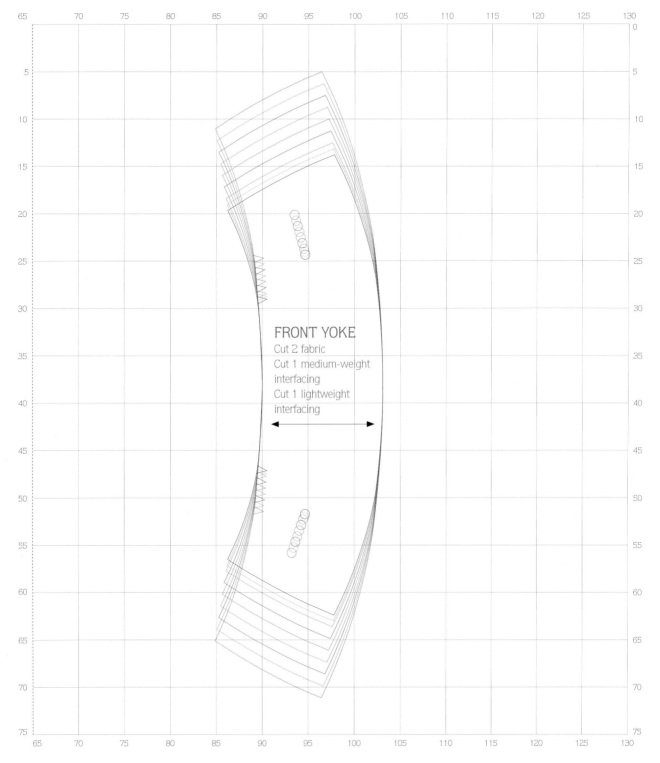 Skirt pattern three **175**

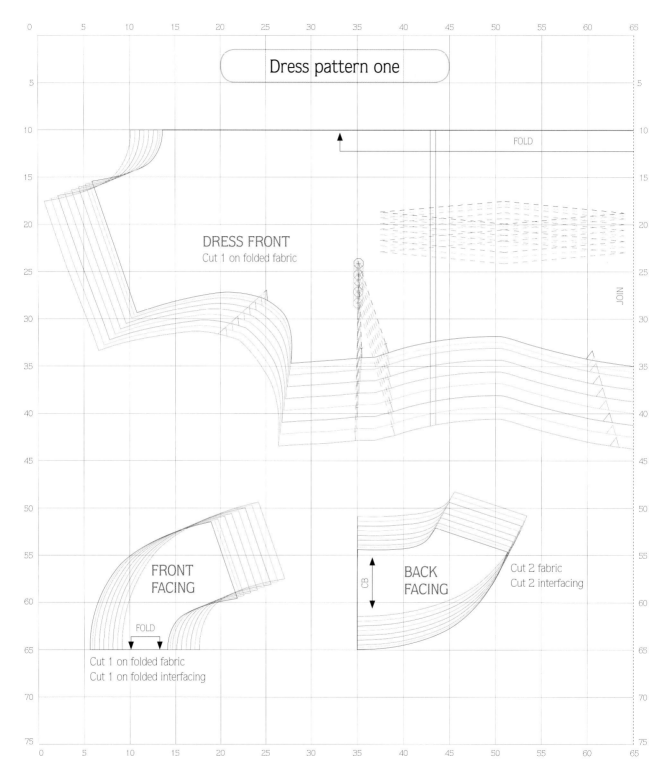

Dress pattern one

DRESS FRONT
Cut 1 on folded fabric

FOLD

JOIN

FRONT
FACING

FOLD

Cut 1 on folded fabric
Cut 1 on folded interfacing

BACK
FACING

CB

Cut 2 fabric
Cut 2 interfacing

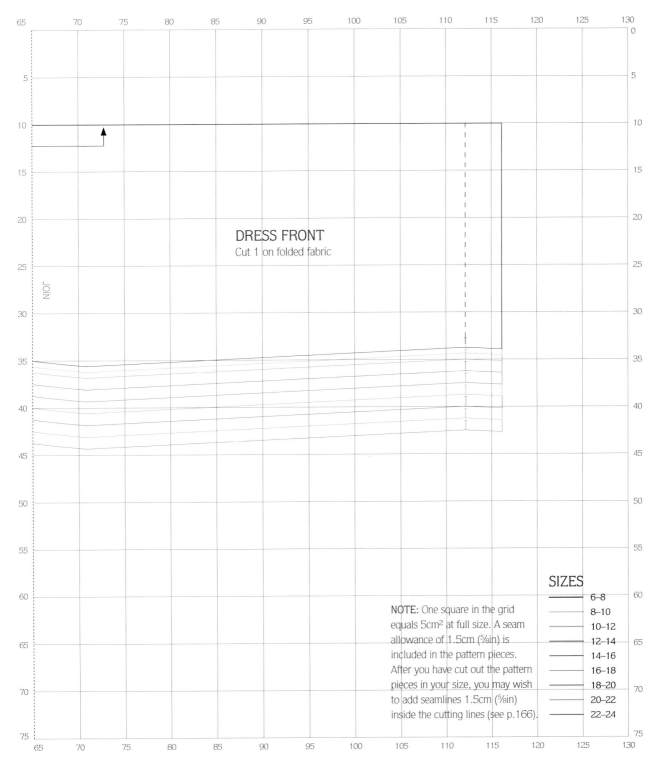

DRESS FRONT
Cut 1 on folded fabric

JOIN

SIZES

———	6–8
———	8–10
———	10–12
———	12–14
———	14–16
———	16–18
———	18–20
———	20–22
———	22–24

NOTE: One square in the grid equals 5cm² at full size. A seam allowance of 1.5cm (⅝in) is included in the pattern pieces. After you have cut out the pattern pieces in your size, you may wish to add seamlines 1.5cm (⅝in) inside the cutting lines (see p.166).

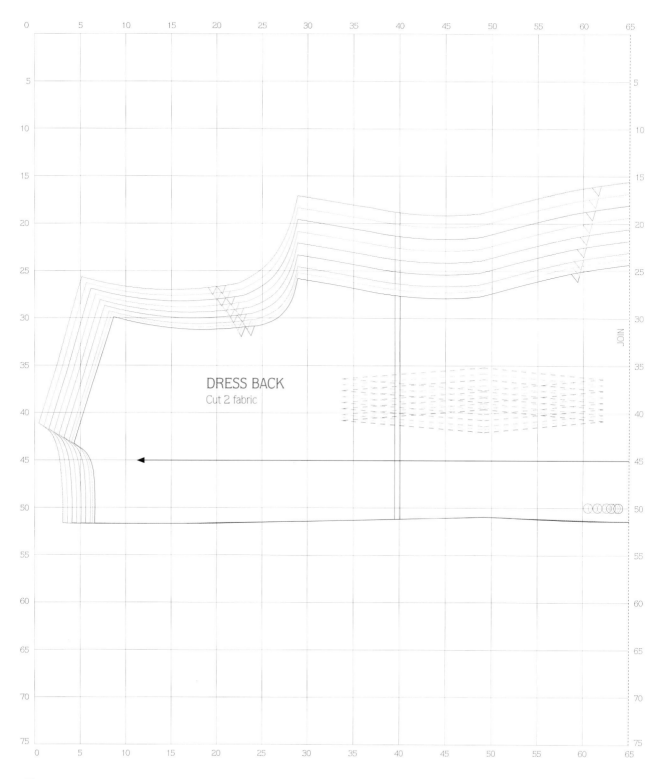

DRESS BACK
Cut 2 fabric

JOIN

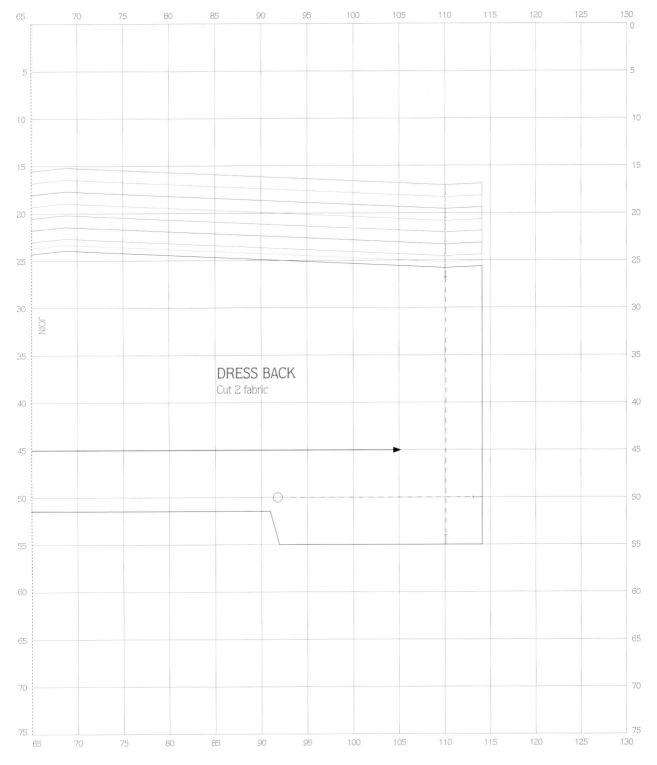

DRESS BACK
Cut 2 fabric

JOIN

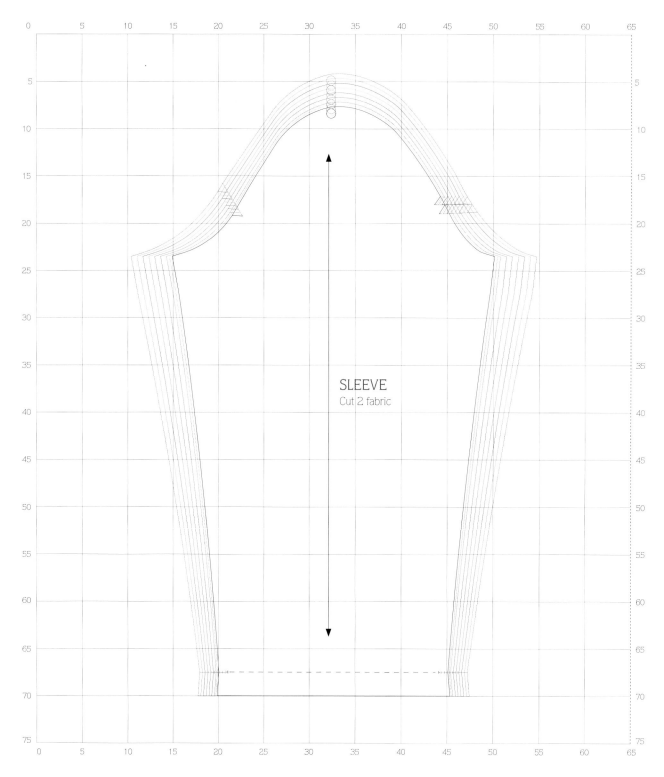

SLEEVE
Cut 2 fabric

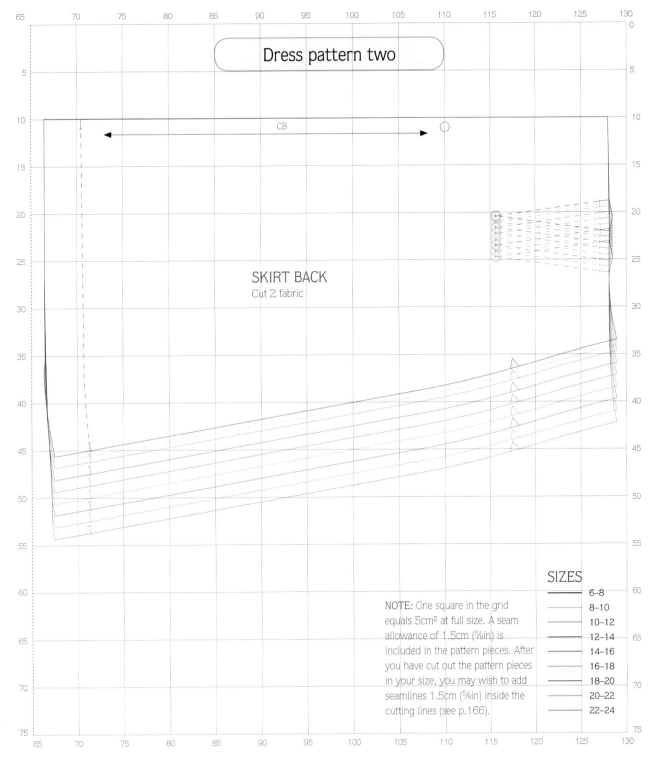

Dress pattern two

CB

SKIRT BACK
Cut 2 fabric

SIZES

	6–8
	8–10
	10–12
	12–14
	14–16
	16–18
	18–20
	20–22
	22–24

NOTE: One square in the grid equals 5cm² at full size. A seam allowance of 1.5cm (⅝in) is included in the pattern pieces. After you have cut out the pattern pieces in your size, you may wish to add seamlines 1.5cm (⅝in) inside the cutting lines (see p.166).

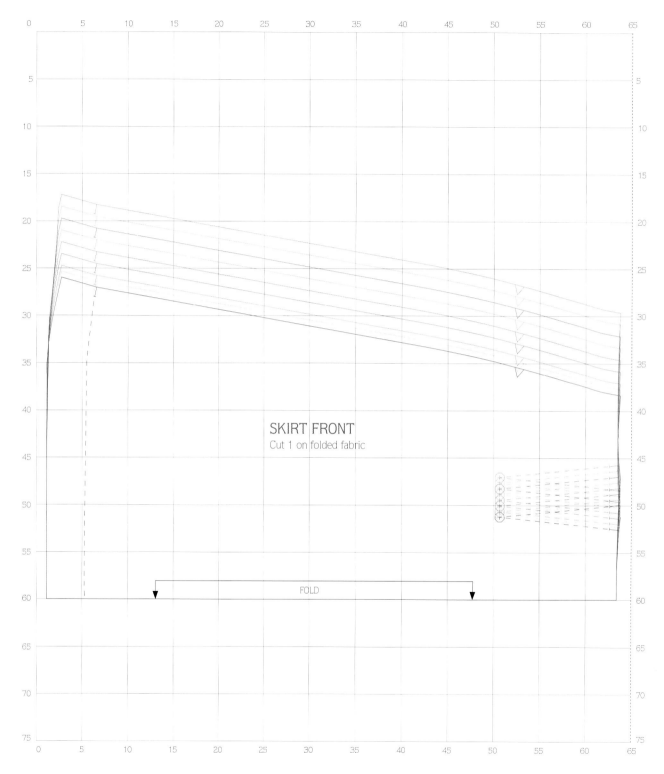

SKIRT FRONT
Cut 1 on folded fabric

FOLD

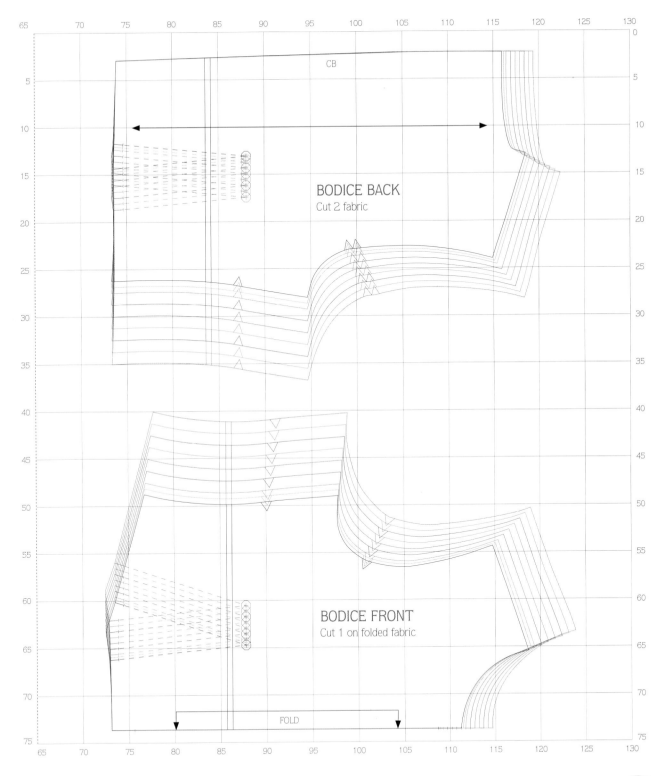

BODICE BACK
Cut 2 fabric

CB

BODICE FRONT
Cut 1 on folded fabric

FOLD

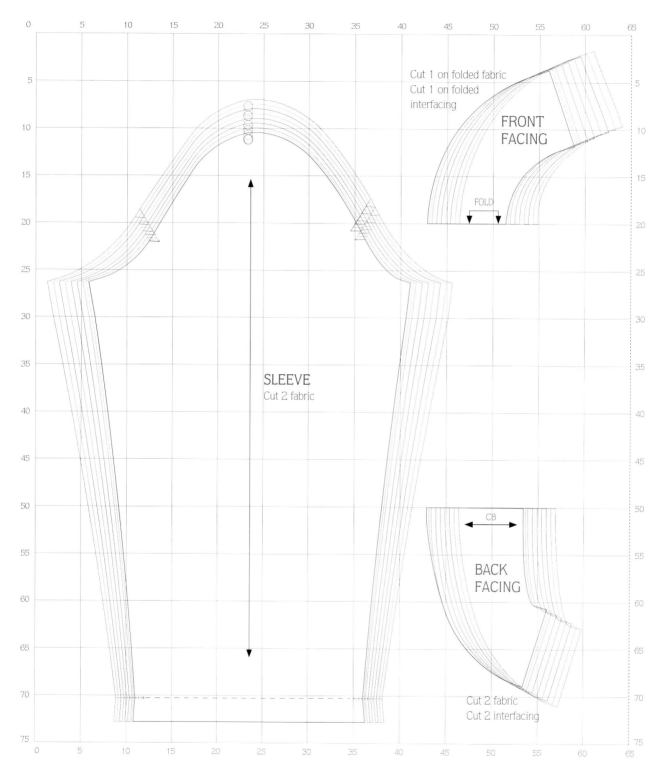

Cut 1 on folded fabric
Cut 1 on folded
interfacing

FRONT
FACING

FOLD

SLEEVE
Cut 2 fabric

CB

BACK
FACING

Cut 2 fabric
Cut 2 interfacing

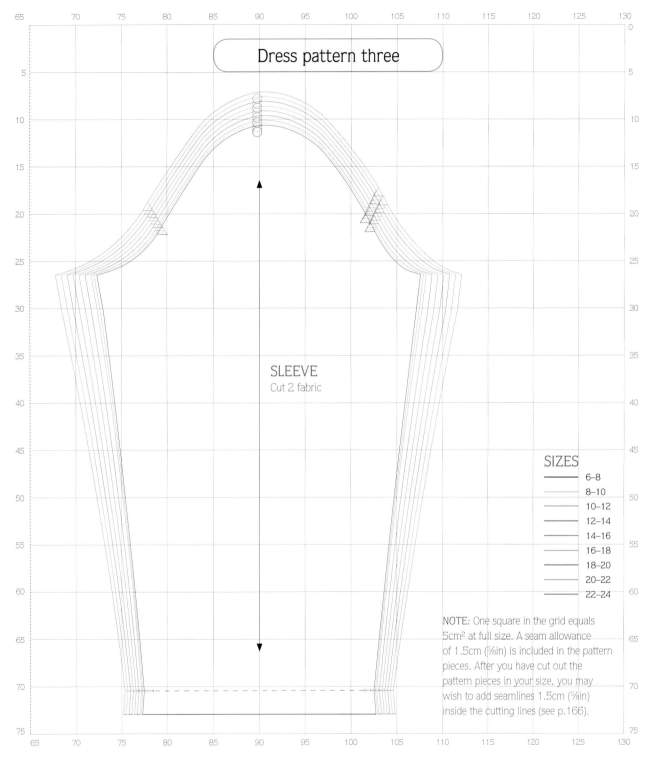

Dress pattern three

SLEEVE
Cut 2 fabric

SIZES
——— 6–8
——— 8–10
——— 10–12
——— 12–14
——— 14–16
——— 16–18
——— 18–20
——— 20–22
——— 22–24

NOTE: One square in the grid equals
5cm² at full size. A seam allowance
of 1.5cm (⅝in) is included in the pattern
pieces. After you have cut out the
pattern pieces in your size, you may
wish to add seamlines 1.5cm (⅝in)
inside the cutting lines (see p.166).

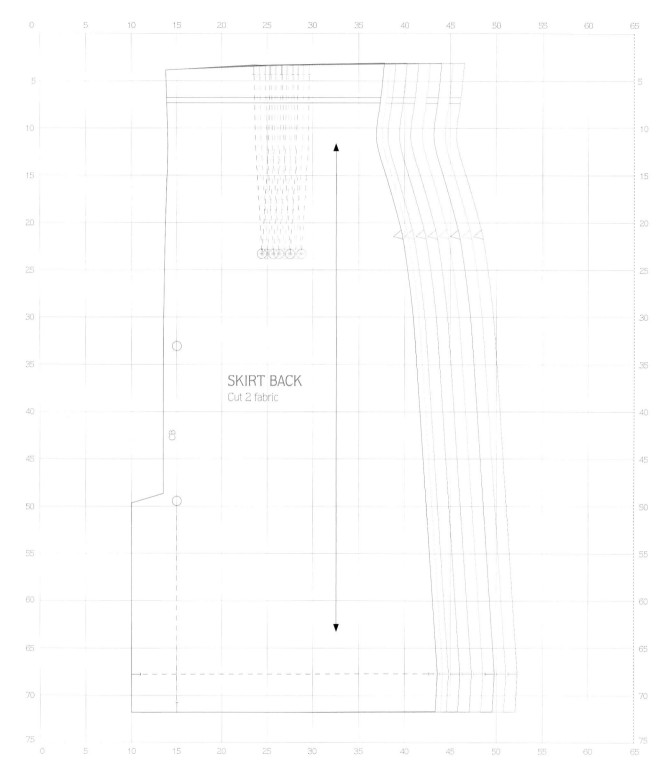

SKIRT BACK
Cut 2 fabric

CB

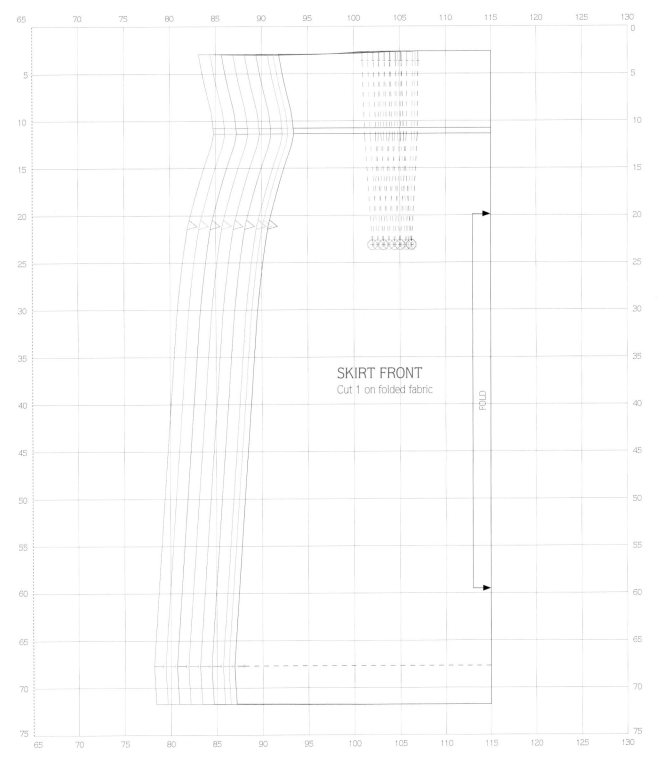

SKIRT FRONT
Cut 1 on folded fabric

FOLD

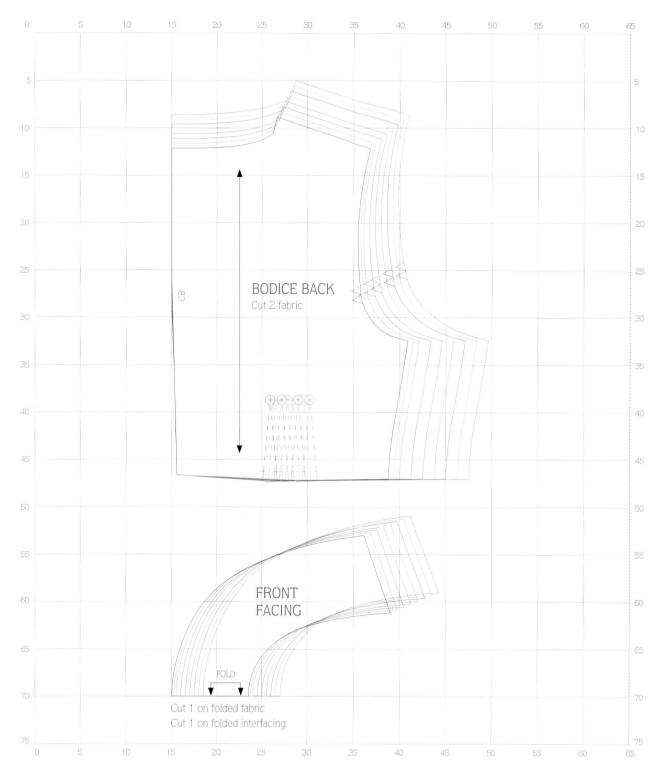

BODICE BACK
Cut 2 fabric

CB

FRONT
FACING

FOLD

Cut 1 on folded fabric
Cut 1 on folded interfacing

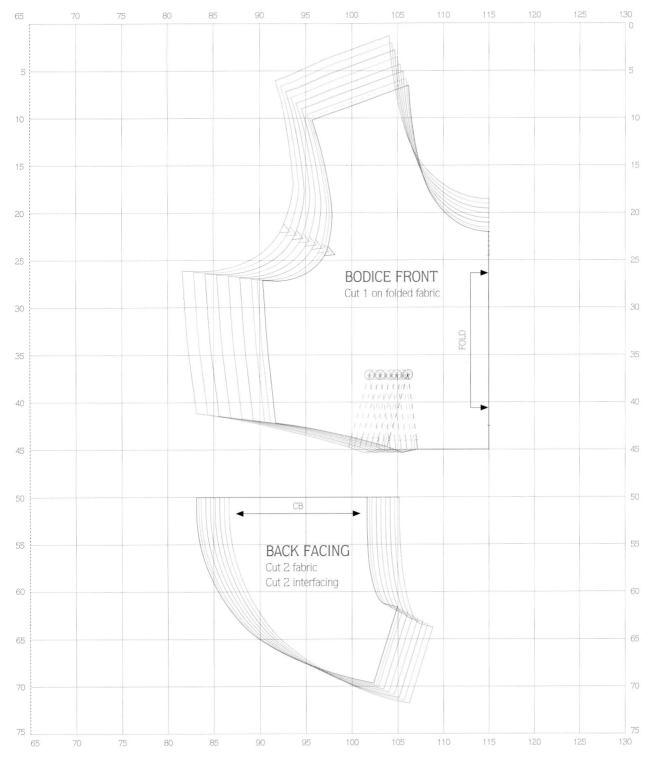

BODICE FRONT
Cut 1 on folded fabric

FOLD

BACK FACING
Cut 2 fabric
Cut 2 interfacing

CB

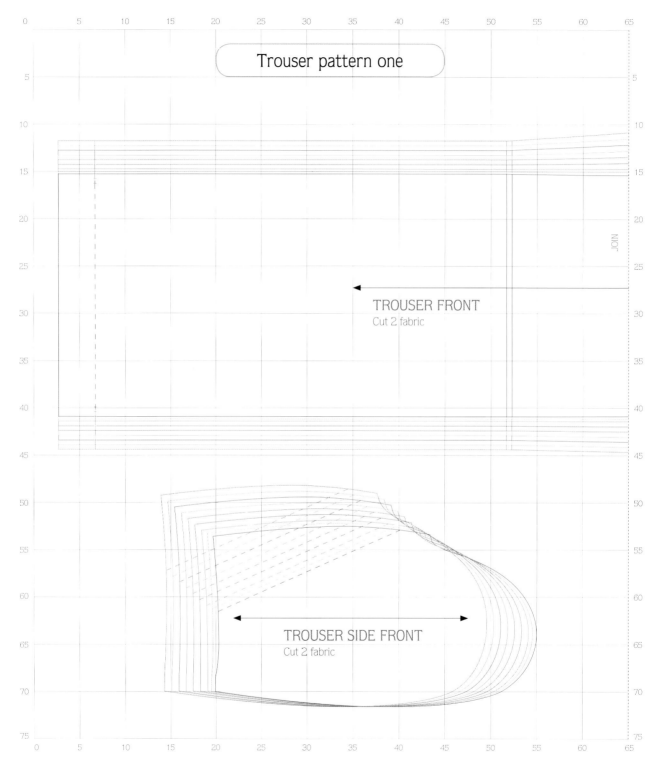

Trouser pattern one

TROUSER FRONT
Cut 2 fabric

JOIN

TROUSER SIDE FRONT
Cut 2 fabric

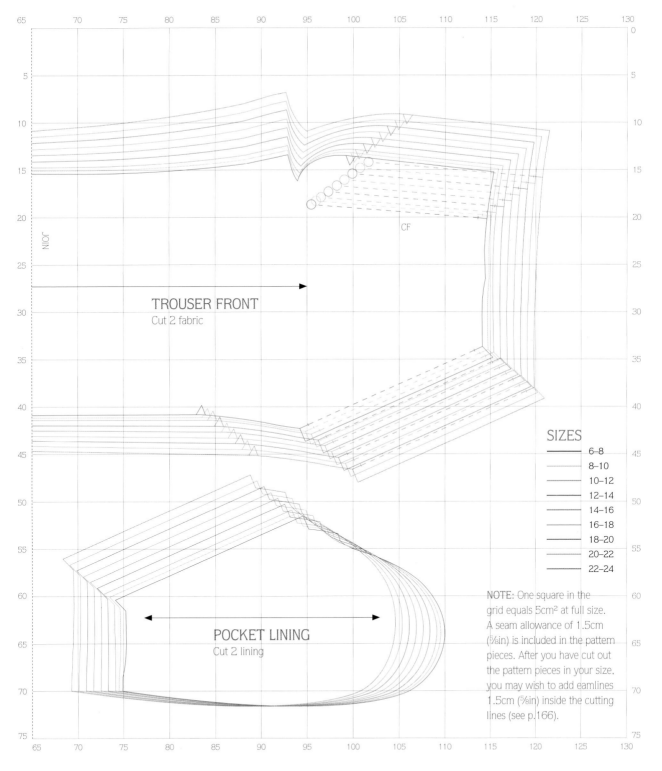

TROUSER FRONT
Cut 2 fabric

CF

JOIN

POCKET LINING
Cut 2 lining

SIZES

——	6–8
——	8–10
——	10–12
——	12–14
——	14–16
——	16–18
——	18–20
——	20–22
——	22–24

NOTE: One square in the grid equals 5cm² at full size. A seam allowance of 1.5cm (⅝in) is included in the pattern pieces. After you have cut out the pattern pieces in your size, you may wish to add eamlines 1.5cm (⅝in) inside the cutting lines (see p.166).

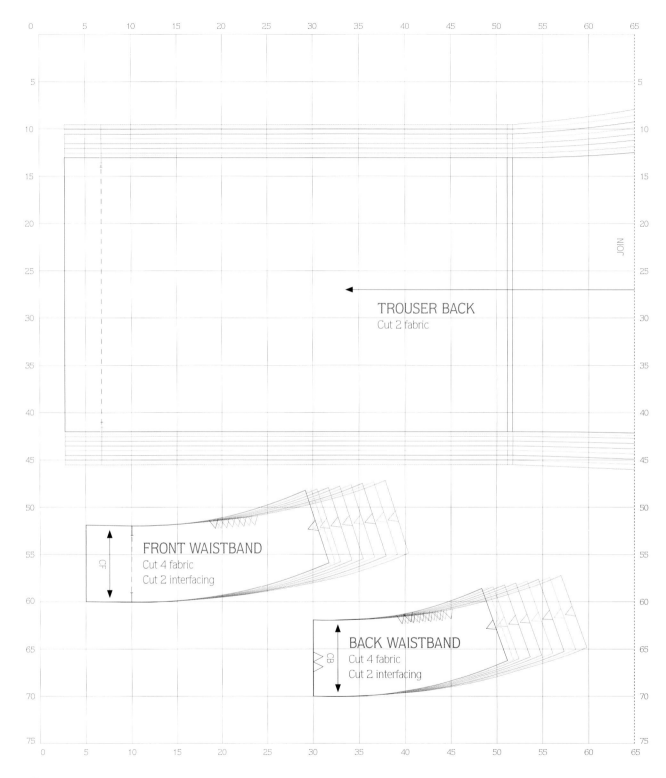

TROUSER BACK
Cut 2 fabric

FRONT WAISTBAND
Cut 4 fabric
Cut 2 interfacing

BACK WAISTBAND
Cut 4 fabric
Cut 2 interfacing

JOIN

CF

CB

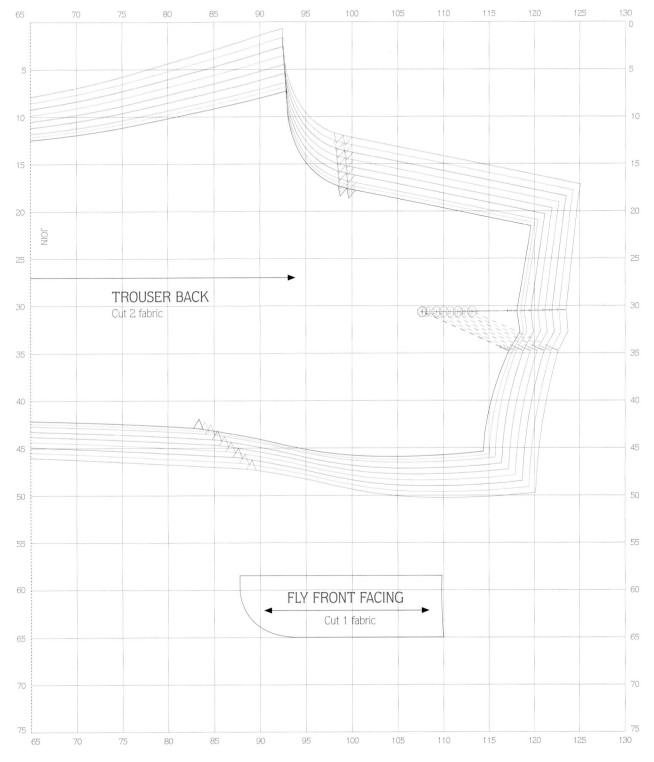

JOIN

TROUSER BACK
Cut 2 fabric

FLY FRONT FACING
Cut 1 fabric

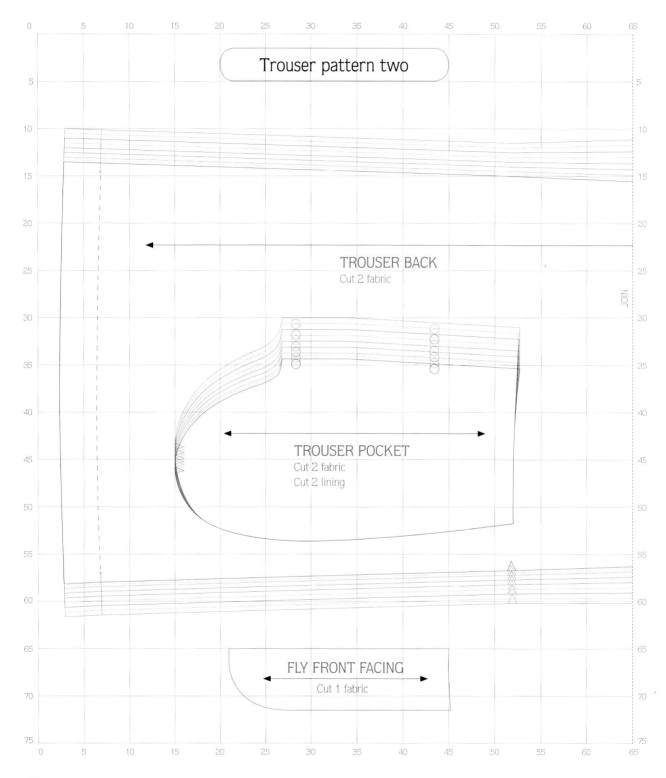

Trouser pattern two

TROUSER BACK
Cut 2 fabric

TROUSER POCKET
Cut 2 fabric
Cut 2 lining

FLY FRONT FACING
Cut 1 fabric

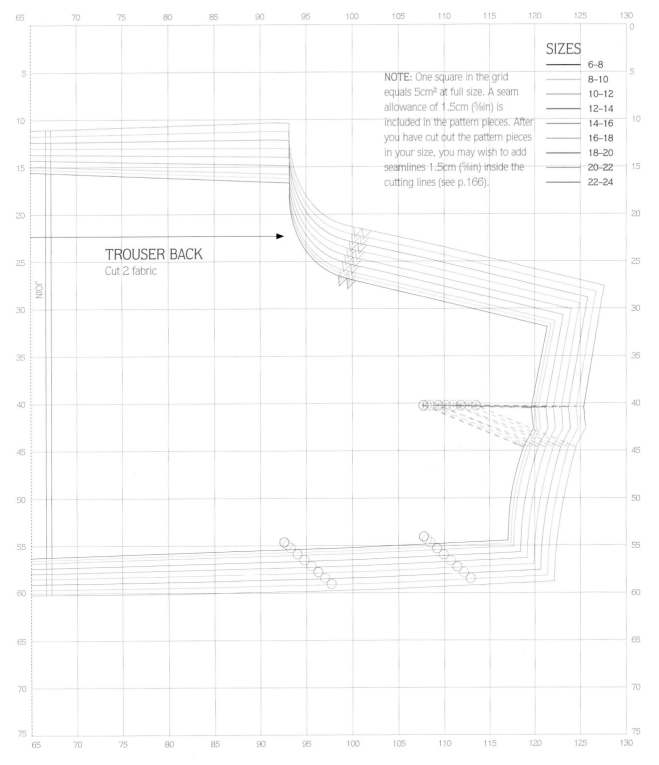

SIZES
6–8
8–10
10–12
12–14
14–16
16–18
18–20
20–22
22–24

NOTE: One square in the grid equals 5cm² at full size. A seam allowance of 1.5cm (⅝in) is included in the pattern pieces. After you have cut out the pattern pieces in your size, you may wish to add seamlines 1.5cm (⅝in) inside the cutting lines (see p.166).

TROUSER BACK
Cut 2 fabric

JOIN

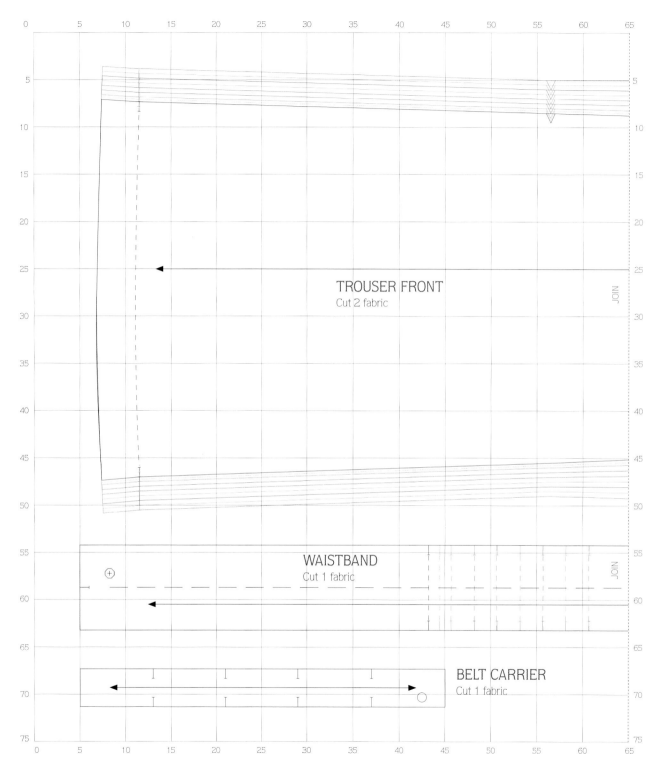

TROUSER FRONT
Cut 2 fabric

JOIN

WAISTBAND
Cut 1 fabric

JOIN

BELT CARRIER
Cut 1 fabric

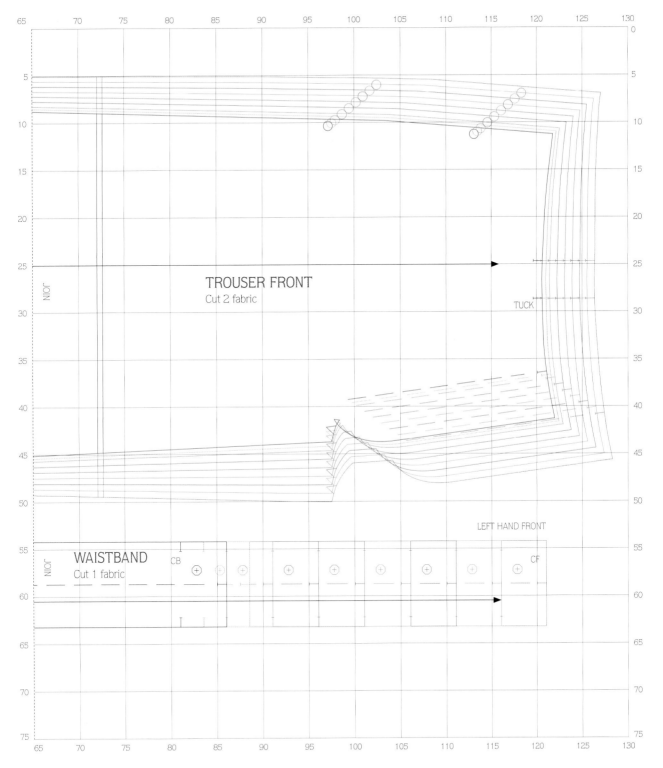

TROUSER FRONT
Cut 2 fabric

JOIN

TUCK

LEFT HAND FRONT

WAISTBAND
Cut 1 fabric

JOIN

CB

CF

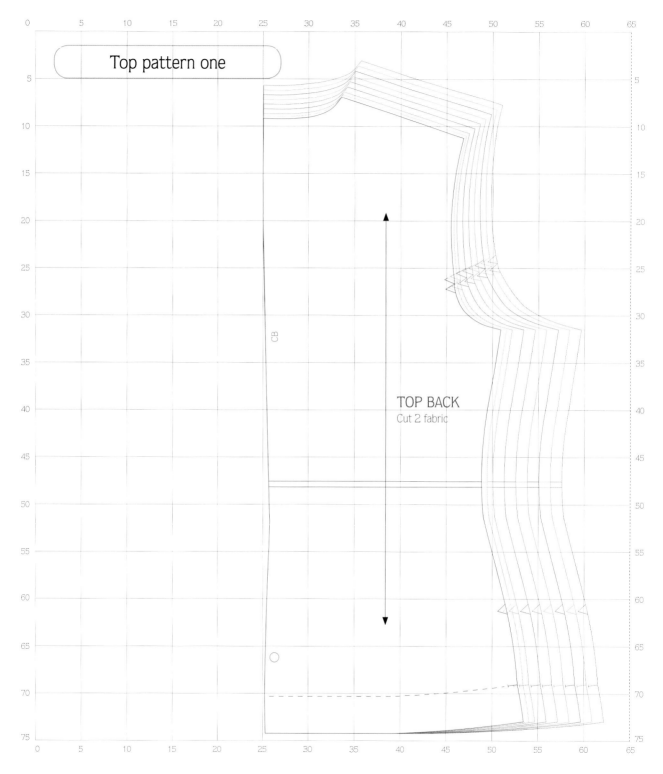

Top pattern one

CB

TOP BACK
Cut 2 fabric

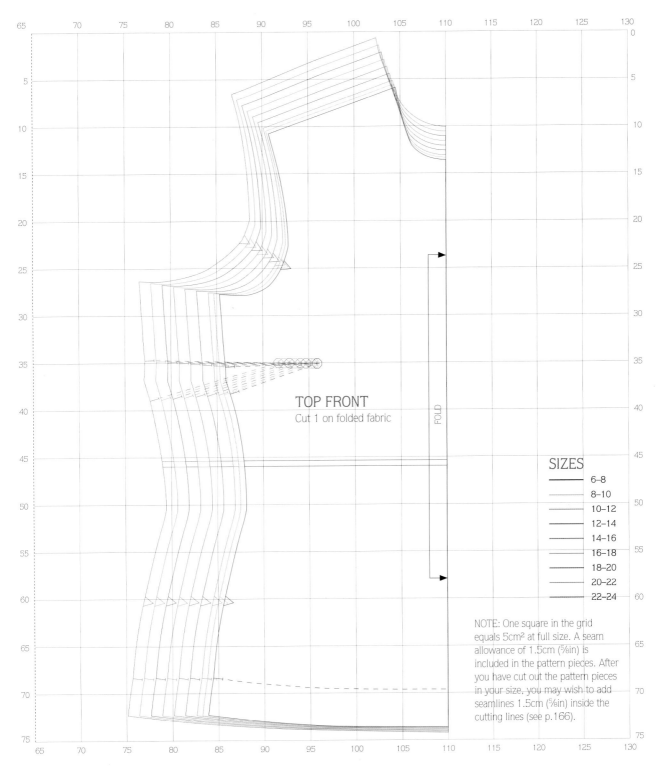

TOP FRONT
Cut 1 on folded fabric

FOLD

SIZES

———	6–8
———	8–10
———	10–12
———	12–14
———	14–16
———	16–18
———	18–20
———	20–22
———	22–24

NOTE: One square in the grid equals 5cm² at full size. A seam allowance of 1.5cm (⅝in) is included in the pattern pieces. After you have cut out the pattern pieces in your size, you may wish to add seamlines 1.5cm (⅝in) inside the cutting lines (see p.166).

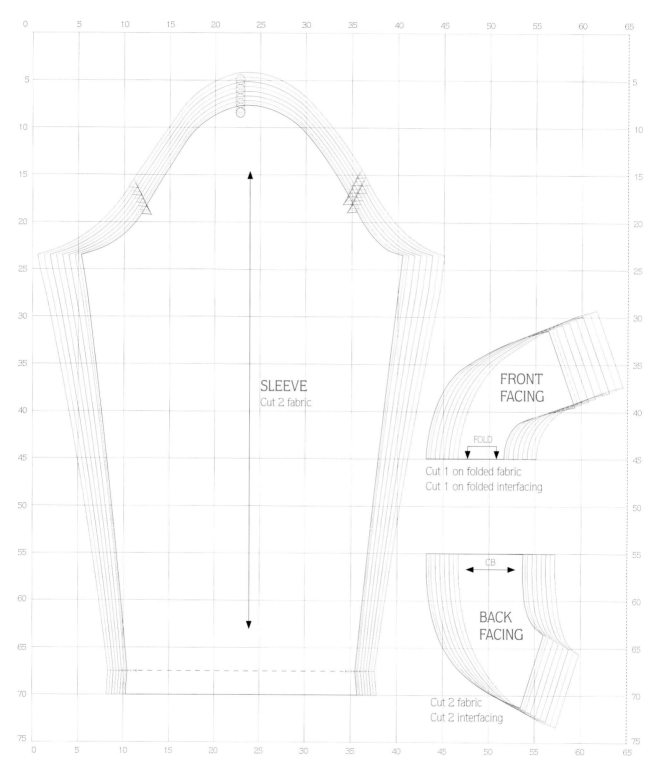

SLEEVE
Cut 2 fabric

FRONT
FACING

FOLD

Cut 1 on folded fabric
Cut 1 on folded interfacing

CB

BACK
FACING

Cut 2 fabric
Cut 2 interfacing

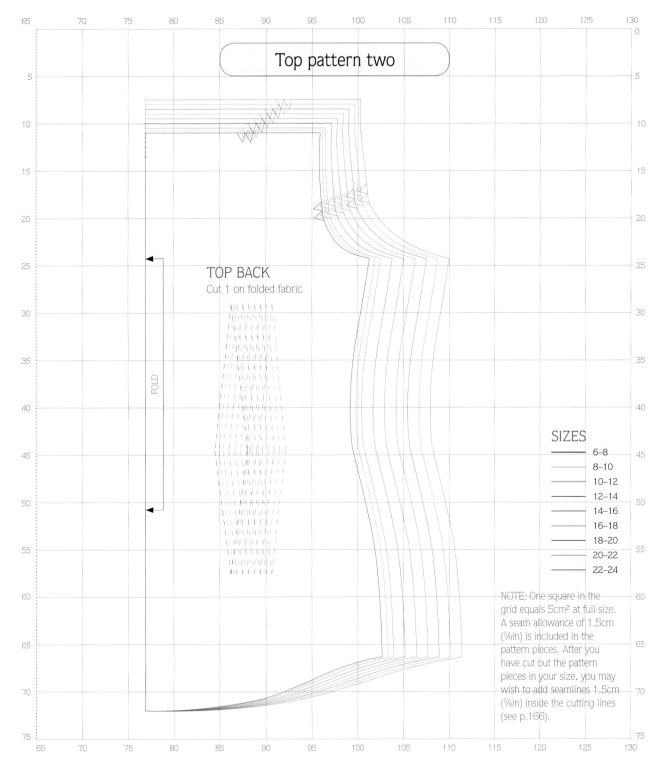

Top pattern two

TOP BACK
Cut 1 on folded fabric

FOLD

SIZES

——	6–8
——	8–10
——	10–12
——	12–14
——	14–16
——	16–18
——	18–20
——	20–22
——	22–24

NOTE: One square in the grid equals 5cm² at full size. A seam allowance of 1.5cm (⅝in) is included in the pattern pieces. After you have cut out the pattern pieces in your size, you may wish to add seamlines 1.5cm (⅝in) inside the cutting lines (see p.166).

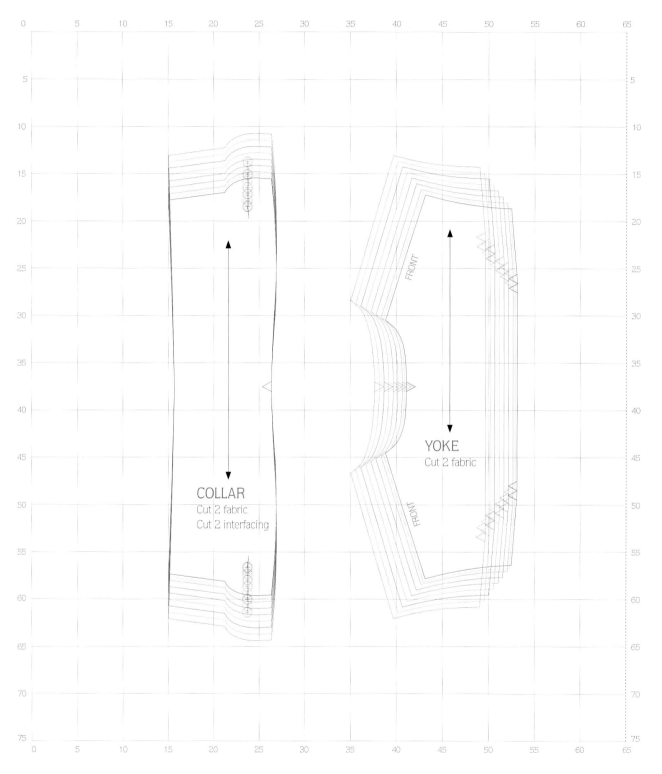

COLLAR
Cut 2 fabric
Cut 2 interfacing

YOKE
Cut 2 fabric

FRONT

FRONT

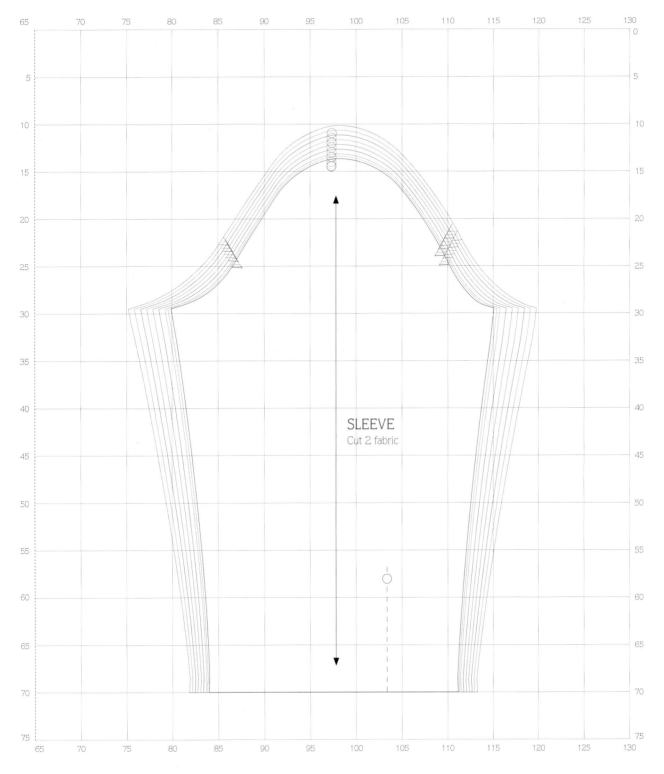

SLEEVE
Cut 2 fabric

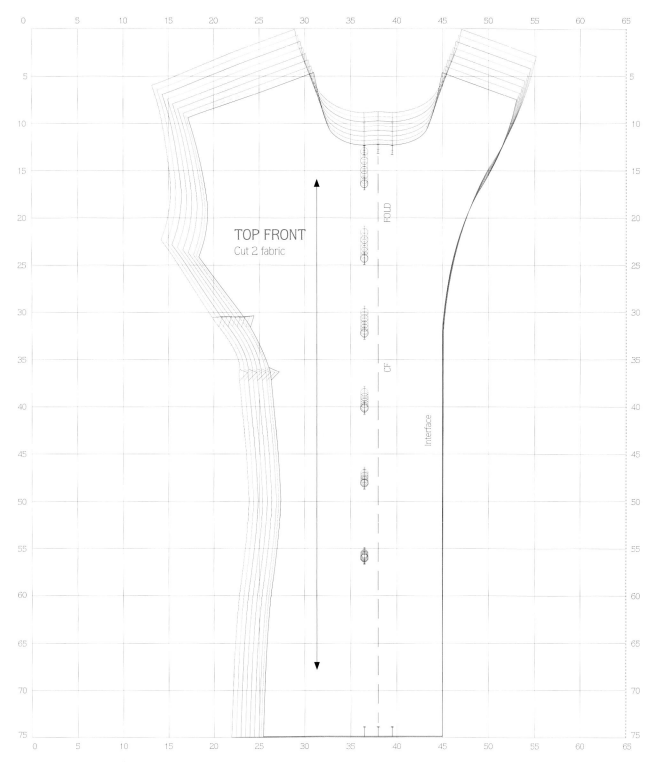

TOP FRONT
Cut 2 fabric

FOLD

CF

Interface

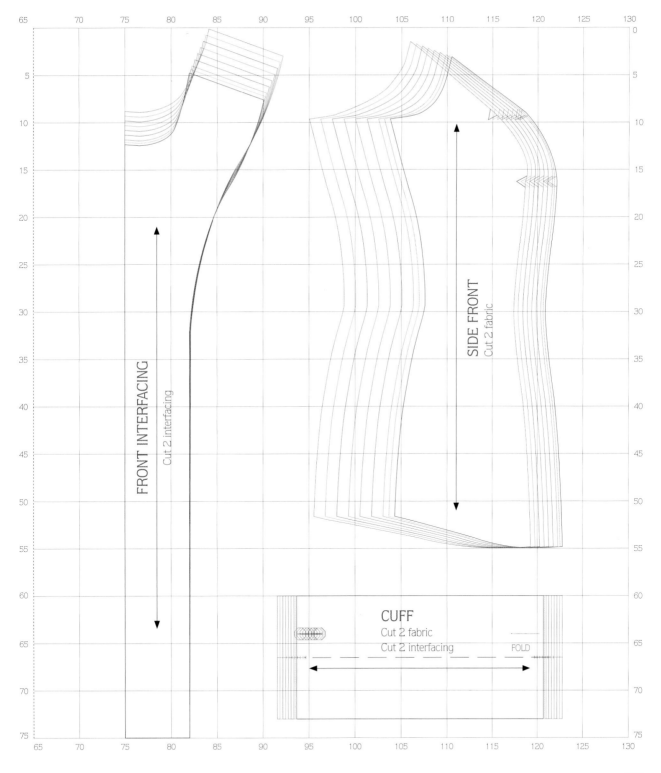

FRONT INTERFACING
Cut 2 interfacing

SIDE FRONT
Cut 2 fabric

CUFF
Cut 2 fabric
Cut 2 interfacing   FOLD

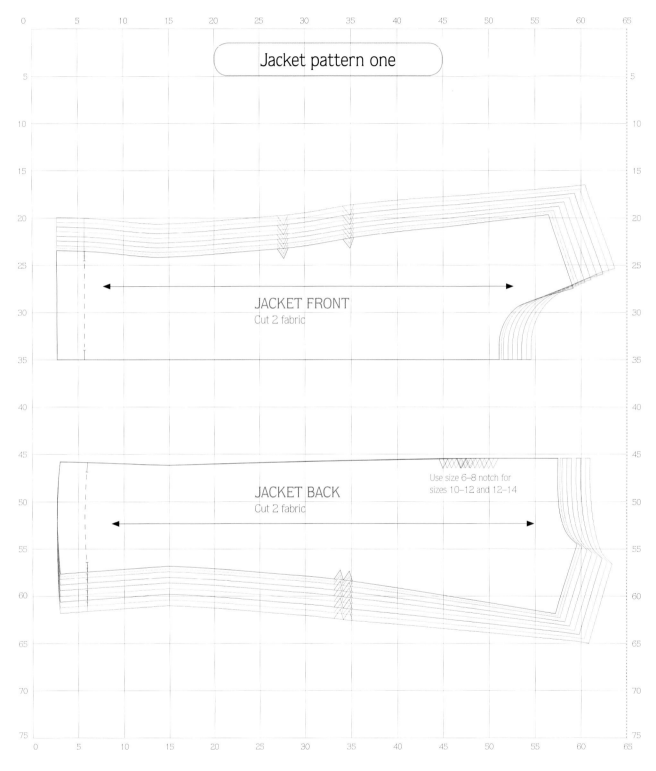

Jacket pattern one

JACKET FRONT
Cut 2 fabric

JACKET BACK
Cut 2 fabric

Use size 6–8 notch for
sizes 10–12 and 12–14

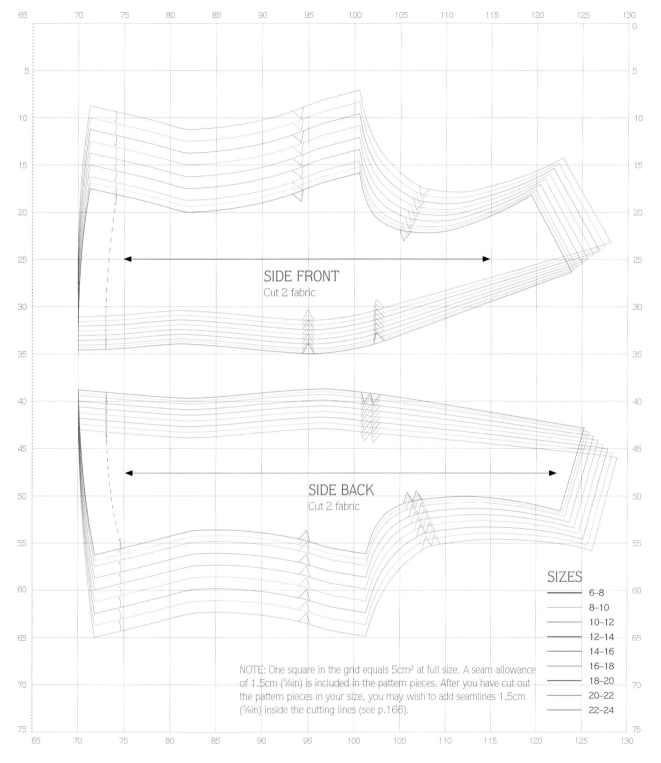

SIDE FRONT
Cut 2 fabric

SIDE BACK
Cut 2 fabric

SIZES
6–8
8–10
10–12
12–14
14–16
16–18
18–20
20–22
22–24

NOTE: One square in the grid equals 5cm² at full size. A seam allowance of 1.5cm (⅝in) is included in the pattern pieces. After you have cut out the pattern pieces in your size, you may wish to add seamlines 1.5cm (⅝in) inside the cutting lines (see p.166).

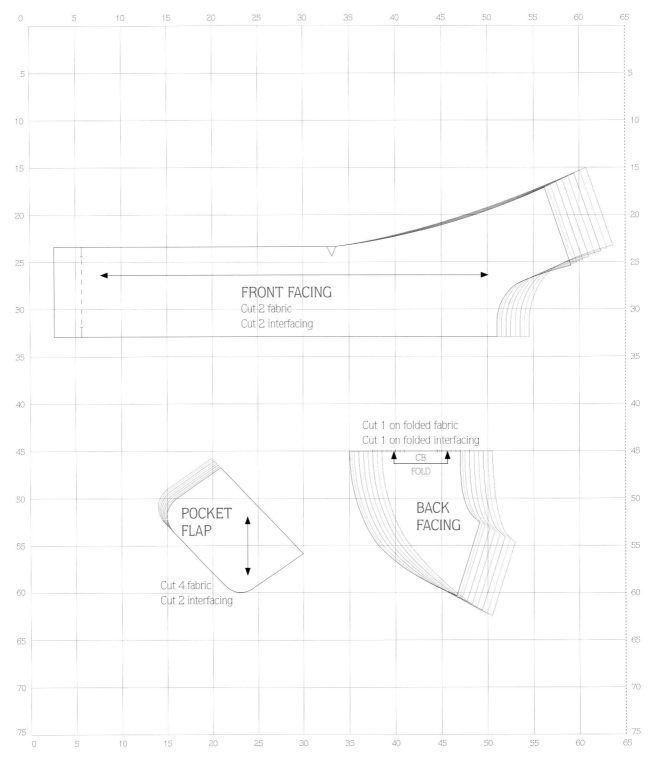

FRONT FACING
Cut 2 fabric
Cut 2 interfacing

POCKET
FLAP

Cut 4 fabric
Cut 2 interfacing

Cut 1 on folded fabric
Cut 1 on folded interfacing

CB
FOLD

BACK
FACING

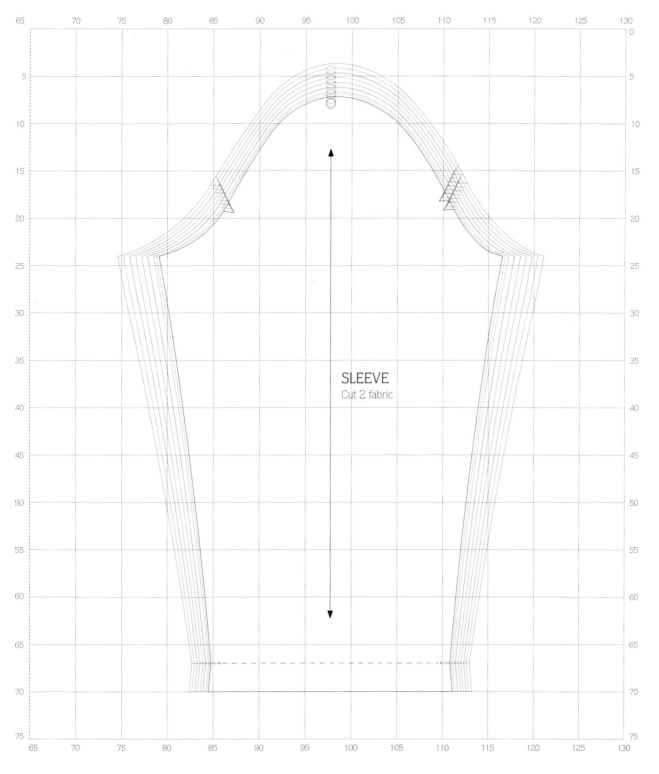

SLEEVE
Cut 2 fabric

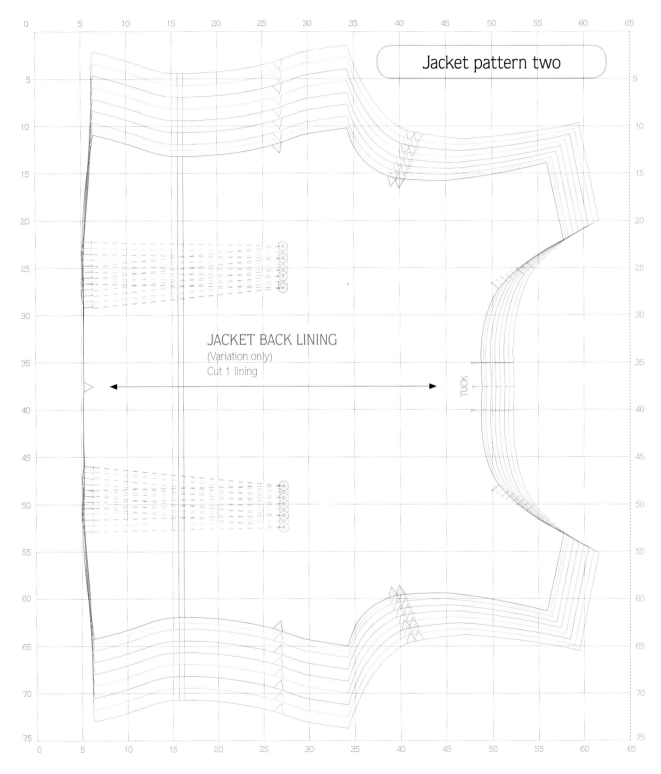

Jacket pattern two

JACKET BACK LINING
(Variation only)
Cut 1 lining

TUCK

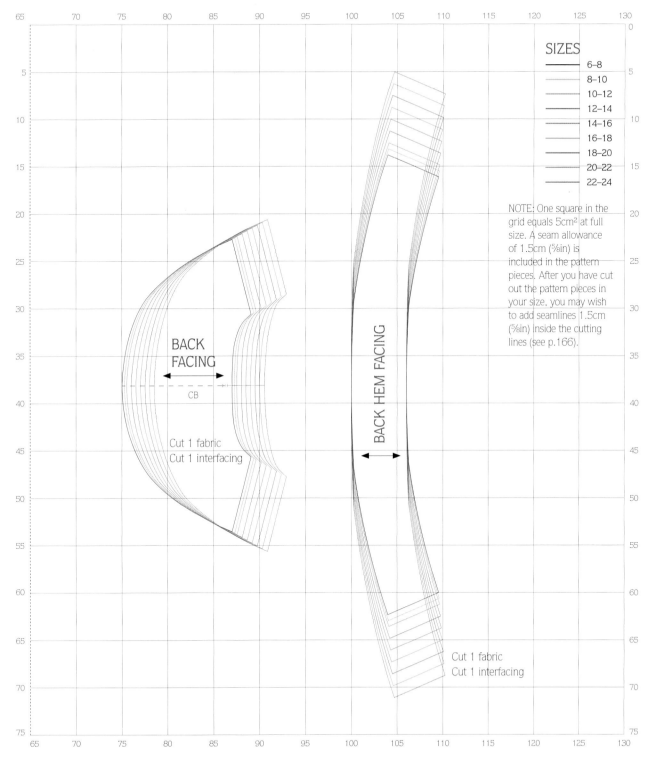

SIZES

———	6–8
———	8–10
———	10–12
———	12–14
———	14–16
———	16–18
———	18–20
———	20–22
———	22–24

NOTE: One square in the grid equals 5cm² at full size. A seam allowance of 1.5cm (⅝in) is included in the pattern pieces. After you have cut out the pattern pieces in your size, you may wish to add seamlines 1.5cm (⅝in) inside the cutting lines (see p.166).

BACK FACING

CB

Cut 1 fabric
Cut 1 interfacing

BACK HEM FACING

Cut 1 fabric
Cut 1 interfacing

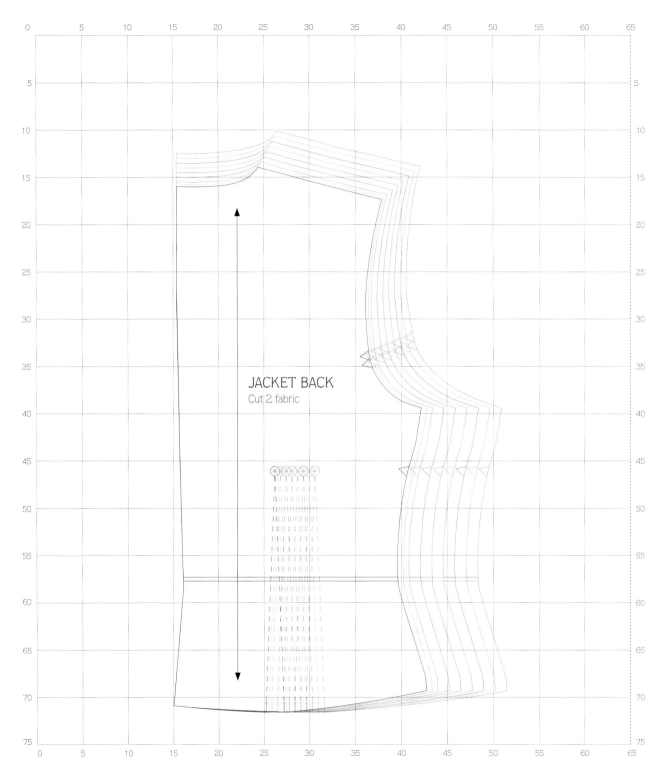

JACKET BACK
Cut 2 fabric

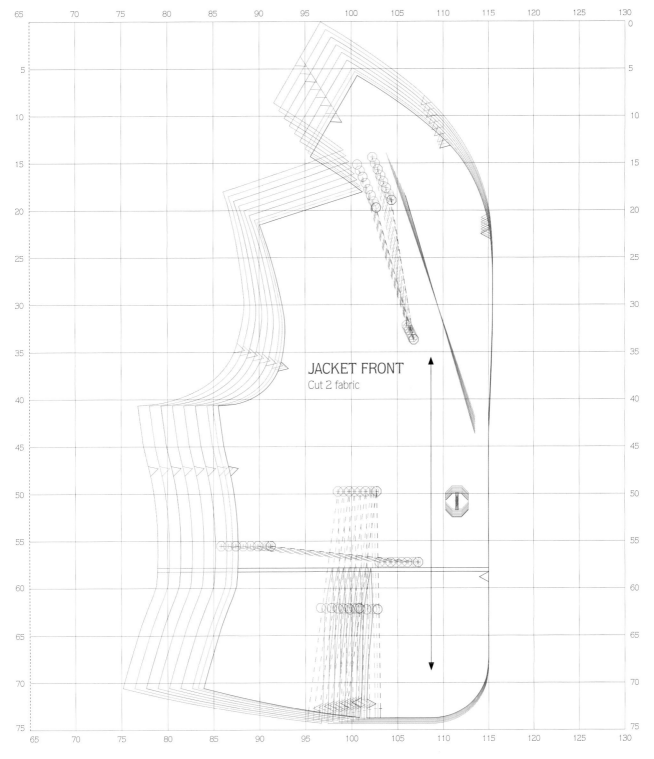

JACKET FRONT
Cut 2 fabric

Jacket pattern two **213**

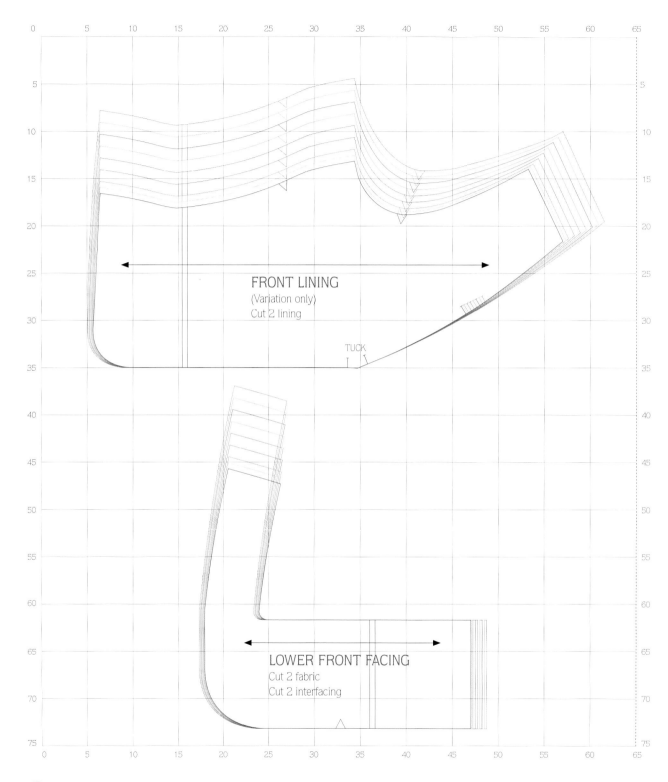

FRONT LINING
(Variation only)
Cut 2 lining

TUCK

LOWER FRONT FACING
Cut 2 fabric
Cut 2 interfacing

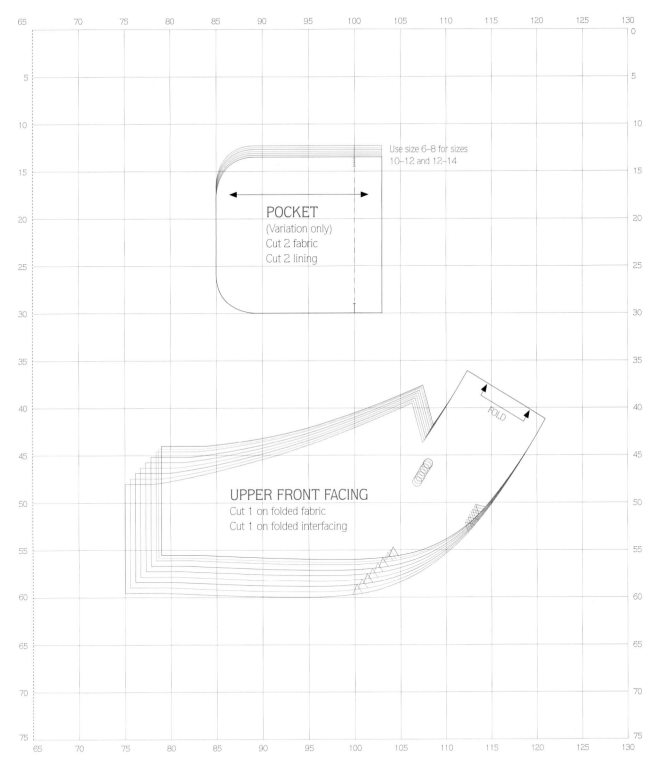

Use size 6–8 for sizes
10–12 and 12–14

POCKET
(Variation only)
Cut 2 fabric
Cut 2 lining

UPPER FRONT FACING
Cut 1 on folded fabric
Cut 1 on folded interfacing

FOLD

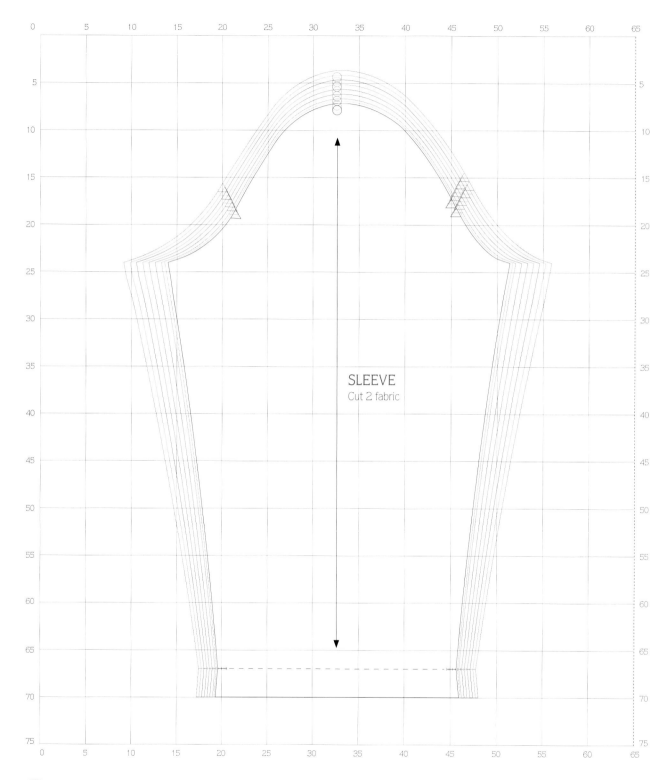

SLEEVE
Cut 2 fabric

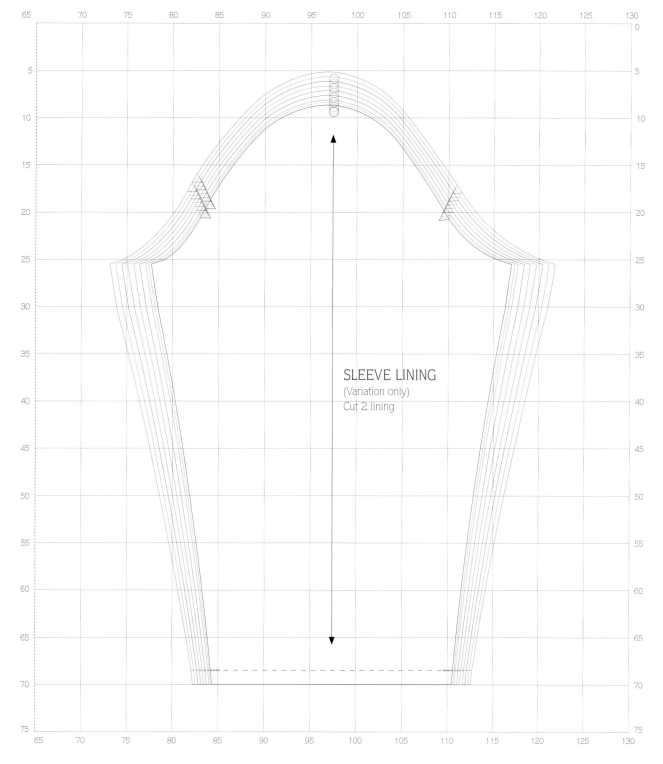

SLEEVE LINING
(Variation only)
Cut 2 lining

Glossary

Armhole Opening in a garment for the sleeve and arm.

Belt carrier Loop made from a strip of fabric, which is used to support a belt at the waist edge of a garment.

Bias 45-degree line on fabric that falls between the lengthways and the crossways grain. Fabric cut on the bias drapes well. See also Grain.

Blind hem stitch Tiny hand stitch used to attach one piece of fabric to another, mainly to secure hems. Also a machine stitch consisting of two or three straight stitches and one wide zigzag stitch.

Bodice Upper body section of a garment.

Box pleat Pleat formed on the wrong side of the fabric, and fuller than a knife pleat. See also Pleat.

Buttonhole Opening through which a button is inserted to form a fastening. Buttonholes are usually machine stitched but may also be worked by hand or piped for reinforcement or decorative effect.

Buttonhole chisel Very sharp, small chisel that cuts cleanly through a machine-stitched buttonhole.

Centre back (CB) The vertical line of symmetry of a garment back piece. Often marked as CB.

Centre front (CF) The vertical line of symmetry of a garment front piece. Often marked as CF.

Contour dart Also known as double-pointed dart, this is used to give shape at the waist of a garment. It is like two darts joined together. See also Dart.

Crease Line formed in fabric by pressing a fold.

Cutting line Solid line on a pattern piece used as a guide for cutting out fabric.

Dart Tapered stitched fold of fabric used on a garment to give it shape so that it can fit around the contours of the body. There are different types of dart, but all are used mainly on women's clothing.

Double-pointed dart See Contour dart

Dressmaker's carbon paper Used together with a tracing wheel to transfer pattern markings to fabric. Available in a variety of colours.

Ease Distributing fullness in fabric when joining two seams together of slightly different lengths, for example a sleeve to an armhole.

Ease stitch Long machine stitch, used to ease in fullness where the distance between notches is greater on one seam edge than on the other.

Facing Layer of fabric placed on the inside of a garment and used to finish off raw edges of an armhole or neck of a garment. Usually a separate piece of fabric, the facing can sometimes be an extension of the garment itself.

Flat fell stitch A strong, secure stitch used to hold two layers together permanently. Often used to secure linings and bias bindings.

French dart Curved dart used on the front of a garment. See also Dart.

Gathers Bunches of fabric created by sewing two parallel rows of loose stitching, then pulling the threads up so that the fabric gathers and reduces in size to fit the required space.

Grain Lengthways and crossways direction of threads in a fabric. Fabric grain affects how a fabric hangs and drapes.

Haberdashery Term that covers all the bits and pieces needed to complete a pattern, such as fasteners, elastics, ribbons, and trimmings.

Hem The edge of a piece of fabric neatened and stitched to prevent unravelling. There are several methods of doing this, both by hand and by machine.

Hem allowance Amount of fabric allowed for turning under to make the hem.

Hemline Crease or foldline along which a hem is marked.

Herringbone stitch Hand stitch used to secure hems and interlinings. This stitch is worked from left to right.

Hook and eye fastening Two-part metal fastening used to fasten overlapping edges of fabric where a neat join is required. Available in a wide variety of styles.

Interfacing A fabric placed between garment and facing to give structure and support. Available in different thicknesses, interfacing can be fusible (bonds to the fabric by applying heat) or non-fusible (needs to be sewn to the fabric).

Keyhole buttonhole stitch A machine buttonhole stitch characterized by having one square end while the other end is shaped like a look to accomodate the button's shank without distorting the fabric. Often used on jackets.

Layering Trimming one side of the seam allowance to half its width to reduce bulk at the seam.

Lining Underlying fabric layer used to give a neat finish to an item, as well as concealing the stitching and seams of a garment.

Locking stitch A machine stitch where the upper and lower threads in the machine "lock" together at the start or end of a row of stitching.

Mitre The diagonal line made where two edges of a piece of fabric meet at a corner, produced by folding. See also Mitred corner.

Mitred corner Diagonal seam formed when fabric is joined at a corner. Excess fabric is cut away before or after stitching.

Multi-size pattern Paper pattern printed with cutting lines for a range of sizes on each pattern piece.

Nap The raised pile on a fabric made during the weaving process, or a print pointing one way. When cutting out pattern pieces, ensure the nap runs in the same direction.

Needle threader Gadget that pulls thread through the eye of a needle. Useful for needles with small eyes.

Notch V-shaped marking on a pattern piece used for aligning one piece with another. Also V-shaped cut taken to reduce seam bulk.

Notion An item of haberdashery, other than fabric, needed to complete a project, such as a button, zip, or elastic. Notions are normally listed on the pattern envelope.

Overlocker Machine used for quick stitching, trimming, and edging of fabric in a single action; it gives a professional finish to a garment. There are a variety of accessories that can be attached to an overlocker, which enable it to perform a greater range of functions.

Overlock stitch A machine stitch that neatens edges and prevents fraying. It can be used on all types of fabric.

Pattern markings Symbols printed on a paper pattern to indicate the fabric grain, foldline, and construction details, such as darts, notches, and tucks. These should be transferred to the fabric using tailor's chalk or tailor's tacks.

Pinking A method of neatening raw edges of fray-resistant fabric using pinking shears. This will leave a zigzag edge.

Pinking shears Cutting tool with serrated blades, used to trim raw edges of fray-resistant fabrics to neaten seam edges.

Placket An opening in a garment that provides support for fasteners, such as buttons, snaps, or zips.

Pleat An even fold or series of folds in fabric, often partially stitched down. Commonly found in skirts to shape the waistline.

Pressing cloth Muslin or organza cloth placed over fabric to prevent marking or scorching when pressing.

Raw edge Cut edge of fabric that requires finishing, for example using zigzag stitch, to prevent fraying.

Reverse stitch Machine stitch that simply stitches back over a row of stitches to secure the threads.

Right side The outer side of a fabric, or the visible part of a garment.

Round-end buttonhole stitch Machine stitch characterized by one end of the buttonhole being square and the other being round, to allow for the button shank.

Running stitch A simple, evenly spaced straight stitch separated by equal-sized spaces, used for seaming and gathering.

Seam Stitched line where two edges of fabric are joined together.

Seam allowance The amount of fabric allowed for on a pattern where sections are to be joined together by a seam; usually this is 1.5cm (⅝in).

Seam edge The cut edge of a seam allowance.

Seamline Line on paper pattern designated for stitching a seam; usually this is 1.5cm (⅝in) from the seam edge.

Seam ripper A small, hooked tool used for undoing seams and unpicking stitches.

Selvedge Finished edge on a woven fabric. This runs parallel to the warp (lengthways) threads.

Set-in sleeve A sleeve that fits into a garment smoothly at the shoulder seam.

Sewing gauge Measuring tool with adjustable slider for checking small measurements, such as hem depths and seam allowances.

Slip hem stitch Similar to herringbone stitch but is worked from right to left. It is used mainly for securing hems.

Snaps Also known as press studs, these fasteners are used as a lightweight hidden fastener.

Snips Spring-loaded cutting tool used for cutting off thread ends.

Stitch in the ditch A line of straight stitches sewn on the right side of the work, in the ditch created by a seam. Used to secure waistbands and facings.

Stitch ripper See Seam ripper.

Straight stitch Plain machine stitch, used for most applications. The length of the stitch can be altered to suit the fabric.

Tacking stitch A temporary running stitch used to hold pieces of fabric together or for transferring pattern markings to fabric.

Tailor's buttonhole A buttonhole with one square end and one keyhole-shaped end, used on jackets and coats.

Tailor's chalk Square- or triangular-shaped piece of chalk used to mark fabric. Available in a variety of colours, tailor's chalk can be removed easily by brushing.

Tailor's ham A ham-shaped pressing cushion that is used to press shaped areas of garments.

Tailor's tacks Loose thread markings used to transfer symbols from a pattern to fabric.

Tape measure Flexible form of ruler made from plastic or fabric.

Thimble Metal or plastic cap that fits over the top of a finger to protect it when hand sewing.

Topstitch Machine straight stitching worked on the right side of an item, close to the finished edge, for decorative effect. Sometimes stitched in a contrasting colour.

Topstitched seam A seam finished with a row of topstitching for decorative effect.

Trace tacking A method of marking fold and placement lines on fabric. Loose stitches are sewn along the lines on the pattern to the fabric beneath, then the thread loops are cut and the pattern removed.

Tracing wheel Tool used together with dressmaker's carbon paper to transfer pattern markings on to fabric.

Understitch Machine straight stitching through facing and seam allowances that is invisible from the right side; this helps the facing to lie flat.

Waistband Band of fabric attached to the waist edge of a garment to provide a neat finish.

Warp Lengthways threads or yarns of a woven fabric.

Weft Threads or yarns that cross the warp of a woven fabric.

Wrong side Reverse side of a fabric; the inside of a garment or other item.

Yoke The top section of a dress or skirt from which the rest of the garment hangs.

Zigzag stitch Machine stitch used to neaten and secure seam edges and for decorative purposes. The width and length of the zigzag can be altered.

Zip Fastening widely used on garments consisting of two strips of fabric tape, carrying specially shaped metal or plastic teeth that lock together by means of a pull or slider. Zips are available in different colours and weights.

Zip foot Narrow machine foot with a single toe that can be positioned on either side of the needle.

Index

About the author

Alison Smith, MBE, trained as an Art and Fashion Textile Teacher before becoming Head of Textiles at one of the largest secondary schools in Birmingham. Alison left mainstream teaching to have a family, but missed teaching so much that she soon established the Alison Victoria School of Sewing. The school is now the largest of its kind in the UK with students attending from all over Europe and beyond. Alison specialises not only in teaching Dressmaking but also Tailoring and Corsetry. In addition to her own school, Alison lectures at Janome in Stockport, and at various sewing shows across the UK. Alison has brought her passion for sewing to TV on series such as **From Ladette to Lady.** Alison lives in Leicestershire with her husband Nigel and has two adult children.

Acknowledgments

AUTHOR'S ACKNOWLEDGMENTS

No book could ever be written without a little help. I would like to thank the following people for their help in making all the garments: Jackie Boddy, Averil Wing, Jenny Holdam, Christine Scott, Angela Paine, and Joan Culver. My darling husband Nigel and our children Kathryn and Oliver for all their support and endless cups of tea! Thanks must also go to the companies who have continued to support me: Janome UK, Coats Crafts, Fruedenberg-nw, Fabulous Fabric, and MIG. Thank you to my editors Laura Palosuo – and Hilary Mandleberg, who I think I have inspired to take up sewing again!

DK ACKNOWLEDGMENTS

DK would like to thank all the people who helped in the creation of this book: Alison Shackleton for art direction, and Paula Keogh for her skills as sewing technician on the first photo shoot; Jane Ewart for art direction on the second photo shoot, Ruth Jenkinson and her assistant Carly for photography, and Rebecca Fallowfield for production assistance. A big thank you goes out to Bob at MIG for demystifying the art of pattern creation. Finally, we would like to thank Claire Cross and Anne Hildyard for editorial assistance, Angela Baynham for proofreading the book, and Marie Lorimer for creating the index.